WHAT
REALLY
WORKS
IN Elementary
Education

This book is dedicated to Steve Holle.

Steve is the Coordinator of Professional Development for the California State University, Northridge (CSUN) Center for Teaching and Learning (CTL). He is also an instructor for the Elementary Education department at CSUN. Steve has been an invaluable member of the CTL for years, bringing our content expertise to the community through practical professional development efforts. He is untiring, always positiv and seems to know everyone. He is truly committed to figuring out "what really works" in education, and we could not do what we do without him. Thank you, Steve.

WHAT REALLY WORKS

IN Elementary Education

Wendy W. Murawski
Kathy Lynn Scott
Editors

FOR INFORMATION:

Corwin
A SAGE Company
2455 Teller Road
Thousand Oaks, California 91320
(800) 233-9936
www.corwin.com

SAGE Publications Ltd.
1 Oliver's Yard
55 City Road
London EC1Y 1SP
United Kingdom

SAGE Publications India Pvt. Ltd.
B 1/I 1 Mohan Cooperative Industrial Area
Mathura Road, New Delhi 110 044
India

SAGE Publications Asia-Pacific Pte. Ltd.
3 Church Street
#10-04 Samsung Hub
Singapore 049483

Printed in the United States of America

A catalog record of this book is available from the Library of Congress.

ISBN: 978-1-4833-8666-9

Acquisitions Editor: Jessica Allan
Associate Editor: Kimberly Greenberg
Editorial Assistant: Cesar Reyes
Project Editor: Veronica Stapleton Hooper
Copy Editor: Beth Hammond
Typesetter: C&M Digitals (P) Ltd.
Proofreader: Dennis W. Webb
Indexer: Jeanne R. Busemeyer
Cover Designer: Gail Buschman
Marketing Manager: Amanda Boudria

This book is printed on acid-free paper.

15 16 17 18 19 10 9 8 7 6 5 4 3 2 1

Contents

Foreword

I remember it like it was yesterday. My first day of teaching, that is. It was September 1996 in Room 323 at John Burroughs High School in Burbank, California. I was ready to face my very own class of real live tenth graders and teach them the mysteries of English. My seating charts, the ones I spent a ridiculous amount of time perfecting, were beautifully printed out. The walls papered in sunny colors with eye-catching posters tacked artfully here and there. In my arms, a sheaf of terrifically important, hot off the copier, papers ready to pass out. On me, a polished, smart-looking outfit with sensible, made-to-last-all-day shoes. I had a megawatt smile and enough enthusiasm to fill a dozen classrooms. I was SO ready. By second period, my naïve ideas of preparedness met the gritty reality of classroom dynamics, and I was exhausted just trying to keep up. By third, I was terrified; by fourth, exhausted; and by sixth, ready to walk out and never return.

If you would have asked me, on the eve of my first day as a real teacher, if I was ready, really ready, I'd have given you a hearty yes. And that's the strange magic of teacher preparation programs. I left mine certain that I'd done the important work of becoming ready to teach. I'd had experiences and opportunities and assignments that had truly shown me not just how to teach, but how to teach skillfully and well. At least, that's what I thought. And I wasn't wrong. You DO walk in ready, but an actual classroom is a remarkable and very real crucible that has its own lessons for you, lessons you cannot learn until you are the teacher.

And here's what's utterly wonderful about being the one in charge in the room. No matter how ready you are, how prepared you feel, you don't really know a thing. But you learn, and you learn fast.

You see, the growth curve in our profession is enormous. You are better at 10:00 a.m. than you were at 8:00 a.m., and by 2:00 p.m. your lesson is amazing. On Tuesday, you're much better than you were on Monday. And Friday? Friday is a gift you give your students . . . you're that good. And don't get me started on the first day of your SECOND year of teaching. On that day, you are truly the rock star teacher you've grown to be. Naturally, as is the order of things in teaching, in walk your new students and a completely new dynamic presents itself. All the skills and talent you brought with you doesn't seem to work the same magic on these kids and back to square one you go trying to figure it all out. It's alarming and wonderful at the same time, which is why our job forces us to stay on our toes every single day.

After 18 years of this, there's only one thing I know for certain, and it's this: I don't know very much for certain. There has not been one way to teach my classes or one strict set of ideas or procedures that worked every year or with every group of students. There just isn't.

What I do know is that I have needed to fill my metaphorical teacher toolbox with every possible tool, tip, technique, idea, and strategy possible so that when new situations in my classrooms arise, I have a deep set of possible options from which to grab as I try to teach my way through. The idea of the teacher's toolbox coupled with the gritty determination to grow and get better by staying open to new ideas and best practices are what turns good teachers into great ones.

And that's where this book comes in.

In the pages ahead, you'll learn from some of the country's best educators about what REALLY works in classrooms. From their experiences comes wisdom along with a whole host of tried and true, practical, hands-on solutions for you to use in your classroom. That's another one of the perks of our professions—our close proximity to other practitioners and our easy access to the greatness that exists in the classrooms right down the hall.

I don't know where I'd be if I didn't have Traci, Karen, Stefanie, Joe, Jim, or Alex to call on for ideas, hope, inspiration, or even just a shoulder to cry on. I am who I am because of the collection of ideas and skills I've gathered from my peers, filtered through my own philosophy and sensibilities, and put to use in my classroom. In that sense, I'm a patchwork quilt of all the great things I've learned from other teachers, but how I patched those pieces together makes me the unique teacher I am proud to be. That's how we grow. Your growth into greatness simply depends on your community of support. This collection of great ideas about what REALLY works in classrooms is another great tool to add to your toolbox; perhaps it's the greatest tool of all. That you can decide for yourself, but it's important you have it as you set out to create or transform your classroom into the vibrant and engaging learning space for all of your students.

I wish I'd had a book like this before I stepped into Room 323 all those years ago. I'm glad I have it now.

Rebecca Mieliwocki

2012 National Teacher of the Year

About the Editors

 **Wendy W. Murawski,** PhD, is the Michael D. Eisner Endowed Chair and Executive Director of the Center for Teaching and Learning at California State University, Northridge. She is a tenured Full Professor in the Department of Special Education, as well as the past President of the Teacher Education Division (TED) of the Council for Exceptional Children (CEC). Wendy is proud to have been the Distinguished Teacher Educator of the Year for the state of California (which is a pretty big state!). She has authored numerous books, chapters, articles, and handbooks in the areas of co-teaching, collaboration, inclusion, and differentiation. Wendy owns her own educational consulting company (2 TEACH LLC), loves to travel and speak nationally and internationally, and is a frequently requested keynote speaker. Wendy would like to publically admit that, although she is keenly aware of the research on child development and best practice, she allows her 10-year-old son Kiernan to eat way too many sweets. She's working on that.

 **Kathy Lynn Scott,** PhD, is the Center Administrative Analyst for the Center for Teaching and Learning (CTL) at California State University, Northridge. Kathy was trained as an "old school" darkroom photographer, but she fell in love with all things to do with education. After conducting research on art education and adult education in England and coordinating research on learning disabilities in New Jersey, Kathy jumped from coast to coast, finding a new home with the CTL where she gets to do a little bit of everything related to education. When not acting as the "glue" for the CTL (as Wendy calls her) and when she finds the time, she collects passport stamps at National Parks. But more often than not, she's just relaxing at home, eating something with entirely too much garlic, watching *Jeopardy!*, and shouting out the (not always correct) answers.

ABOUT THE CTL

The CSUN Center for Teaching and Learning (CTL) is the research and professional development hub of the California State University, Northridge's Michael D. Eisner College of Education. The CTL was created through a generous endowment by the Eisner Foundation in 2002. The CTL's focus continues to be improving the education of all learners through the betterment of preservice and inservice teachers, counselors, administrators, educational therapists, and other educational specialists. The CTL provides local, state, and national professional development across a variety of topics and is dedicated to bringing the best evidence-based practices to educators in a practical manner. The CTL is committed to "what really works" in education!

About the Contributors

Making Math Meaningful

Nancy O'Rode, PhD, is an Associate Professor in the Michael D. Eisner College of Education at California State University, Northridge. When she is not teaching mathematics methods and curriculum for elementary schools, she is Zumba dancing, kikoy collecting, bird watching, chocolate inhaling, and is a life-time member of the Jane Austen Society.

Rewarding Reading Practices

Renee Ziolkowska, EdD, is an Associate Professor at California State University, Northridge. She has worked as a classroom teacher and a reading specialist. Her teaching and research interests center around literacy. She enjoys traveling, trying new foods, and devouring books. She maintains a fitness program by attempting to keep up with her 6-year-old daughter, Sophia.

Teaching Writing Right

Kathleen Dudden Rowlands, PhD, teaches in the Department of Secondary Education and directs the Cal State Northridge Writing Project. When she can sneak away for a few days, she enjoys camping and hiking in Death Valley or Joshua Tree, spoiling her grandchildren, or checking up on the school of Humuhumunukunukuapua'a (reef trigger fish) that live in Shark's Cove on Oahu.

Successful Social Studies

Joyce H. Burstein, EdD, is a Professor of Social Studies Education and the Director of Community Engagement at California State University, Northridge. She is the recipient of the university's Distinguished Teaching Award and author of several works on social studies and arts education. After hours, you can catch her in her role as party mixologist.

Greg Knotts, PhD, is an Associate Professor of Elementary Education and the Director of the Queer Studies Program at California State University, Northridge. He has published and presented extensively on social studies, the arts, and LGBT (Lesbian, Gay, Bisexual, and Transgender) issues in elementary education. He dreamed of being a Solid Gold Dancer; okay . . . he's still dreaming . . . but now it's for *So You Think You Can Dance.*

Stellar STE(A)M Strategies

Erica Rood is a veteran teacher who is convinced that all children can learn and deserve to learn. As a national finalist for the Presidential Awards for Excellence in Mathematics and Science Teaching (we'll find out in 2016!), Ms. Rood is currently continuing her education as a member of NASA's Endeavor Leadership program through California State University, Northridge's STEM Masters Program. She is currently researching arts integration in a variety of STEM areas and one day hopes to be the first ballerina to travel to space!

Awe-Inspiring Arts Integration

Mary Wolf, PhD, is the Director and Assistant Professor of Art Education at Daemen College. For 20 years, she's taught art and advocated for the arts at a variety of levels in a variety of settings including elementary, middle, high school, magnet school, alternative school, home school, adult education, higher education, and at international, national, state, and local conferences. She secretly wants to teach and represent the arts as a professor on the sitcom, The Big Bang Theory.

Ann Fontaine Lewis, MEd, K–12 Content Specialist and Professional Developer in Delaware, is a former classroom teacher, administrator, curriculum supervisor, and a current adjunct professor who presents nationally on literacy, curriculum and instruction, assessment, classroom management, and arts integration. She spends her "spare" time training and riding horses, feeding her addiction to reading and writing, and enjoying her family, farm, and friends.

Beth Thompson is a visual arts teacher at Dundalk Elementary School in Baltimore County and has taught visual art education in Maryland for over 30 years. She's presented at state and national conferences advocating for S.T.E.A.M. and was named Maryland State Art Educator of the Year, 2014. On a daily basis, Beth captures the imagination and energy of children of all ages—including her husband Albert.

Tuning in With Technology

Lisa A. Dieker is a Pegasus Professor and Lockheed Martin Eminent Scholar Chair at the University of Central Florida. In addition, she directs the doctoral program in special education and is one of the creators of the virtual classroom TeachLivE. She has no spare time these days even as an empty nester, but when she does, she enjoys her two crazy cats (one will ignore you, and the other will attack you)—noting her failure in behavior management with her pets.

Lauren Delisio is a doctoral candidate in Exceptional Education at the University of Central Florida. She is a native New Yorker with 9 years of teaching experience in both general and special education classrooms. Her areas of research interest include identifying effective academic interventions for students with disabilities in inclusive classrooms, especially in STEM content areas. A true Type-A personality, Lauren enjoys creating to-do lists, cleaning, and waiting on the prince of the house, her tiny, pampered Pomeranian.

Caitlyn A. Bukaty is a doctoral scholar of Exceptional Education at the University of Central Florida. A native of Buffalo, New York, she's still thawing out! As a professional educator and former ballet dancer, Caitlyn infuses her passion for the arts with her commitment to students. She is especially interested in postsecondary transition for students with disabilities. The rest of Caitlyn's time is consumed by catering to the every whim of her two rescue dogs, Giselle and Bukets.

Perfectly Positive Behavior

Brittany Hott, PhD, is an Assistant Professor of Special Education at Texas A&M University-Commerce. While Dr. Hott spends much of her time focused on developing and testing interventions to support secondary students, with or at-risk for, learning and behavioral disabilities, she has been observed running in circles—literally! Dr. Hott is a Boston and New York marathon qualifier and multiple ironman finisher.

Laura Isbell, PhD, is an Assistant Professor at Texas A&M University-Commerce. Her research interests include curriculum development and the impact of RTI on students and teachers. When she is not busy working, Laura enjoys watching the Green Bay Packers. Go Pack go!

Jennifer Walker, PhD, is an Assistant Professor at the University of Mary Washington in Virginia. Her research interests include students with emotional and behavior disabilities and positive behavior supports. Recently, Jennifer moved to a house on 11 acres where she is trying to figure out how to raise chickens without actually having to touch them or clean their coop.

Classy Classroom Management

Luisa Palomo Hare is a kindergarten teacher in a high-poverty urban school in Omaha, Nebraska. She is endorsed in English as a Second

Language and has her masters in Educational Administration. Luisa has been recognized by Warren Buffet as a recipient for the Buffet Outstanding Teacher Award and is the 2012 Nebraska Teacher of the Year. Luisa's biggest surprise of all came when she adopted her Goldendoodle, Sadie, and promptly fell head over heels in love with all things dog!

Wendy W. Murawski, PhD, is a Professor in Special Education and the Executive Director and Eisner Endowed Chair for the Center for Teaching and Learning at California State University, Northridge. She's published and presented extensively on co-teaching, but when she's not traveling or working, she is creatively decorating cupcakes.

Cool Cooperative Learning

Scott Mandel, PhD, has been a classroom teacher for 30 years. A National Board Certified Teacher, he has written 11 teacher education books, including *Cooperative Work Groups: Preparing Students for the Real World* and *Improving Test Scores: A Practical Approach for Teachers and Administrators*. He wants to write a book about champion sports teams in his hometown of Cleveland, but he's still waiting for material.

Unique Universal Design for Learning

Tamarah M. Ashton, PhD, is a Professor in the Department of Special Education at California State University, Northridge and a frequent presenter for the Speakers Bureau through CSUN's Center for Teaching and Learning and with 2Teach LLC. When not running the graduate program in Special Education, Dr. Ashton is on stage in numerous theatrical productions waiting to be discovered. Still . . . waiting. . . .

Incredible Inclusion

Amy Hanreddy, PhD, is an Assistant Professor in the Department of Special Education at California State University, Northridge where she teaches classes related to inclusive and collaborative practices that benefit all students. Amy has worked as a special education teacher and an administrator at an inclusive school and has presented on a range of topics related to inclusive education with a particular focus on students with significant support needs. When she is avoiding deadlines, Amy is busy posting cat and kid pictures on Facebook.

Erin Studer, EdD, is the Executive Director of CHIME Institute in Los Angeles, California. CHIME is a national model for inclusive education and serves over 700 children from the Los Angeles area each year. Dr. Studer has taught special education and general education in K–12 and also has taught preservice educators at the university level. He hails from the great state of Iowa and, like many from his native state, spent many years wrestling. Though he no longer grapples, he enjoys wearing his wrestling shoes around the house because of how cool they look.

Creative Co-Teaching

Wendy W. Murawski, PhD, is the Executive Director and Eisner Endowed Chair for the Center for Teaching and Learning at California State University, Northridge. She's written four books, as well as chapters, articles, and software . . . all on co-teaching. In fact, she and her coauthors, Tamarah Ashton, Claire Hughes, Sally Spencer, and Lisa Dieker, have been extending the co-teaching culture to co-shopping, upon which they are intent on becoming experts.

Amazing Assessment

Brooke Blanks, PhD, is an Assistant Professor of Special Education at Radford University. She is particularly interested in inclusive classrooms in rural schools. When she is not teaching, writing, or supervising interns, Dr. Blanks enjoys running (slowly) and learning to play more than three chords on her guitar.

Great Gifted Education

Claire E. Hughes, PhD, lives her life in twos: She is an Associate Professor at the College of Coastal Georgia in a dual-certification Elementary/ Special Education teacher preparation program and received her doctorate in both gifted education and special education from the College of William and Mary. She specializes in twice-exceptional children; lives on St. Simons Island, but works in Brunswick on the mainland; and has two children, two dogs, two cats, two fish and is one half of a two-parent team.

Engaging English Language Learners

Shartriya Collier, PhD, is currently an Associate Professor, Director of the Los Angeles Times Literacy Center and Graduate Advisor in the Department of Elementary Education at California State University, Northridge. Dr. Collier's personal teaching motto is, "transform the world, one mind at a time." When she is not teaching students or working with families in the community, she is a professional deejay and backup singer at local lounges and events in and around the Los Angeles area.

Addressing Autism Spectrum Disorder

Emily Iland, MA, is an award-winning author, advocate, filmmaker, researcher, and leader in the autism field. She travels extensively conducting training in English and Spanish on almost every autism-related topic. When she is not exhausted from doing all that stuff, she loves to research family history, which is not as boring as it sounds, honest!

Developing Deaf Education

Flavia Fleischer, PhD, is currently the Chair of the Deaf Studies Department at California State University, Northridge. She is an activist who is very interested in fighting against oppression of all minorities, especially oppression of Deaf people through her research and teaching. When Flavia is not handling department needs, teaching, or presenting, she is either out on her crazy training runs or in the kitchen experimenting with new recipes.

Will Garrow, PhD, is from upstate New York, where he was first introduced to the Deaf community through his career as a professional snowboarder. As a faculty member at California State University, Northridge his teaching mainly focuses on how oppression works in American society, Deaf culture, and ASL linguistics. When Will is not teaching, he can be found either on the snow in the mountains or splatting balls on the racquetball court.

Rachel Friedman Narr, PhD, is a Professor in Special Education/Deaf Education at California State University, Northridge. She's published and presented nationally on reading with DHH students and parent-to-parent support for families raising DHH children. She's best known for her truthiness and well . . . her husband's amazing skills in the kitchen.

Superb Social Skills Instruction

Michelle Dean is an Assistant Professor in Special Education at California State University, Channel Islands. She received her PhD from the University of California, Los Angeles. Michelle's research focuses on the social engagement of children with disabilities at school. At home, Michelle changes diapers, plays "I'm gonna get you," and cooks in real and pretend kitchens. Prior to becoming a professor and a mom, Michelle was a special education teacher for the Los Angeles Unified School District.

Fantastic Family Collaboration

Susan Auerbach, PhD, is a Professor in the Educational Leadership and Policy Studies Department at California State University, Northridge. She's published and presented extensively on family engagement, school leadership, and school-community partnerships. She enjoys relaxing with [free range] chicken TV in the backyard—the curious antics of Buffy, Little Red, Skittery, and Peck.

Introduction

What you have at your fingertips is a compilation of chapters written by individuals who not only know the theory and research in their various fields of expertise, but also know teaching *and* teachers. They are in classrooms across the nation, learning and adding to our knowledge of what really works—and unfortunately what does not work—with students today. There are so many experts nationally and internationally who write about and study different areas of education. What was important to us as we invited authors to write for this book is that they provide us with work that is timely, practical, to the point, and written so that you would want to pick it up and use it time and time again. We asked authors to talk to you, not to preach or write as if this were a research journal. We wanted humor and realism throughout the best practices and substantive content. And we think we got it!

You may notice that there are some areas of redundancy. For example, many authors ask teachers to stop talking so much, to give students more choice, to individualize and differentiate, and to connect with parents. Rather than pulling these items out, we left them to help emphasize and highlight tips that experts from differing frames of reference share. On the other hand, you might notice some discrepancies among chapters. While person first language (e.g., "the boy with the learning disability" as opposed to the "learning disabled boy") is important for many of the authors (and honestly, for us as the editors), we respected the fact that fields such as Deaf education and Gifted education don't use person-first language and instead refer to the Deaf child or the gifted student. We left those also to depict the variety in the field.

How do you use this book? That's up to you. You can read it from beginning to end or you can pick and choose. We organized it so that our content areas are first, followed by instructional strategies and pedagogy. In the third section, we include information on special populations. While some chapters may be more or less relevant to you and your teaching, we hope you consider reading them all. You may be surprised what you pick up in a chapter on working with English language learners, even if you haven't yet had any of those students in your class yet!

We'd also like to point out that we have interspersed quite a few "Making Connections" boxes throughout the chapters. This is so you can see how all of these chapters interrelate and support one another. If you want, you can make this a "Choose-Your-Own-Adventure" book and follow the Making Connections boxes throughout the text! Want to keep learning? We certainly hope you do. If so, please look at the plethora of references our authors have included and cited from. In many cases, we also provide a "Recommended Readings" section but be aware, if an item was cited in the References section, it is not in the Recommended Readings section as well. We hope you will know the author recommends it by the fact that it was important enough to reference.

We must thank each and every one of our authors for their hard work on this book. When we approached them and said, "We want you to write a practical chapter on your topic, but please keep it mainly focused on bulleting the Do's and Don'ts . . . oh right, and keep it really short," we had mixed responses. Some replied, "Heck yeah! I could do that in my sleep," while others said, "Just a few pages? On this huge topic? Are you crazy?" But they all took up the challenge and came through! They, like us, felt this book was important enough to get out there. They, like us, knew that teachers are busy and are understandably looking for something short and sweet that boils down the key information in a quick to grab format. They, like us, are passionate about education and improving what we are doing for all kids. All of them. So we thank our authors. (And yes, we owe you all a drink!)

We must also thank the Eisner Foundation for creating and supporting the Center for Teaching and Learning (CTL) at California State University, Northridge (CSUN). Their vision of ongoing professional development for urban education has enabled us to create this book in the first place. Our Dean at the CSUN Michael D. Eisner College of Education, Dr. Michael Spagna, also continues to constantly encourage us to pursue cutting edge practices in education and to remain the professional development and research hub of the college. We would like to make a "shout out" to Rick Goldman, Marcia Rea, and Amy Sheldon, who were with the CTL when we first conceptualized "What Really Works"—we hope you three are proud of where we've come! Last, but never ever least, we both would like to thank our CTL student assistants, Ashot Nikoyan and Timothy Nang, for their incredible support as we worked diligently on this text (while trying to concurrently run about 17 other projects and events). Special thanks to CTL student assistant Sam Garley, for providing indispensible behind-the-scenes help. You three are amazing, and we are grateful you have joined our CTL family.

Randy J M__ski and *Kath__ftdt*

SECTION I

What Really Works in Content

1

Making Math Meaningful

Nancy O'Rode

California State University, Northridge

WHAT REALLY WORKS IN MATH IN THE ELEMENTARY CLASSROOM

Understanding for Every Child

The last 25 years have brought a universe of changes to the field of mathematics education. We need to stop and celebrate the accomplishments of so many educators working together to improve outcomes for children. We have moved a mountain here. Rather than continuing the disagreements from the 1980s and 1990s between reform mathematics and back to basics, international studies have pushed U.S. educators to agree on higher standards for all students. Yay for us!

The 1990s ushered in a series of important international studies that scraped the skin off the notion that the United States was leading the world in producing talented mathematicians. There are many brilliant teachers and students in the United States, but we now know it is a fallacy to state that we are providing a first-rate education to our children when compared to the top-ten high-performing nations. International studies, most notably, the TIMSS (Trends in International Mathematics and Science Study), looked closely at U.S. classrooms and found several factors that need to be improved (National Center for Education Statistics, 2013; Schmidt, McKnight, & Raizen, 1996; Stigler & Heibert, 1999). But rather than pack it up and go home, we have, as a group of educators, come up with a vision and a plan for improvement. Double-yay.

Equity is the overarching goal in teaching and learning mathematics because no matter how many research studies and findings are published, it will not make a difference in the lives of children if they have not been given an opportunity to learn mathematics with understanding. The *Principles and Standards for School Mathematics* (National Council of Teachers of Mathematics, 1989, 2000) is a clarion call for educators to pay attention and work toward mathematical understanding for all children.

We need to provide high-quality, worthwhile tasks for learning mathematics for every child and at every grade level (Stein, Smith, Henningsen, & Silver, 2000). Teachers can hardly be asked to change the way they teach if they continue to use the same materials that were used when they were children. We need high-quality resources that help teachers deliver demanding lessons that require students to explain solutions. Superficially, it seems that we now have many technologies to improve children's mathematical understanding, but most of these applications are only flashier flashcards. We need to have children practice the basic facts, but only after they have explored and understood the concepts. The essence of good teaching is providing engaging lessons that facilitate learning mathematical concepts before learning the procedures.

Assessments are another key to improving mathematics learning. In the last decade when high-stakes assessments were created to evaluate learning and teaching, we went off the rails in teaching to the test. Teachers, with the pressures of testing and the resultant evaluation, left what they knew to be solid pedagogical ideas to instead cram procedures into their students' heads. This was unfortunate because many research studies showed that children do as well or better if activities that introduce and extend concep-

Making Connections

Check out Chapter 14 on Assessment

tual ideas are provided rather than beginning with the procedures (National Council of Teachers of Mathematics, 2000; see also Grouws & Cebulla, 2000; Hiebert, 2003). Feeding students math facts without the *why* is like giving a daily survival diet of crumbs without the enjoyment of the feast. Many school districts around the country have subsequently signed up for new 21st century assessments that ask children to explain their thinking rather than pick one choice out of four on a multiple-choice test. The new assessments focus on the big picture rather than a diet of crumbs.

The current trends in mathematics teaching and learning tell us that we need to change the way we are teaching, which will change the way children are learning mathematics. We also need to change the way we assess learning (Hertzog & O'Rode, 2011). Ultimately, the underlying principle of every teacher who teaches math needs to be that of ensuring every child has an understanding of rigorous, useful, connected mathematics. Though we now have principles, standards, and priorities that are integrated, rigorous, and meaningful, teachers need to be able to implement these ideals each day in the classroom. We each need to take a long hard look at what we, as individuals, are doing in the classroom, and it will take brutal honesty to evaluate and change the way we teach. To move forward will require collaboration, the sharing of ideas, and lots of trial and error. We can do this.

KEY RESEARCH YOU NEED TO KNOW ABOUT TEACHING ELEMENTARY MATHEMATICS

Common misconceptions about math are that it is cut and dried and easy to teach, that it is a universal language and has to do with correct answers, or that anyone can teach math if they like numbers. Not so fast! The following research-based ideas are being used successfully in elementary classrooms today and should cause many to rethink what math teaching is about.

Deborah Ball and her colleagues got it right when they wrote *Knowing Mathematics for Teaching: Who Knows Mathematics Well Enough to Teach Third Grade and How Can We Decide?* (Ball, Hill, & Bass, 2005). They break down the work of teaching and pinpoint various tasks that successful teachers need to accomplish in everyday lessons, such as analyzing errors, choosing representations, evaluating mathematical explanations, designing homework and quizzes, and evaluating student work, to name a few. Who better to define the work that teachers do than teachers, the authors ask. They call for a professional knowledge base that is backed with evidence of what it means to know mathematics for teaching (Ball, 1993; Ball & Bass, 2003). When teachers have this specialized knowledge for mathematics teaching, findings show student achievement scores increase significantly (Hill, Rowan, & Ball, 2005). This specialized knowledge includes using invented strategies, open-ended questions, high-cognitive demand tasks, and discussing concepts before procedures, which are discussed here. Other important techniques, such as using a diversity of representations and energizing classroom discourse are critical as well, and teachers are encouraged to research these ideas in *Putting Research Into Practice in the Elementary Grades* (National Council of Teachers of Mathematics, 2002).

Invented strategies are procedures that children create or invent without the teacher directly instructing the child. Children have traditionally learned procedures for carrying out calculations from step-by-step instruction led by the teacher. Because standard algorithms are conceptually dense procedures created over many, many years, students (and adults) often have a difficult time understanding why the algorithm works. Carpenter, Franke, Jacobs, Fennema, and Empson (1998) studied children in Grades 1 through 3 over several years and found that almost all children could invent strategies. The children who used invented strategies before learning about the standard algorithm gained a deeper understanding of place value, were more successful in carrying out the calculations, and made fewer errors. Students were flexible in using a variety of strategies to solve problems, using both the standard algorithm and invented strategies. One important tool students can use is an Empty Number Line to illustrate their invented strategies. (See page 14 for examples.) Teachers should promote the use of invented strategies in their classrooms by asking children to solve problems in two or more ways and highlighting different strategies during class discussions. Note that the word *algorithm* is not found in the Common Core Standards until Grade 3, which reflects recent research on invented strategies.

Open-ended problems are problems that can be solved in more than one way. There are many ways to provide open-ended questions: create questions with more than one solution, ask for two or more strategies to solve the problem, require an explanation, or ask for two ways to represent the solution. If you allow students to make sense of a problem in their own way, they feel capable of doing math. Open-ended problems are also a good way to differentiate so that the gifted children and students with disabilities can be successful. If this is new to your classroom, persevere. Students will push back because it is so much more comfortable to follow someone else's thinking than to produce your own. When we focus the attention on students' various ideas, they are less fearful of making mistakes. (See page 12 for examples.)

High-cognitive demand tasks are worthwhile, high-level, challenging problems for the mathematics classroom that are important to develop students' ideas of what it means to do mathematics. Henningsen and Stein (1997) identify classrooms that scaffold learning, build upon prior knowledge, and have sustained pressure for explanation and meaning when using high-level tasks. In other classrooms, where the challenging parts of the problem were removed, or the focus shifted to the correctness of the answer, students' thinking declined toward using procedures and the classwork had little connection to the mathematical concepts. Complexity of a task is often reduced when students press teachers for the procedure and teachers respond by showing students how to do the difficult parts of the task (Henningsen, 2000). High-cognitive demand tasks should require student accountability, encouraging students to explore and use relevant knowledge in appropriate ways, and may create some anxiety for the student because of the creative nature of the solution process (Smith & Stein, 1998). (For self-reflection guide on teaching mathematics, see page 14.)

Pesek and Kirshner (2000) showed that we do have the time to *teach for understanding*. In an experimental study, these researchers gave half of the fifth-grade classrooms an extra five lessons for procedural skill development in area and perimeter. These students then joined the other classrooms, which were given three conceptual lessons on area and perimeter. After assessing all students through interviews and written tests, they found that students who had only three conceptual lessons knew area and perimeter concepts far better than the students who were given an extra five procedural lessons in addition to the three conceptual lessons. What? Three lessons can be more effective than eight lessons? The take away here is that teaching concepts *before* procedures improves understanding, ultimately saving time. We *do* have the time to teach for conceptual understanding. You can build a sandcastle every day, but it is gone in 12 hours. We need to do the hard work of building concrete foundations if we want something permanent. So dig deep, concentrate on the concepts first, and teach for understanding.

WHAT YOU NEED TO AVOID AT ALL COSTS IN TEACHING MATHEMATICS IN ELEMENTARY SCHOOL

If I had a magic wand, I would wave it around and shout, "*Expelliarmus*" every time a teacher does any of the following.

Teachers

- ✗ **STOP telling children how to solve math problems.** Giving students the steps to solve a problem does not produce understanding. Research shows that when teachers give the steps, it produces very limited memorized procedures without understanding. What, you say? I learned math this way. Yes, me too. But we need to stop this self-perpetuating cycle of innumeracy. Math should make sense to children and big people too.
- ✗ **STOP relying on math textbooks.** Textbooks have low-level, irrelevant problems, or, I should say, practice exercises that do not give children rigorous math problem-solving situations called for in today's Common Core era. That's the hard part; as teachers, we are trying to up the game here, but most of us learned math by the *gorge and regurgitate* method. We need to seek materials elsewhere and create our own teaching communities by sharing what works.
- ✗ **STOP telling children if they are right or wrong.** Once you admit that a solution is correct, children stop thinking about the

mathematics involved. Don't be the all-knowing source for correctness—children need to make sense of the mathematics and determine for themselves if their answers are right or wrong.

✗ **STOP giving fill-in-the-blank worksheets.** Yes, students need to practice basic number facts—but find enjoyable ways for children to practice. Engage children in activities that reveal concepts and procedures rather than individual worksheets. Think about it—which would you rather do?

✗ **STOP giving timed tests.** As Marilyn Burns (2000) says, "Timed tests make no instructional sense" (p. 157). Timed tests do not promote sense-making approaches. Most adults begin their negative associations with math at third grade timed tests. I have asked over 2,000 preservice teachers about their experiences with mathematics, and timed tests in third grade is the number one reason they loathe mathematics, with ability grouping coming in a close second. The new 21st century achievement tests will not have strict time limits.

✗ **STOP wasting time on chapter tests and reviewing for chapter tests.** Some teachers give up 2 days a week to testing and review rather than learning. Give short, matter-of-fact quizzes or short tests. Short evaluations that are framed as: "Here is what I want you to learn. Have you learned it? Tomorrow I will be asking you to do this. Let's find out if you can." Then ask students how confident they are that they can solve or explain the idea. This is not to say that you only want quizzes. Good teachers integrate valuable and varied assessments into the work that the students are already doing.

Administrators

✗ **STOP looking for quiet classrooms where children are completing worksheets.** Teachers and children need to be engaged in solving problems—and this is a messy, noisy process.

✗ **STOP micromanaging the length of daily math lessons.** Give teaching professionals the courtesy of being able to spend 1 hour and 15 minutes on a math lesson, if it is called for, and making up the time for other subjects in the next few days. Flexibility is the key.

✗ **STOP focusing on scores.** You are a manager of people, not test scores. So concentrate on the humans under your care. Feed. Water. Provide support. Prune when needed. Celebrate growth and good teaching. Increases in test scores only come from effective teaching.

✗ **DON'T even think about equating scores from your state accountability assessments to the new assessments for Common Core.** Higher performance standards. Different test quality, testing methods, and proficiency levels. They are not comparable—so don't go there.

STRATEGIES FOR SUCCESS
IN TEACHING ELEMENTARY MATHEMATICS

"Be careful what you teach children—they will learn it." This is a quote from a math educator and dear friend. If we teach children to solve simplistic, mind-numbing exercises, that is what they will learn to do. If we teach children to fill in the blanks, that is what they will learn. If we teach children to choose the best answer out of four choices, that is what they will become good at doing. If we want critical thinkers who can creatively find solutions to complex problems, then we need to ask students to solve high-cognitive demand problems.

Teachers, DO This

- ✓ **CELEBRATE divergent thinking by asking all students to find another way to solve a problem.** Asking students to listen to and accept other's solutions, or argue and disagree, emphasizes reasoning. This strengthens the caliber of connections needed for deeply understanding a math concept (Fosnot, 1996).
- ✓ **USE open-ended questions, and make solving the problem the feature of the math lesson.** Feature multiple ways of knowing so students will concentrate on the process of solving rather than the product. Ask for other ways to solve a problem. "Does anyone have a different way to solve this problem? Let's hear from you."
- ✓ **ASK for explanations and don't give up. It is easier if you begin the year demanding explanations.** And, of course, an explanation for 5 + 1 isn't the point. High-cognitive demand, rigorous problems for all age groups will lead to several solution strategies and hence explanations will be a natural part of classroom discussions.
- ✓ **ENCOURAGE argument.** Yes, argument. The best classes occur when students are investing an effort to find out who is right. These can be edge-of-seat discussions. Who really *is* correct? Can both solutions be right? How can that be?
- ✓ **USE blank paper.** Hold students responsible for organizing their own thinking. We do too much for students sometimes. Giving out pages that have predetermined work spaces or blanks to fill in answers does not allow children to develop their own way to show solutions—ownership of the solution is then transferred to the teacher or worksheet.
- ✓ **If you use a traditional textbook, USE it as a resource for exercises and homework practice.** Traditional texts are set up for minimal thinking and minimal student responsibility for learning. (There are also minimal difficulties for teachers.) Excellent teachers go beyond the minimal expectations and work at creating lessons

that push students' thinking. Parents expect practice, and children do need accuracy and fluency for number facts, so have students practice at home.

✓ **SUBSTITUTE appreciation in place of praise.** Substitute "thank-you" in place of "great work." Excellent teachers bite their tongue before saying "good job" or "right." The children, for the most part, ignore and dismiss meaningless praise and stop thinking about the mathematics. An appreciation of the effort children give in solving problems has more lasting importance than evaluating the correctness of the answer (Willingham, 2009).

✓ **FINALLY, one of the most demanding aspects of teaching mathematics is tying the divergent ideas from students together to summarize the learning.** This is when you make explicit connections from students' ideas to the learning objective. You mention ideas from each group and restate explicitly how each idea fits into the overall learning objective. It's powerful and satisfying for students to know that their efforts had a purpose. This is also time to introduce ideas for tomorrow's problem-solving!

Administrators, DO This

✓ **SUPPORT your district, teachers, and parents by explaining upfront how the new state assessments will not be comparable to the old state assessments.** Tell all constituents to expect an increase in rigor, an increased focus on conceptual understanding, and many hours of work to meet these new standards. It will take time and resources to prepare students for the new assessment format. Children who excel at drill and practice may not do well on assessments that ask for explanations. Parents need to hear this. Have high expectations and give strong support to teachers during this transition and innovation. Encourage your teachers. Perseverance in problem-solving isn't only for students; everyone needs to persevere to support these new rigorous standards (Larson & Leinwand, 2013).

WHY USE OPEN-ENDED PROBLEMS IN MATHEMATICS?

- Provide Multiple Entry Points for students
- Differentiate Instruction for many developmental levels
- Meet needs of both struggling learners and promising students who need challenges

The following chart gives 17 examples of Open-Ended Problems.

	Type of Open-Ended Problem	*Example*
1	Ask for more than one strategy	"Can you show two different ways to add 24 and 37?"
2	Show more than one representation	"Use numbers, pictures, and words to show your answer."
3	Require an explanation	"Please explain how you know you have the correct solution."
4	Ask for more than one solution	"Find three ways that the sisters can spend $10."
5	Ask for a story problem and solution	"Write a story problem using the numbers 3, 5, and 15. Solve the problem."
6	Begin with the answer and ask for possibilities	"Find all the number combinations that make 16," or "What are three different ways that Henrietta could spend $15 on carnival rides?"
7	Create many possibilities by using dice, number cards, or spinner	"Use two dice and three number cards to make an addition problem. Solve the problem."
8	Put a constraint on the problem	"How could you find the area of a trapezoid without using the formula?" or "The 6 key on the calculator is broken. How could you solve the problem without using the 6 key?"
9	Use a range of numbers in the problem	"Use the numbers 4, 5, 6, and 7 to make as many addition problems as you can. Solve."
10	Use a developmental progression in the problem	"First draw a picture of the shape, identify the shape by name, and describe the shape using as many properties as you can."

	Type of Open-Ended Problem	Example
11	Connect problem situation to real world and ask for expertise	"Design three different sized boxes to hold 24 chocolate candies. Tell which box is the best design and why."
12	Ask for similarities and differences	"How are the numbers 75 and 100 alike? How are 75 and 100 different?" "How are the numbers 3.007 and 8.002 alike? Different?"
13	Replace a number with a blank	"Mr. Reynoldo's class has ____ students. Ms. Chen's class has ____ students. How many students are there altogether?"
14	Ask for a number sentence	"Use the numbers 8 and 7 as well as the words 'product' and 'equal' to create a number sentence. Can you find more than one sentence?"
15	Change a textbook question	*Textbook:* "What number has 4 hundreds, 5 tens, and 3 ones?" *Change to:* "You can use 8 base ten blocks to model a number. What could the number be?"
16	Student choice in working with numbers	"The diameter of a chocolate cookie is between 2 and 3 inches. Give the diameter as a fraction using two different ways."
		"You multiply two numbers and the product is almost 600. What could the numbers have been? Explain."
		"Choose a fraction and a percentage. Tell which is greater and how you know."
17	Use parallel tasks that explore the same idea but fit different developmental levels	"What coin combinations can you use to show your amount?" *Option 1:* 12 cents; *Option 2:* 60 cents

Resources

Kiberi, M. S., & Smith, N. L. (2003). Turning traditional textbook problems into open-ended problems. *Mathematics Teaching in the Middle School, 9*(3), 186–192.

Myren, C. (2013). *Posing open-ended questions in the primary math classroom.* Bellingham, WA: Math Perspectives.

Small, M. (2009). *Good questions: Great ways to differentiate mathematics instruction.* New York, NY: Teachers College Press.

SO HOW AM I DOING? A SELF-REFLECTION ON TEACHING MATHEMATICS

Provide specific examples from a math lesson you recently taught for the questions below.

	What Really Worked?	*Shoulda/Coulda*
Problem-Solving Did I actively engage students in problem-solving?		
Explanations Did I have students make sense of math by explaining & reasoning?		
Representations Did the class use multiple ways to represent ideas?		
Connections Did you make real-world connections?		

THE EMPTY NUMBER LINE

The *Empty Number Line* is a tool that supports children's invented strategies. Using an empty number line, children can illustrate and explain their way of thinking about solving addition or subtraction problems (Klein, Beishuizen, & Treffers, 1998). It is empty because it is a simple line without numbers and evenly spaced hash marks (which often confound children). In the Netherlands, where the research was conducted, children begin with a length of 100 beads on a string, which alternate color every 10 beads (e.g., 10 white beads alternating with 10 green beads). When using the bead string, children familiarize themselves with numbers as tens and ones and also become familiar with the positions of numbers from 1 to 100. Children then transfer these ideas to the empty number line by placing a number on the line and then jumping up the number line by ones, tens, or eventually multiples of tens. Children must make decisions on how to solve the addition or subtraction problems and actively show these decisions by drawing them on the number line. The transparent character of the moves shown on the number line helps children develop their own strategies and communicate their solutions and, in doing so, also develop a deep understanding of the concepts of addition and subtraction.

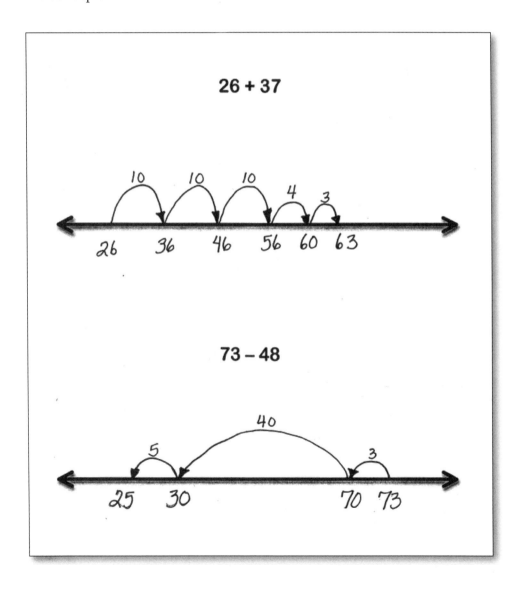

REFERENCES

Ball, D. L. (1993). With an eye on the mathematical horizon: Dilemmas of teaching elementary school mathematics. *Elementary School Journal, 93,* 373–397.

Ball, D. L., & Bass, H. (2003). Toward a practice-based theory of mathematical knowledge for teaching. In B. Davis & E. Simmt (Eds.), *Proceedings of the 2002 annual meetings of the Canadian Mathematics Education Study Group* (pp. 3–14). Edmonton, Alberta, Canada: Canadian Mathematics Education Study Group.

Ball, D. L., Hill, H. C., & Bass, H. (2005). Knowing mathematics for teaching: Who knows mathematics well enough to teach third grade, and how can we decide? *American Educator, 29*(1), 14–17, 20–22, 43–46.

Burns, M. (2000). *About teaching mathematics.* Sausalito, CA: Math Solutions.

Carpenter, T. P., Franke, M. L., Jacobs, V. R., Fennema, E., & Empson, S. B. (1998). A longitudinal study of invention and understanding in children's multidigit addition and subtraction. *Journal for Research in Mathematics Education, 29,* 3–20.

Fosnot, C. T. (1996). Constructivism: A psychological theory of learning. In C. T. Fosnot (Ed.), *Constructivism: Theory, perspectives, and practice* (pp. 8–33). New York, NY: Teachers College Press.

Grouws, D. A., & Cebulla, K. J. (2000). *Improving student achievement in mathematics.* Geneva, Switzerland: International Academy of Education.

Henningsen, M. (2000). Triumph through adversity: Supporting high-level thinking. *Mathematics Teaching in the Middle School, 6,* 244–248.

Henningsen, M., & Stein, M. K. (1997). Supporting students' high-level thinking, reasoning, and communication in mathematics. In J. Sowder & B. Schappelle (Eds.), *Lessons learned from research* (pp. 27–35). Reston, VA: National Council of Teachers of Mathematics.

Hertzog, H., & O'Rode, N. (2011). Improving the quality of elementary mathematics student teaching: Using field support materials to develop reflective practice in student teachers. *Teacher Education Quarterly, 38*(3), 89–111.

Hiebert, J. (2003). What research says about the NCTM standards. In J. Kilpatrick, W. G. Martin, & D. Schifter (Eds.), *A research companion to principles and standards for school mathematics* (pp. 5–23). Reston, VA: National Council of Teachers of Mathematics.

Hill, H., Rowan, B., & Ball, D. (2005). Effects of teachers' mathematical knowledge for teaching on student achievement. *American Educational Research Journal, 42*(2), 371–406.

Klein, A. S., Beishuizen, M., & Treffers, A. (1998). The empty number line in Dutch second grades: Realistic versus gradual program design. *Journal for Research in Mathematics Education, 29,* 443–464.

Larson, M. R., & Leinwand, S. (2013). Prepare for more realistic test results. *Mathematics Teacher, 106*(9), 656–659.

National Center for Education Statistics. (2013). *United States mathematics and science achievement in 2011* [Data file]. Retrieved from http://nces.ed.gov/timss/results11_states11.asp

National Council of Teachers of Mathematics. (1989). *Curriculum and evaluation standards for school mathematics.* Reston, VA: Author.

National Council of Teachers of Mathematics. (2000). *Principles and standards for school mathematics.* Reston, VA: Author.

Pesek, D. D., & Kirshner, D. (2000). Interference of instrumental instruction in subsequent relational learning. *Journal for Research in Mathematics Education, 31,* 524–540.

Schmidt, W. H., McKnight, C. C., & Raizen, S. A. (1996). *A splintered vision: An investigation of U.S. science and mathematics education.* Boston, MA: Kluwer.

Smith, M. S., & Stein, M. K. (1998). Selecting and creating mathematical tasks: From research to practice. *Mathematics Teaching in the Middle School, 3,* 344–350.

Stein, M. K., Smith, M. S., Henningsen, M., & Silver, E. A. (2000). *Implementing standards-based mathematics instruction: A casebook for professional development.* New York, NY: Teachers College Press.

Stigler, J., & Heibert, J. (1999). *The teaching gap: Best ideas from the world's teachers for improving education in the classroom.* New York, NY: Simon & Schuster.

Willingham, D. (2009). *Why don't students like school? A cognitive scientist answers questions about how the mind works and what it means for the classroom.* San Francisco, CA: Wiley & Sons.

RECOMMENDED READINGS

* Carpenter, T. P., Franke, M., & Levi, L. (2003). *Thinking mathematically: Integrating arithmetic and algebra in elementary school.* Portsmouth, NH: Heinemann.

* Myren, C. (2013). *Posing open-ended questions in the primary math classroom.* Bellingham, WA: Math Perspectives.

* National Council of Teachers of Mathematics. (2002). *Putting research into practice in the elementary grades: Readings from the journals of the National Council of Teachers of Mathematics.* Reston, VA: Author.

* Sowder, J., & Schappelle, B. (2002). *Lessons learned from research.* Reston, VA: NCTM.

* Van de Walle, J. A., Karp, K., & Bay-Williams, J. M. (2010). *Elementary and middle school mathematics: Teaching developmentally* (8th ed.). Boston, MA: Pearson.

GO EVEN FURTHER WITH THIS TOPIC ON THE WORLD WIDE WEB

- www.illuminations.nctm.org
- www.nlvm.usu.edu/en/nav/vlibrary.html
- www.corestandards.org
- www.robertkaplinsky.com/lessons
- www.myboe.org/
- ime.math.arizona.edu/progressions/
- www.scoe.org/pub/htdocs/ccss-mathematics.html
- www.engageny.org/
- www.bowlandmaths.org.uk/index.html
- www.illustrativemathematics.org

THE Apps WE LOVE

- Math Concentration
- Pick-a-Path
- Deep Sea Duel
- Grouping and Grazing
- Isometric Drawing Tool

2

Rewarding Reading Practices

Renee Ziolkowska

California State University, Northridge

WHAT REALLY WORKS IN READING IN THE ELEMENTARY CLASSROOM

Why Do We Read?

What comes to mind when you hear the word *reading?* Is it an image of relaxing with a good book, or is it something that produces anxiety? For many of us, as teachers, we enjoy reading and are probably good at it. That is one reason some of us became teachers—we were successful in reading and in school. However, many students struggle with reading and do not find it enjoyable, which is difficult for some of us to understand. In this chapter, you will find suggestions on how to help students learn to read and enjoy it, too!

Why do we read? Well, there are many reasons, such as enjoyment, entertainment, to gain information, to be able to do certain things, and so on. Reading is an important skill for success in our society. When children cannot read, it limits what they can do and the opportunities they have.

We know that teaching reading is complex. There are various perspectives on how best to teach children to read. Some of these perspectives are in conflict with each other (e.g., holistic vs. skill-based reading approaches), which makes it more challenging for teachers to make the best decisions related to reading in their classrooms. In addition, our classrooms are now more diverse and more students with special needs are identified, thus making the teaching of reading even more challenging.

In the following pages, suggestions are listed for the teaching of reading to elementary school children—what really works and what does not.

WHAT IS READING?

What is reading? Is it simply decoding the words on a page or is there more to it? A standard dictionary definition of reading (or to read) might sound something like this: "To examine and grasp the meaning of written or printed characters, words, or sentences." This definition is not sufficient because without understanding what we read, there is little or no purpose for reading. In the next several pages, essential components of an effective reading program will be discussed.

In the past, the focus of reading was on the mechanics. We now know that the main goal is for students to construct meaning as they interact with text (Pearson, Roehler, Dole, & Duffy, 1990). Reading should always be an active process! Students need instruction as well as opportunities to practice what they have learned in the following areas: phonemic awareness, phonics, high-frequency words, vocabulary, comprehension, and fluency.

It is important to remember that there needs to be balance in a literacy program: modeled reading/reading aloud, shared reading, guided reading, and independent reading as well as modeled writing, shared writing, guided writing, and independent writing. Students who do much reading tend to be very good readers. Students who read more books and are given a choice in what to read have a positive attitude toward reading (Cline & Kretke, 1980).

Teachers also need to differentiate instruction. Students benefit from flexible grouping, especially those who struggle with reading. It is especially important to meet the needs of beginning readers. "Researchers agree that if instruction for struggling students is to be beneficial, that support needs to begin early, as soon as difficulties emerge. It is much harder to help children if problems are detected later . . . early intervention and quality instruction are the key to helping more learners be successful" (Ziolkowska, 2007, p. 76). Not all students are the same kinds of readers or have the same affinity or skill toward reading; differentiation encourages teachers to recognize this diversity and mix it up as needed.

It is important to value the experience and knowledge that students bring to the classroom. Our schools tend to be more individualistic and value students doing things independently. However, children who are Hispanic, African American, and American Indian come from families that value collectivism or are group oriented (Trumbull, Rothstein-Fisch, & Greenfield, 2000). Teachers need to be aware that there may be differences between what families value and what schools value. It is common to sometimes feel overwhelmed when you cannot reach all the students in your diverse classrooms. Don't give up! Instead, search for ways that will support the learning needs of all your students. Teachers can have a profound impact on the literacy lives of their students. Remember, you can make a difference!

One last thing—teacher quality is the most important factor in determining how well students learn (Vandevoort, Amrein-Beardsley, & Berliner, 2004). Teachers need to understand what reading is and how best to teach children to read. They need to be aware that what worked in the teaching of reading years ago may not be best practice today. Effective teachers of reading need to stay current and familiar with research on the teaching of reading and make decisions that are best for their students . . . because reading is a skill students will use throughout their lives!

 ## INEFFECTIVE STRATEGIES FOR TEACHING READING IN THE ELEMENTARY CLASSROOM

- ✗ **STOP using the words *reading* and *decoding* synonymously.** They are not the same. Decoding is sounding out the letters/letter patterns in a word, whereas reading means that there is an understanding of the text. We need to get our students to do more than decode; they need to *read!*
- ✗ **STOP using Round Robin (the practice of students taking turns reading one by one out loud) in class.** Most students will stop listening to their peers reading. Instead, they will try to figure out what section they will need to read and practice their part so that they do not embarrass themselves in front of their peers. By not paying attention to those who read before them, they miss out on a learning opportunity.
- ✗ **STOP asking questions that have only one possible correct answer.** Instead, ask questions that promote discussion. Don't simply ask *what* questions, integrate *why, how,* and *what if* questions. Also, encourage students to pose their own questions. Harvey and Goudvis (2007) explain that very young children have many questions; however, by the time they reach upper elementary grades, they hardly ask any questions. They state, "Schools do not foster questions. Schools demand answers—answers to teachers' questions . . . " (p. 18). In addition, promote thinking at different levels.

- ✖ **STOP doing timed reading/fluency tests.** These tests give children the wrong message—that students who read the fastest are the best readers. Of course, we know that is not always true. Sometimes when students read too quickly, they do not have enough time to process what they read, and therefore, they do not comprehend what they just read. Fluency means that students can decode words easily and accurately, chunk words into meaningful phrases, and use appropriate intonation and expression.

- ✖ **STOP teaching a skill or strategy just once and assuming that the students understand.** Most often students need multiple exposures and practice before they fully understand a new concept. The key is to reteach and practice the skill or strategies in various ways . . . so students don't get bored. Incorporate fun activities and games when reviewing.

- ✖ **STOP using the one-size-fits-all model.** Students have different needs—some are reading at grade level, while others are reading above or below grade level. Doing only whole class reading will not meet their needs. Small group instruction, such as guided reading (Fountas & Pinnell, 1996), is much more effective. The purpose of reading groups is to meet the reading needs of all the students in the classroom. Guided reading is different than the traditional basal reading groups where students tend to stay in the same group throughout the year (and often beyond). Guided reading groups are flexible, and the student composition in these groups changes throughout the school year based on their needs. The benefit of guided reading is that students read text at their level or slightly above with the support of a teacher. Learn more about guided reading at the URL in the Plugged In box.

Plugged In

www.readwritethink.org/

rmsra.wikispaces.com/file/view/Student+reading+survey.pdf

www.professorgarfield.org/

- ✖ **STOP reading from only one text.** Instead, use multiple texts such as fiction, nonfiction, magazines, articles, and books of varying difficulty, as well as electronic texts. By doing this, you will meet the interests and needs of all your students.

- ✖ **STOP over-assessing students.** When used appropriately, assessments can be beneficial (they can inform your teaching). However, too much time spent on assessment takes time away from instruction. Observations and reflections on what students do on a daily basis can be extremely informative.

- ✖ **STOP reteaching the same concepts in the same exact way.** If students did not learn it the first time, it is most likely they will not get it the second time if it's taught in the same exact way. It is crucial to reteach, but do so in a variety of ways. You may even want to ask students to explain their understanding to their peers.

✘ **STOP using rote memorization/drilling of facts for everything—it's ineffective.** Students may recall the information for the test but will most likely not retain it. Instead, teach it in a way that relates to the students' lives or allows them to experience it in some way. They will learn it more deeply that way and remember it better.

✘ **STOP asking students to look up and write definitions for a long list of vocabulary words.** This is an ineffective way to learn new words because students are simply copying words and not thinking what the words mean.

✘ **STOP teaching vocabulary words for only the length of the unit and never returning to review these words.** Children need multiple exposures to words before they really own them (using the words in their speech and writing).

✘ **STOP asking students to respond to readings with only book reports.** There are so many different and engaging ways to respond to readings.

✘ **STOP making reading boring or a task.** Show your enthusiasm for books . . . it will be contagious!

✘ **STOP talking so much.** Many children are passive and bored in schools. One of the reasons is that teachers do most of the talking and doing. Let's rethink how learning occurs in the classroom. Wong and Wong (2001) state:

The reason teachers are so tired at the end of the school day is that they have been working. If I worked as hard as many teachers do, I'd be tired, too. But have you ever noticed what happens at 3 o'clock when the students leave? "Yea, yea, yea!" Why are they so full of energy? Because they have been sitting in school all day doing nothing while the teacher is doing all the work. The person who does the work is the only one doing any learning! (p. 205)

IDEAS AND STRATEGIES TO CREATE EFFECTIVE READING INSTRUCTION FOR ELEMENTARY STUDENTS

✓ **CREATE a classroom community.** Create a classroom climate/ environment where all students feel welcomed, respected, and part of a community of learners. Get to know your students by asking them what they are good at and what is important to them. You may want to ask students (or their parents) to write you a letter introducing themselves (or their child) at the beginning of the school year.

✓ **ADMINISTER a reading survey.** Find out your students' attitude toward reading by creating or using a premade reading interest/attitude survey or questionnaire, such as the Elementary Reading Attitude Survey (McKenna & Kear, 1990). You may want to visit the websites identified in the Plugged In box.

✓ **OBSERVE your students.** Become good at *kid watching* (Goodman, 1978). Learn to closely observe them in the classroom, and take anecdotal notes on their strengths and needs.

✓ **TAKE TIME to build motivation.** Share with students your passion for reading. This can be very motivating for some students. Also, provide opportunities for students to read highly engaging, motivating material. You may also want to display books all over the classroom. Interesting books may inspire students to want to read more. Bring in a new book from time to time and read a little from it (a few pages or a chapter). Then leave it on the chalkboard ledge . . . you'll be surprised how many students will be curious and pick it up to read.

✓ **BUILD phonemic awareness.** When working with younger students, devote time to phonemic awareness (the ability to manipulate the sounds in words). This can be done in fun and engaging ways: Use a puppet and ask students to blend the sounds (e.g., /sh/ /i/ /p/), or segment sounds in a word (e.g., *sun*). Play and sing songs, such as *Down by the Bay, Willoughby Wallaby Woo,* or *Apples and Bananas,* and ask students to make up rhyming words or manipulate sounds. Bring a yoga mat and explain to the students that they are going to stretch their body, then explain how they are going to stretch words and listen for all the sounds (e.g., s-w-i-m). Play a bean bag toss game where students toss a bean bag for each sound they hear in a word. Some other ideas you may want to try: read Dr. Seuss books, bring in lots of rhyming books, use nursery rhymes, share texts that contain alliteration, bring in alphabet books, use tongue twisters, share and create rhymes, clap syllables in someone's name, read or chant poems, and so on. Keep in mind that researchers have concluded that phonemic awareness is a powerful predictor of later reading achievement. So be sure to devote time to it!

✓ **START with a morning message.** Write a morning message each day to help beginning readers learn concepts about print (basic understandings about the way print works, such as: direction of print, what is a letter/word). If you can, make it funny or interesting or have it incorporate your students' names and interests. A morning message can be written by the teacher or together by the teacher and students. Some teachers make purposeful mistakes on the morning message and when students come into the classroom they are asked to be detectives and search for the mistakes . . . they love this!

✓ **USE the Language Experience Approach (LEA).** Children have many wonderful stories in their head, but the minute you ask them to write it down, some children don't know what to write. LEA is beneficial to all students, but especially English language learners and struggling writers, by allowing children to dictate their stories or experiences while someone else writes their words down. Later, the story is read by the students and the teacher. This promotes reading, writing, and vocabulary development. LEA can be done one-on-one with a student, in small groups, and as a whole class. The story can be written on chart paper, on the board, on PowerPoint, on an interactive whiteboard, a laptop, or on other electronic formats. Don't forget to use technology if you are too busy to have students dictate to you! Students can use Dragon Dictate or other speech to text software, videotape themselves on a smart phone or iPad, or import photos and music to enhance their writing.

✓ **TEACH phonics.** Devote time to teaching phonics (the relationship between letters and sounds). You can use flip books, cube words, alphabet books, tongue twisters, Elkonin boxes, and Making Words (Cunningham & Cunningham, 1992). With younger students, you can do a beginning of the year activity by exploring student names. For example, if you have students with the names *Sophia* and *Sam*, ask students how the two names are similar and different.

✓ **TEACH, use, and review high-frequency words (on the Word Wall).** Teach high-frequency words (words that appear often in print) in the lower grades because some of these words are difficult to decode (e.g., *the, of, have*) and children encounter them often in text. Make a high-frequency word wall (words displayed on a wall or the board) and refer to these words often. Tips for doing a word wall: (a) be selective about what words go up on the word wall, (b) add words gradually, (c) make the words accessible by placing them where everyone can see them easily, (d) practice the words in different ways (e.g., chanting and writing them), (e) review the words frequently (e.g., playing games), and (f) make sure that word wall words are spelled correctly in student writing. Want to make it really fun? Use Murawski's (2010) Magic Tablecloth to have a dynamic word wall. Tape a plastic tablecloth to a wall or window and spray it with adhesive spray. Then students can put their words up on paper, index cards, paper plates, or any other light material without sticky notes or other adhesive. Goes up easily and can be quickly changed around, sorted, and used for activities.

✓ **BUILD your students' vocabulary/word knowledge.** Vocabulary knowledge is the most important predictor of reading comprehension. Wide reading is the most common way children learn vocabulary. Students who have difficulty with reading may not learn words as easily on their own and will need direct instruction. Teach vocabulary words in relationship to other words and ideas in the text. In addition, using a word map (see page 32) and other graphic organizers as well as word sorts will allow students to gain a better understanding of words. Discussions should be a component of all vocabulary instruction. Display the words in the classroom for at least the length of the instruction unit, if not longer (adding an image next to the word is very helpful). Children need many exposures to words so they can learn them deeply enough to comprehend reading and to use them in speaking and writing. Word activities and games (e.g., Bingo, Jeopardy, Hedbanz, Twister, Taboo, Memory, Pictionary, Vocabulary Parade, and Charades) are good ways to provide exposure to new words . . . plus, they are fun!

✓ **MONITOR comprehension.** The goal of reading is to understand what is read. Simply sounding out words on a page without understanding them is not *reading,* it's *decoding.* Comprehension is a complex process where the reader constructs meaning by interacting with the text. Reading comprehension is a critical component to being successful in school and the workplace. Work on comprehension strategies with the students, and be sure to explain what each strategy is and why it's important. Also, model how to use the strategy in context, and finally, provide opportunities for guided practice (with a partner or in small group) and independent practice.

✓ **DON'T FORGET to teach and use graphic organizers.** Use graphic organizers (e.g., Venn diagram, story map, fact and opinion, KWL, flow chart, and other webbing charts and maps) to help students organize material more clearly. Graphic organizers can be used before reading, during, and/or after reading a text. One of the most effective ways to prepare students to focus on what they are about to read is to use an Anticipation Guide—Agree/Disagree Chart (see the end of this chapter for an example). Remember, organizers and maps should not be used as worksheets; their purpose is to help students see connections. Make sure to model all organizers before asking students to do them on their own, and then later encourage them to create their own. Keep in mind that organizers are also helpful when students want to organize their thoughts before writing.

✓ **PROMOTE fluency.** Model what fluent reading sounds like. For example, try chunking words into meaningful parts, pausing in appropriate places, reading with intonation and expression, and at an appropriate pace. It's important to remember that you first want to read the book, discuss it, and do activities with it before practicing fluency. Students can become more fluent by participating in readers' theater. (In the beginning, you can provide the students with the script, later they can create their own scripts after reading a text.) To become more fluent, students can also reread with a partner, participate in choral reading, listen to an audio of the story and read along with it, read stories they wrote, read books of interest, and read independently. Rasinski (2004) suggests poetry, scripts, speeches, monologues, dialogues, jokes, and riddles. Now, doesn't this sound more fun (and consequently more engaging) for students than a timed fluency test?

✓ **INTEGRATE writing to improve reading.** One way to respond to reading is through writing. This may include double or triple journal entries or making class books, shape books, quickwrites, journals/diaries, and so forth. By integrating writing, teachers are promoting reading. Connect with others so that you can be more creative and think outside the box. For example, organize a pen pal project (Ziolkowska, 2010). Your students will love writing and getting mail to read if there is an actual person on the other end responding to them. Authentic writing can be very motivating for students—they have a real audience and a real reason for writing (not just for the teacher for a grade).

✓ **INCORPORATE different kinds of texts.** Read a variety of materials including fiction, nonfiction, realistic fiction, biography, fantasy, sports, Internet information, humor, joke books, comics, magazines, and poetry. Know your students' interests, and integrate them as often as you can. Infuse multicultural literature into the curriculum (by doing this, you demonstrate that you value your students' heritage). And be sure to include high-quality reading material. Research suggests that the kind of texts teachers select can make a difference. When teachers choose books that are on unfamiliar topics and have challenging words, they are more likely to promote vocabulary and language learning (Paratore, Cassano, & Schickedanz, 2011). Have high expectations for your students (without being overwhelming), and help them achieve this!

✓ **PROMOTE different kinds of reading.** Encourage independent/self-selected reading, partner reading, and buddy reading programs (with older students) as well as reading in small groups. Be sure to provide differentiated instruction. Working in small groups with students is very beneficial—you will get to know the students' reading abilities much better and provide the instruction they need at their level, there is more active student involvement, the teacher provides immediate feedback to students, and it allows the teacher to monitor and assess students on a regular basis and address those needs immediately. Many students are very social and learn better (gain a deeper understanding) when they work with others. You may also want to have literature circles or hold literature discussions. Invite guest/mystery readers into the classroom to read a book (and explain why or how reading is important in their daily lives). Remember children learn to read by reading. When students are engaged in independent reading, such as Drop Everything and Read (DEAR), stop what you're doing and read a book, too. Often children are encouraged to read, but don't see the adults in their lives reading. By stopping what you're doing to read a book, you demonstrate that reading is important!

✓ **FACILITATE deeper discussions.** It is important to have deep discussions with students. I would encourage you to put the teacher manual away and have authentic discussions. Ask questions, especially those that do not have an answer. You will be surprised by the meaningful discussions you will have. Let students take the lead in these discussions.

✓ **ASK for various responses to reading.** Children are creative! Provide them with multiple opportunities to respond to the books they read with accordion books, flip-flaps, murals, poof books, pop-up books, postcards, step books, travel guides, advertisements, conducting interviews, writing letters, giving speeches, writing/performing songs, cartoons/comic strips, and so on. Not sure what some of these are? Google them!

✓ **TEACH content area reading.** Many students assume that all material is read in the same way. However, we may need to reread parts of a textbook several times because it tends to be dense with information and include specific academic vocabulary. Also, teachers sometimes assume that if students do well in reading fiction, they will also be equally successful with nonfiction texts. However, this may not always be true. The Common Core State Standards call for an increased reading of informational text. So, take the time to teach effective strategies to comprehend informational material. Here are just a few ideas you can start with to help your students with nonfiction texts: preview the text; ask students to generate questions before/during/after reading the text; use anticipation guides; have class discussions; create concepts maps/graphic organizers (such as a KWL); do Think, Pair, Share; build vocabulary; do word sorts, and so on. Remember, you can enhance the understanding of the textbook by using multiple texts on the subject, using short video clips, periodicals, the Internet, and other materials that help make the content more comprehensible and interesting to students.

✓ **TEACH critical literacy.** Teachers need to encourage students to be critical readers and consumers of information by analyzing texts and authors' perspectives. Critical literacy means that students need to approach a text and look at power, inequity, and injustice in the world. It is important that students challenge what they read (they do not have to agree with someone else's perspective).

✓ **MONITOR struggling readers.** Some students begin to struggle in lower elementary grades, while others develop difficulties in upper elementary grades. Helping students who struggle requires effective classroom instruction and personalized intervention (Allington, 2012). You may want to implement some of these ideas to help your struggling readers: differentiate instruction (in small groups or one-on-one; a tutor or a reading specialist is helpful, if there's one available at your school), encourage parents to read to their child at home, and teach skills and strategies explicitly.

Making Connections

Check out Chapter 16 on English Language Learners

✓ **SUPPORT English language learners.** Try using visuals (such as pictures, diagrams, charts, and graphic organizers) and realia. Encourage students to work with others, scaffold, preteach vocabulary, give enough response time, provide engaging and challenging material to read, assess the students and provide instruction where the child is, label objects in the classroom in English (and if possible, in the students' native language), have a bilingual dictionary, pair the students with other bilingual students who are more proficient, and make the necessary modifications so the students can be successful. The nice thing is that most of these strategies are supportive of all students, not just those who are not native English speakers.

✓ **DO carefully select your assessments.** When assessing student reading, use both informal and formal assessments. Doing a running record, which is an informal assessment of a student's reading (Clay, 1997) and following this up with questions to check the student's comprehension can provide information about their reading ability and how to meet their individual needs. For more detailed assessments, use an Informal Reading Inventory, such as the Qualitative Reading Inventory (Leslie & Caldwell, 2011) or the Basic Reading Inventory (Johns, 2012). Remember to gather information about your students using ongoing assessments that inform your instruction.

Making Connections

Check out Chapter 7 on Engaging With Technology

✓ **INTEGRATE technology and reading.** Students can use the Internet to do research; digital software or apps to reinforce certain skills; computers to type reports or develop PowerPoint, Prezi, or PowToon presentations; programs like Kidblog to write blogs; interactive whiteboards; and digital cameras to create documentaries. Students are very interested in using technology in the classroom to learn and sometimes feel more comfortable using it than their teachers do.

✓ **DON'T forget family involvement.** Encourage parents and care-givers to be your partners in promoting reading. Invite parents to help in the classroom (especially when you are doing guided read-ing with each group). Parents can help at centers, read books to students, and monitor student writing, or they can assist students with other work. Whether they themselves are readers or not, they can still help support the reading and learning of children. Oftentimes, they just need your guidance and suggestions.

✓ **EXPLORE what good readers do.** Instead of having a premade poster on What Good Readers Do, discuss with the students what it means to be a good reader and create a poster together (adding more information as the year progresses).

✓ **OBSERVE educators teaching reading.** Take time to observe other highly effective teachers of reading to get ideas, ask questions, and collaborate on projects that will support you in becoming a fabu-lous reading teacher that promotes a love of reading!

Currently, there is an emphasis on preparing students to be college and career ready. It is not enough to simply have students participate in low-level tasks/skills/thinking. We need to engage our students in higher level thinking (that is the expectation of colleges and employers). Remember: It's not the program or the materials you use or the technology you have, but it's teacher effectiveness that determines student success. So always keep this in mind: YOU, the teacher, are the key to effective reading instruction. Finally, make every effort to promote reading and show stu-dents how enjoyable it can be. It begins with you! If you demonstrate your love and passion for reading, most likely it will be contagious. Create a classroom environment where students get excited about reading!

ANTICIPATION GUIDE
(AGREE/DISAGREE CHART)

Before Reading			After Reading	
Agree	Disagree	Reading Topic: *Cesar Chavez*	Agree	Disagree
		Migrant workers travel from farm to farm picking crops.		
		A union is an organized group of workers.		
		Mexican-American farmworkers in the 1960s made good money and had good working conditions.		
		A fast is a period of time when you eat more than you normally do.		

Steps in Developing an Anticipation Guide

1. Identify the major concepts related to the reading.

2. *Develop a list of four to six statements.* The teacher writes statements on chart paper or on the board, or the students can each have their own sheet of paper with the statements on it. This activity is done before reading. It can be done together as a whole class, in small groups, or independently. As each statement is read, students decide if they agree or disagree.

3. *Discuss the anticipation guide.* Once the students have decided whether they agree or disagree with each statement, bring the discussion to the whole class.

4. *Read the text.* As students read the text, they should be thinking about statements on the anticipation guide.

5. *Discuss each statement again.* After reading the text, students return to the anticipation guide and fill out the "after" column, compare their answers before and after reading, and then discuss it as a whole class, with a partner, or in a small group.

Note: This anticipation guide can be modified. An additional column may be inserted on the far right stating, "If you disagree, explain why. Find evidence in the text, write it, and include the page number(s)."

One last thing: Anticipation guides tend to work best with informational texts (Head & Readence, 1986).

WORD MAP ON A VOCABULARY WORD

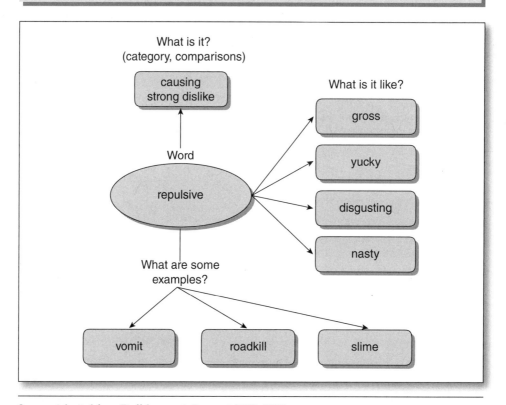

Source: Adapted from Duffelmeyer & Banwart (1992–1993).

When introducing new vocabulary words, study them in depth together with your students.

Step-By-Step Procedure for Doing a Word Map

1. Write the vocabulary word in the middle of the word map.

2. Look up the word in the dictionary. If the definition is difficult to understand, rephrase it and write it in the "What is it?" box.

3. Ask the students to think of other words similar to it (synonyms) and write these words in the "What is it like?" section.

4. Ask students to think of examples and record their responses in the "What are some examples?" section.

After the completion of this activity, most students will have a much better understanding of this word.

Of course you can modify this Word Map by including some of these: synonyms, antonyms, part of speech, write the sentence where the word appears in the text, write your own sentence with it, connect it to your life, make up a story with the word, draw a picture of it, etc.

PAIRED READING

Steps in Paired Reading

1. Two students read silently a portion of an assignment. One student is a designated *reteller* while the other student is a designated *listener*.

2. After reading (a small portion/paragraph), both students put the material out of sight. If one student finishes the portion before the other student, the student goes back and reads the portion again until the partner finishes.

3. When both have finished reading, the reteller orally retells what has been read without referring to the text.

4. During the retelling, the listener should only interrupt to get clarification.

5. After the retelling, the listener should point out and correct any ideas that were summarized incorrectly and add any ideas that were not included in the retelling, but should have been.

6. Students should alternate roles after reading each portion/paragraph.

The strategy above was developed by Don Dansereau. (The basic outline of the procedure was modified.)

Tips to Make Paired Reading Successful in Your Class

- Because partners are retelling after each portion/paragraph, it's very easy to hear others talking/retelling and this may be distracting (and it may get a little noisy). I would recommend that you utilize your whole room and have the students spread out around the whole class (perhaps some can even go out in the hallway).
- Please model Paired Reading very carefully before having students try this on their own.
- First time you implement this, give the students a very short text.
- After the students try Paired Reading, reflect with them—what worked and what changes could be made for a better experience next time?
- Match a strong reader with an average reader and an average reader with a struggling reader. Try not to pair up a strong reader with a struggling reader.

Adapting Paired Reading for the Needs of Your Students

You don't have to follow the procedure exactly the way it's outlined in steps 1 to 5. Remember, you know your students and their needs best . . . so feel free to make the changes you need. Here are some possible modifications:

- Students who struggle with reading may need to see the text as they retell their portion/paragraph, or perhaps they can highlight important information in the text or take notes to help themselves retell.
- If retelling is challenging for your students, perhaps both students can do the retelling.

(Continued)

(Continued)

- Some students can handle one paragraph at a time, others may be able to do more. It also depends on the kind of reading they are doing. I would keep it to one paragraph with an informational text because there are more facts the students need to recall.
- Perhaps you can have the paired students write a summary about what they learned from the reading and share it with the whole class or just have a class discussion about the assigned reading.
- You could also ask your students to come up with questions they have about the text that they may want to explore on their own.

Paired Reading can be extremely beneficial for several reasons:

- Unlike Round Robin Reading and Popcorn Reading, which can embarrass weak readers, Paired Reading engages all the students. They are all actively involved and responsible for the reading and retelling.
- Students discuss the reading with each other. We know that the more students talk about the reading, the more likely they will learn.

HELPFUL WEBSITES FOR READING INSTRUCTION

What for	*Website*
Building phonemic awareness	blog.maketaketeach.com/8-great-ideas-for-teaching-segmenting-and-blending/#
Elkonian boxes	www.readingrockets.org/strategies/elkonin_boxes
Teach and reinforce phonics	www.starfall.com/ www.internet4classrooms.com/kplus_phonics.htm
Reinforce high-frequency words	www.sightwords.com/sight-words/games/fishing/ www.bluemangollc.com/beyond-flashcards-how-to-teach-sight-words-creatively/
Vocabulary instruction	www.edutopia.org/blog/vocabulary-instruction-teaching-tips-rebecca-alber
Review comprehension strategies	buxton.theeducationcenter.com/print/editorial_content/35692
Graphic organizers	www.eduplace.com/graphicorganizer/ www.teach-nology.com/worksheets/graphic/
Readers Theater	www.teachingheart.net/readerstheater.htm www.aaronshep.com/rt/index.html
Pen pals	www.epals.com/#!/main
Help struggling readers	www.scholastic.com/teachers/article/how-can-i-help-my-struggling-readers

REFERENCES

Allington, R. (2012). *What really matters for struggling readers: Designing research-based programs.* Boston, MA: Allyn & Bacon.

Clay, M. M. (1997). *Running records for classroom teachers.* Portsmouth, NH: Heinemann.

Cline, R., & Kretke, G. (1980). An evaluation of long-term SSR in the junior high school. *Journal of Reading, 23,* 503–506.

Cunningham, P., & Cunningham, J. (1992). Making words: Enhancing the invented spelling-decoding connection. *Reading Teacher, 46*(2), 106–116.

Duffelmeyer, F. A., & Banwart, B. H. (1992–1993). Word maps for adjectives and verbs. *The Reading Teacher, 46,* 351–353.

Fountas, I. C., & Pinnell, G. S. (1996). *Guided reading: Good first teaching for all children.* Portsmouth, NH: Heinemann.

Goodman, Y. M. (1978). Kid watching: An alternative to testing. *National Elementary Principal, 5*(4), 41–45.

Harvey, S., & Goudvis, A. (2007). *Strategies that work: Teaching comprehension for understanding and engagement.* Portland, ME: Stenhouse.

Head, M. H., & Readence, J. E. (1986). Anticipation guides: Meaning through prediction. In E. K. Dishner, T. W. Bean, J. E. Readence, & D. W. Moore (Eds.), *Reading in the content areas: Improving classroom instruction* (2nd ed., pp. 229–234). Dubuque, IA: Kendall/Hunt.

Johns, J. L. (2012). *Basic reading inventory: Pre-primer through grade twelve and early literacy assessments.* Dubuque, IA: Kendall/Hunt.

Leslie, L., & Caldwell, J. (2011). *Qualitative Reading Inventory.* Boston, MA: Pearson.

McKenna, M. C., & Kear, D. J. (1990). Measuring attitude toward reading: A new tool for teachers. *Reading Teacher, 43*(9), 626–639.

Murawski, W. W. (2010). *Collaborative teaching in elementary schools: Making the co-teaching marriage work!* Thousand Oaks, CA: Corwin.

Paratore, J. R., Cassano, C. M., & Schickedanz, J. A. (2011). Supporting early (and later) literacy development at home and at school: The long view. In M. L. Kamil, P. D. Pearson, E. B. Moje, & P. P. Afflerbach (Eds.), *Handbook of reading research* (Vol. IV, pp. 107–135). New York, NY: Routledge.

Pearson, P., Roehler, L., Dole, J., & Duffy, G. (1990). *Developing expertise in reading comprehension: What should be taught? How should it be taught?* Technical Report No. 512. Champaign, IL: Center for the Study of Reading.

Rasinski, T. (2004). Creating fluent readers. *Educational Leadership, 61*(6), 46–51.

Trumbull, E., Rothstein-Fisch, C., & Greenfield, P. (2000). *Bridging cultures in our schools: New approaches that work* [Knowledge Brief]. San Francisco, CA: West Ed.

Vandevoort, L., Amrein-Beardsley, A., & Berliner, D. (2004). National board certified teachers and their students' achievement. *Education Policy Analysis Archives, 12*(46). Retrieved from http://epaa.asu.edu/ojs/article/view/201

Wong, H. K., & Wong, R. T. (2001). *The first days of schools: How to be an effective teacher.* Mountain View, CA: Harry K. Wong.

Ziolkowska, R. (2007). Early intervention for students with reading and writing difficulties. *Reading Improvement, 44*(2), 76–86.

Ziolkowska, R. (2010). "I love the story so much I cry:" A literature pen pal project. *Illinois Reading Council Journal, 38*(3), 3–10.

RECOMMENDED READINGS

* Bennett, B., & Rolheiser, C. (2008). *Beyond Monet: The artful science of instructional integration.* Toronto, Ontario, Canada: Bookation.

* Cunningham, P. (2009). *Phonics they use: Words for reading and writing* (5th ed.). Boston, MA: Allyn & Bacon.

* Evans, J. (2005). *Literacy moves on: Popular culture, new technologies, and critical literacy in the elementary classroom.* Portsmouth, NH: Heinemann.

* Keene, E. O., & Zimmerman, S. (2007). *Mosaic of thought: The power of comprehension strategy instruction.* Portsmouth, NH: Heinemann.

* Marzano, R. J. (2009). *Teaching basic and advanced vocabulary: A framework for direct instruction.* Boston, MA: Heinle/Association for Supervision and Curriculum.

GO EVEN FURTHER WITH THIS TOPIC ON THE WORLD WIDE WEB

- www.readwritethink.org/
- www.reading.org/
- www.ncte.org/
- www.rakisradresources.com/2013/07/top-10-reading-students-for-elementary.html
- www.readingrockets.org/
- www.smartteaching.org/blog/2008/08/100-awesome-free-web-tools-for-elementary-teachers/

THE Apps WE LOVE

- BiblioNasium
- Chicktionary
- Dictionary.com
- BrainPop
- Free Audiobooks
- Kidblog
- iBooks
- Sight Words List
- Powtoon

3

Teaching Writing Right

Kathleen Dudden Rowlands

California State University, Northridge

WHAT REALLY WORKS IN WRITING IN THE ELEMENTARY CLASSROOM

Don't Underestimate Short People

Donald Graves (1983) opens his groundbreaking book *Writing: Teachers and Children at Work* with the following claim:

> Children want to write. They want to write the first day they attend school. This is no accident. Before they went to school they marked up walls, pavements, newspaper with crayons, chalk, pens, or pencils . . . anything that makes a mark. The child's marks say, "I am." (p. 3)

Watching children and carefully recording their growth as writers, Graves and his research team learned that children as young as 6, when given time and opportunity, could do a great deal more as writers than adults had expected or believed. So how do we get to the place where kids all of a sudden start moaning when you ask them to take out a pencil?

Indeed, Graves found that most (well-intended) approaches to teaching writing "take the control away from children and place unnecessary road-blocks in the way of their intentions" (p. 3).

Graves and his co-researchers discovered that not only did the children want to write, but they wanted to write well. The children adopted and developed remarkably sophisticated ways of revising their writing. They were able to talk about their work and their processes as writers with surprising maturity. What Graves and his team discovered was that the biggest error writing teachers can make is to underestimate students' abilities and potential for development—no matter how young they are. In a nutshell, don't underestimate short people!

KEY RESEARCH ON WRITING INSTRUCTION

The craft of teaching writing develops with reflective use and with attention to what the writers in our classrooms have to teach us. Even our littlest writers can show us what they can do and what they need to learn next. As we learn to teach writing, our best, and most influential, instructors are teachers and writers themselves. By observing themselves and their students, these gurus were able to extract general principles about writing and then use them to guide writing instruction. Want your students to learn how to write and even to come to *love* writing? Then embrace the following principles when teaching writing.

Writing generates thinking. The human mind is never quiet. One thought leads to the next thought, which leads to the next, and so on. Peter Elbow's (1973) initial difficulties with his own writing led him to experiment with *freewriting,* a process for generating ideas where a writer begins writing on a topic and continues to write steadily for an established period. Freewriting uses the generative power of the mind, making the writer's thinking concrete and available for discussion, revision, and extension. If you want students to think, ask them to write.

Asking even the youngest children to write helps them generate ideas and capture them for later reflection and use. If we understand the youngest child's scribbles as containing meaning and ask the scribblers to tell us about their "story," they explain the meanings embodied in those scribbles. If we learn to talk about scribbles and later combinations of drawing and letters as "writing," we can help students develop their thinking. The act of writing—even in its most primitive forms—not only generates, but shapes thinking.

Fluency, form, correctness. Writers need to develop fluency—the ability to get language into print smoothly and quickly. Fluency develops when writers have lots of repeated practice without concern for form or correctness. Young children begin with pictorial or pretend writing, combining a picture with random letter-like forms sometimes interspersed with numbers. Fluent writing displays multiple sentences arranged in a chronological or logical sequence with emerging control over conventional use. As they develop, writers are able to consider both audience and purpose as they organize content. Even very young writers are able to begin editing their writing using appropriate and conventionally correct language. Certainly development of fluency, form, and correctness is recursive and interwoven, but without fluency, it is difficult for the writer (or the teacher) to have much to work with.

Writers need time to develop their thinking. Writers need content—things to write about. Pulitzer Prize winning journalist, Donald Murray (1978) advocated that 85% of a writer's time should be spent in prewriting—discovering and developing that content. To begin, writers need to find topics. Common classroom practice often spoon-feeds students with topics, story starters, and even beginning paragraphs or sentences. This writer's "welfare" (Graves, 1984) leads to learned helplessness. Students who have been overly supported are at a loss when invited to write about a topic of their own choosing. Teaching students to identify topics and expand their thinking on those topics is central to effective writing instruction. When the teacher owns all the topics, students lose interest in writing. They write less. They lose any motivation to write well. Plus, think about it. Do you *really* know all the interests of your first graders?

Effective writing depends upon revision. Donald Murray (1998) wrote, "All writers write badly—at first. . . . Then they rewrite" (p. 1). Donald Graves (1983) and his research team learned that the youngest students would do extensive revisions in order to "get the information the way they want it" (p. 4). Calkins (1983) found that children need "permission to mess up [their] paper[s]" (p. 44), and they need to be taught how to scratch out words, add material, or move things around by drawing arrows or taping new pages onto existing work (pp. 44–48).

Linda Flower (1979) labeled early draft writing "writer-based prose" and saw it as an essential part of the writing process. Ideas are not fully developed, logically arranged, or clearly presented. Flower noted that, "effective writers do not simply express thought but transform it in certain complex but describable ways for the needs of a reader" (p. 19). That is, they transform writer-based prose into "reader-based prose." Transforming writing from egocentric writer-based prose to reader-based prose is the focus of revision.

Reflective practice—for both writing teachers and writers—is central to writing improvement. Just as there is craft to writing, there is craft in teaching writing. George Hillocks (1995) argues that, "effective . . . writing [instruction] is reflective, continually reexamining assumptions, theories, and their practical implications at every stage from developing knowledge for practice, to planning, interactive teaching, and evaluation" (p. xvii). That is, writing teachers must constantly test theoretical knowledge against practical applications. They must assess their pedagogies against their success with students. Is what you learned in your teacher training program working with your group of students? If not, why not? What else can you try? Many writing teachers follow the lead of National Writing Project teachers (www.nwp.org) and use their own experiences as writers to guide instruction.

Plugged In

www.nwp.org

Another way to learn the craft of teaching writing is by listening to what children tell us and letting them show us how they need to be taught (Calkins, 1994; Graves, 1983). As good "kid watchers" (Short, Harste, & Burke, 1996), writing teachers view student performances as instructional starting points. Effective writers are reflective and mindful of their processes. Learning to reflect on both writing products and writing processes accelerates children's development as writers and teachers' development as writing teachers.

Making Connections

Check out Chapter 2 on Reading

Connecting reading and writing instruction improves both. Graham and Hebert (2010) tell us that writing can potentially enhance reading in three ways. Exactly. *Writing* can help kids improve their *reading!* First, writing about something that was read empowers reading comprehension. Second, reading and writing are both meaning-making processes by which the reader/writer creates understandings. Finally, "writers . . . gain insight about reading by creating their own texts" (p. 4). Understanding texts as writers—from inside particular forms—empowers students when they become readers of similar forms. Writing about reading can be as brief as creating written questions or taking notes or might be more extended writing such as responses or summaries, depending on the age of the child.

Effective teachers of writing write. The practitioner tradition in writing instruction is strong. Thousands of National Writing Project teachers share a belief that writing teachers should write. Although some teacher-writers share what they have learned from students in their many articles and books, writing teachers need not publish to understand the craft of writing from the inside. If you find writing daunting, how can you expect your students to embrace it? So blog, journal, write short stories, or create the next great novel . . . as long as you are writing.

STOP INSTRUCTIONAL PRACTICES TO AVOID

Here is the bad news. In spite of what some textbooks might suggest, there are no formulas for either writing or writing instruction. That said, there is a great deal of solid research-based information about effective practices for teaching writing. While much has been published summarizing effective practices, little available advice suggests practices to avoid. The list that follows is grounded in more than 30 years of my personal experience as both a writer and a writing instructor and lists common practices of many well-intentioned (but ineffective) teachers.

- ✗ **STOP making all the decisions and doing all the thinking about the writing.** Don't choose all the writing topics. Don't tell students how many words or paragraphs or pages their writing needs to be. Don't tell them how to make their writing better without asking what they think will make it better, even for the youngest students.
- ✗ **STOP limiting children's writing to "stories."** Out of school, children write in many genres. The Common Core State Standards (National Governors Association, 2010) also broaden children's writing beyond stories, asking that K–5 students write in three text types: opinion (which becomes argument in Grades 6–12), explanation, and narrative.
- ✗ **STOP asking students to write before they have something to say.** Writers need to develop a rich bank of material upon which they can draw while composing. Even when writing about areas of expertise such as their own lives where they have much to say and the confidence to say it well, children need time to rehearse and develop their ideas.
- ✗ **DO NOT ask students to write in forms they have no experience with as readers.** If the only reading students have experienced is fiction, they won't know how to explain the life cycle of a frog or how to give directions for making cupcakes. They may not even know how to write a thank-you note.
- ✗ **STOP accepting first drafts as finished work.** Few—if any—experienced writers produce decent work on the first try. Why should students expect to produce quality writing in a first draft? Why should teachers encourage those expectations?
- ✗ **STOP acting as the only reader of students' writing.** If you are the only audience for students' writing, they waste precious time trying to determine what will please you instead of focusing on how to present content in a clear, interesting manner to an authentic audience.
- ✗ **STOP collecting and grading everything students write.** For students to develop necessary fluency, they need to produce two or three times more writing every week than even the most dedicated writing teacher possibly has time to read. The football coach doesn't grade practices. Don't grade rehearsals. Save your scoring for game day.
- ✗ **STOP teaching grammar out of context and expecting student writing to improve.** More than 150 years of research demonstrates

little or no transfer between isolated grammar instruction and writing improvement. Some studies even suggest that such instruction makes writing worse (Durst, 1984).

✖ **STOP marking or correcting every mechanical error.** Correcting is not teaching. Marking errors after writing is finished does nothing to improve students' use of conventional English.

✖ **STOP just assigning writing.** Writing with no guidance leads to little improvement except, perhaps, in fluency. With instruction, student writing should show considerable growth at the end of each school year.

GO INSTRUCTIONAL STRATEGIES TO EMBRACE

Helping children develop into fluent writers, capable of producing clear, interesting, and purposeful texts that are respectful of the needs and interests of many different audiences, is possible . . . if you slow down. Think about the year as a whole. What do these students need to know and know how to do by spring? Writing development is a slow process; improvement requires explicit instruction and regular opportunities for safe practice. Plan sequences of writing experiences (Moffett, 1965, 1968) and conversations around those experiences (Calkins, 1983; Graves, 1983) that will help student writers develop.

✓ **USE a Writer's Workshop model for explicit writing instruction.** For more than 40 years, writer's workshop (or reader's-writer's workshop) has been proven an effective way to increase student literacies. It is flexible enough to be adapted to individual teaching styles and student populations, yet its regular structure promotes writing growth. Typically, writer's workshop begins with a 5- to 10-minute mini-lesson, followed by a 40- to 50-minute workshop for writing and conferences, and ends with sharing work in process, either in groups or to the whole class via an Author's Chair.

✓ **LET students write.** Make writing an integral part of every class. Donald Graves (1994) tells us "if students are not engaged in writing at least four days out of five, and for a period of thirty-five to forty minutes . . . they will have little opportunity to learn to think through the medium of writing" (p. 104). The National Commission on Writing (2003) recommends that schools double the time students spend writing. In K–5 classrooms, this could be 40 to 60 minutes daily. Use writing throughout the day as a tool for learning and thinking to teach content and develop fluency. Encourage students to write out of school by helping them connect with pen pals or write letters to friends and family members. Give each student a fresh writer's notebook and new pencils as he or she leaves for the summer.

✓ **GIVE students choices and ownership.** Writers need choices about both content and form. When children have topic choice, they are more engaged in their writing and more willing to invest the time and energy into producing their best work. Offer possibilities within a broad subject range. If the class is studying a particular topic, provide a list of writing choices, or invite children to determine a topic for your approval. Use RAFT prompts to provide choices (ReadWriteThink, n.d., Using the RAFT writing strategy.) (See page 47.) Instead of telling students what they need to do to make their writing better, invite them to set goals. Include space for student-determined goals on assessment rubrics.

✓ **TEACH WRITING!** Teach students to consider purpose and audience as they develop and organize content. Help them explore different ways of organizing their material when writing for different purposes and audiences. Find many ways to teach and reteach these principles. Use every writing task as an instructional opportunity to help students develop writer's craft. Develop a systematic plan for teaching skills. Use mini-lessons to teach children how to find topics to write about, how to expand their writing, how to revise, and how to use dialogue or specific conventions (see page 49 for a list of possible mini-lessons).

✓ **TEACH writing as a process, and teach writing processes.** Teach students that writing is a messy, recursive process and that multiple drafts have value. Teach children about prewriting (choosing a topic, getting and organizing information), drafting, revising, editing, and publishing.

✓ **TEACH invention.** Writers must have something to say. Young writers move from scribbles to drawing. Children who are writing just with pictures can be coached to add more details to their writing, blurring the distinctions that adults make (but young children don't) between pictures and words. Suggest to young writers that they interview one another about their topics before they write. Use modeling to demonstrate how to identify topics to write about. Let them role-play, then write. Use inquiry to generate content (Short et al., 1996).

✓ **TEACH drafting.** Writers don't have to draft in the order in which readers will eventually read. Teach children to write easy chunks first. Sometimes it is helpful to craft the title or the introduction after writing most of a piece. Teach students that a first draft is a beginning, not an end.

✓ **TEACH revision.** The real work of writing for most practiced writers comes with revision. Teach four basic revision strategies: addition, subtraction, substitution, and reordering content. Show students how to use the caret for insertion (^), and how to staple or tape new paragraphs to existing text in the old-school cut/paste format. Have students apply these strategies to any draft moving toward publication. Create a revision corner in the classroom where writers can go during workshop to get feedback on their writing. Use questions during conferences to help writers discover opportunities and directions for revising their writing.

✓ **TEACH editing in order to develop student control over conventional language use.** If students don't identify and correct their punctuation and grammatical errors, they make no improvement. Use errors instructionally. Discuss grammatical constructions and punctuation in the context of writing. Teach students editing responsibilities. Respond selectively to drafts. Create checklists for common spelling or mechanical errors for writers to use at the editor's table. Are there patterns that students can identify and learn to edit for (Andrasick, 1993)? Once children serve as outside editors for other writers, they begin to do more self-editing. Students who receive praise on their work develop positive attitudes toward writing and increase their efforts to improve.

✓ **USE mini-lessons to develop writer's craft** (Calkins, 1994; Ray, 2002, 2010). Use short (10–15 minute), targeted direct instruction as needed for the whole class or a small group of students. Choosing topics and developing content are subjects for early mini-lessons in a writing class. Teach *show, don't tell.* Teach style. Teach students to craft titles and opening paragraphs. The list goes on. See page 49 for a full list of possible mini-lessons.

✓ **CONNECT reading to writing and writing to reading** (Biancarosa & Snow, 2006). For far too long, reading and writing have been taught as separate skills. No longer. Current research suggests that they are learned (and should be taught) in a holistic, integrated way. Having students write about the texts they read is one of three writing practices that enhance students' reading. The other two are teaching students writing processes and skills and simply having students write more. Better writers tend to be better readers, and better readers write more syntactically mature writing than poorer readers (Stotsky, 1983).

✓ **USE mentor texts** (Fletcher, 2011). Use reading selections as mentor texts to teach writing strategies, text structures, genres, and language use. Have students imitate mentor passages to explore a writer's structure, syntax, and stylistic choices (Butler, 2002; ReadWriteThink, n.d., Literary parodies). Use mentor texts to explore unusual or dramatic uses of punctuation. Use reading selections as mentor texts to teach students about genres and the multiple possibilities they offer writers. Be sure to find a mentor text that the students will actually enjoy reading; it's no fun to imitate a reading you didn't like or couldn't connect with at all!

✓ **DO have students read and write in many forms and many genres.** Thomas Newkirk (1989) discovered that children's self-selected writing included a broad range of genres not necessarily privileged in classrooms, including notes (to the Tooth Fairy, among others), letters (including letters to Santa), signs, lists, jokes, and party invitations. The Common Core State Standards expect students to develop proficiency in three text types: opinion/argument, informative/exploratory texts, and narrative. These three types are broadly categorized by rhetorical purposes and in no way limit the genres or text structures that writers might use. A poem (in the broadest sense of the genre) might present an opinion or argument, might inform or explain, or might present a story. Proscribing particular structures (yes, even such as five-paragraph essays!) not only misrepresents the ways in which forms grow organically from purpose and audience but can inhibit writers and their development. Expand students' understanding of genres to include digital writing and possibilities such as blogs, podcasts, and digital stories.

✓ **TEACH students to reflect on their own progress.** Help students participate in their learning, at every age. Ask what they were trying to accomplish with a piece, why they chose a particular title, and what other titles they considered. If you have a large class, put reflection questions on the board and have student pairs ask and answer the questions themselves. Trust students (and teach them to trust themselves) to choose topics and set goals. Ask for a weekly reflection: "What did you learn as a writer this week? What will you work on next week?" Help students see their progress. Have students date everything they write. Save their writing for them. Several times during the year, ask them to review past work and choose pieces that demonstrate an aspect of their writer's craft: their use of dialogue, show, don't tell, or powerful titles, for example. Families will love to see these concrete examples of their children's progress!

✓ **USE brief conferences to coach student writers.** Circulate around the workshop observing what children are doing and asking them to tell you about their work. Identify what the writer is doing well (specifically) in a particular piece; suggest one or two things to work on. Effective writing classrooms provide safe opportunities for rehearsal—practice designed for low-stakes experimentation with style or form. Offer feedback, not assessment, at these developmental stages.

✓ **PROVIDE authentic writing tasks and authentic audiences.** Arthur Applebee's work (1981, 1984) provides solid evidence for the value of providing students with authentic audiences beyond the teacher. Writers need feedback from a number of readers. A single teacher, however well intentioned, simply cannot meet that need. Furthermore, if students are dependent only on the teacher for approval or disapproval of their writing, they become dependent on what Donald Graves (1984) called teacher *welfare* (pp. 43–51). Such dependency is crippling; students never learn how to make the independent choices all writers must make for themselves. Use peer response. Have students read their work aloud (or parts of it) to peers. Set up situations wherein older elementary students can read their work to younger students. Reading aloud develops voice.

✓ **TEACH conventional language use in context.** Have students fix the mechanical errors on their work and identify patterns of spelling and conventional misuse in order to edit for several patterns until they are mastered. Make catching grammar and punctuation mistakes as engaging as possible. Use different colored pens or highlighters or stickers. Create spelling sticky notes with frequently misspelled words. On each sticky note, write the word correctly, emphasizing the trouble spot by size or color. Students keep these reminders where they will be seen often (on binders or a bathroom mirror) until they have mastered the spelling (Andrasick, 1993).

RAFT ASSIGNMENTS

Use RAFT to design writing tasks that provide students with choices while keeping their writing on a particular topic. RAFT tasks can be designed for use in all content areas.

R = Role

A = Audience

F = Format

T = Topic

Here are some sample RAFT assignments to use as models:

The Three Little Pigs

Role	Audience	Format	Topic
Farmer	Potential customers	Poster	Straw for sale!
Second pig (twig house)	His fiancé	Poem	Buying good sticks to build their house
A brick layer	Third pig	Top-ten reasons why list	Bricks make the best houses
Third pig (brick house)	One of his brothers	A letter	Three things that are wrong with a house made of straw (or twigs)
Builders' supply store	House builders	Brochure	Home improvement materials
Wolf	A judge and jury	A defense speech in court	Why he should not be sent to prison
Newspaper reporter	Village citizens	Front page news story	The wolf's acquittal

Jon Scieszka's *The True Story of the Three Little Pigs* ostensibly written by A. Wolf (Puffin, 1996) is a wonderful mentor text to use with this tale as you are introducing RAFT.

David Wiesner's *The Three Pigs* (Clarion, 2001) changes the ending to suit the pigs.

Cinderella

Role	Audience	Format	Topic
Cinderella's best friend	Cinderella	Letter of support	The Stepmother
Cinderella	The Prince	Thank-you note	I had a lovely time . . .
Stepmother	Herself	Interior monologue	Explaining why she treats Cinderella cruelly
Godmother	Cinderella	Song	How to behave and when to leave the ball
A lady guest at the ball	Her mother	Dramatic monologue	Cinderella arriving at the ball
Prince	Citizens of the village	30-second commercial	Help me find the owner of the glass slipper

The RAFT writing strategy is explained at ReadWriteThink: www.readwritethink.org/professional-development/strategy-guides/using-raft-writing-strategy-30625.html

The Writing Fix website has a RAFT builder to help you develop RAFT tasks for content classes: www.writingfix.com/wac/RAFT.htm

Douglas Fisher and Nancy Frey have a list of RAFT assignments based on picture books available online: docs.google.com/document/d/1FzUgftgJ040Frik0dBVVUH7GlLDG3wc69GY28C5JBFw/edit?pli=1

MINI-LESSON TOPICS

Mini-lessons take between 10 to 15 minutes and should be targeted to specific students' needs. An Internet search for *mini-lessons* leads to many useful examples crafted for classroom use. The following list should not be thought of as comprehensive.

Procedures for Writer's Workshop

Writing folders

Keeping a list of ideas

Choosing a topic

Four ways to revise (addition, substitution, subtraction, reordering)

Crossing out instead of erasing

Adding to a piece of writing (tape or staple a new page or part of a page; use arrows)

Writing conferences

Keeping a "Strategies for Me to Try" list

What to do when you're stuck

Using mentor texts

Effective leads

Effective closings (on beyond summary)

Effective titles

Show, don't tell in narrative

Show, don't tell in nonfiction writing

Empty words (e.g., very, really, nice, fun, good, I think, etc.)

Effective verbs

Long and short sentences

Loose and periodic sentences

Transitions

Paragraphing

Author's chair

REFERENCES

Andrasick, K. D. (1993). Independent repatterning: Developing self-editing confidence. *English Journal, 82*(2), 28–31.

Applebee, A. N. (1981). *Writing in the secondary school: English and the content areas* (Research Monograph 21). Urbana, IL: National Council of Teachers of English.

Applebee, A. N. (1984). *Contexts for learning to write: Studies of secondary school instruction.* Norwood, NJ: Ablex.

Biancarosa, C., & Snow, C. E. (2006). *Reading next—A vision for action and research in middle and high school literacy. A report to the Carnegie Corporation of New York* (2nd ed.). Washington, DC: Alliance for Excellent Education.

Butler, P. (2002). Imitation as freedom: (Re)forming student writing. *The Quarterly, 24*(2). Retrieved from http://www.nwp.org/cs/public/print/resource/361

Calkins, L. (1994). *The art of teaching writing* (new ed.). Portsmouth, NH: Heinemann.

Calkins, L. M. (1983). *Lessons from a child: On the teaching and learning of writing.* Portsmouth, NH: Heinemann.

Durst, R. K. (1984). The development of analytic writing. In A. N. Applebee (Ed.), *Contexts for learning to write* (pp. 79–102). Norwood, NJ: Ablex.

Elbow, P. (1973). *Writing without teachers.* New York, NY: Oxford University Press.

Fletcher, R. (2011). *Mentor author, mentor text: Short texts, craft notes, and practical classroom uses.* Portsmouth, NH: Heinemann.

Flower, L. (1979). Writer-based prose: A cognitive basis for problems in writing. *College English, 41*(1), 19–37.

Graham, S., & Hebert, M. A. (2010). *Writing to read: Evidence for how writing can improve reading. A Carnegie Corporation Time to Act report.* Washington, DC: Alliance for Excellent Education.

Graves, D. H. (1983). *Writing: Teachers and children at work.* Exeter, NH: Heinemann.

Graves, D. H. (1984). *A researcher learns to write: Selected articles and monographs.* Exeter, NH: Heinemann.

Graves, D. H. (1994). *A fresh look at writing.* Portsmouth, NH: Heinemann.

Hillocks, G., Jr. (1995). *Teaching writing as reflective practice.* New York, NY: Teachers College Press.

Moffett, J. (1965). I, you, and it. *College Composition and Communication, 16*(5), 243–248.

Moffett, J. (1968). *A student-centered language arts curriculum K–13: A handbook for teachers.* Boston, MA: Houghton Mifflin.

Murray, D. M. (1978). Write before writing. *College Composition and Communication, 29*(4), 375–381.

Murray, D. M. (1998). *The craft of revision* (3rd ed.). Fort Worth, TX: Harcourt Brace College.

National Commission on Writing in America's Schools and Colleges. (2003). *The neglected "R," The need for a writing revolution.* New York, NY: The College Board.

National Governors Association Center for Best Practices, Council of Chief State School Officers. (2010). *Common core state standards.* Washington, DC: Author.

Newkirk, T. (1989). *More than stories: The range of children's writing.* Portsmouth, NH: Heinemann.

Ray, K. W. (2002). *What you know by heart: How to develop curriculum for your writing workshop.* Portsmouth, NH: Heinemann.

Ray, K. W. (2010). *In pictures and in words: Teaching the qualities of good writing through illustration study.* Portsmouth, NH: Heinemann.

ReadWriteThink. (n.d.). Literary parodies: Exploring a writer's style through imitation. Retrieved from http://www.readwritethink.org/classroom-resources/lesson-plans/literary-parodies-exploring-writer-839.html

ReadWriteThink. (n.d.). Using the RAFT writing strategy. Retrieved from http://www.readwritethink.org/professional-development/strategy-guides/using-raft-writing-strategy-30625.html

Short, K. G., Harste, J. C., & Burke, C. (1996). *Creating classrooms for authors and inquirers* (2nd ed.). Portsmouth, NH: Heinemann.

Stotsky, S. (1983). Research on reading/writing relationships: A synthesis and suggested directions. *Language Arts, 60*(5), 627–643.

RECOMMENDED READINGS

* Culham, R. (2014). *The writing thief: Using mentor texts to teach the craft of writing.* Newark, DE: International Reading Association.
* Fletcher, R. (2013). *What a writer needs* (2nd ed.). Portsmouth, NH: Heinemann.
* Fletcher, R., & Portalupi, J. (2001). *Writing workshop: The essential guide.* Portsmouth, NH: Heinemann.
* National Council of Teachers of English's Assembly for the Teaching of English Grammar. (2002). Guidelines on some questions and answers about grammar. Retrieved from http://www.ncte.org/positions/statements/qandaabout-grammar
* Newkirk, T., & Kittle, P. (Eds.). (2013) *Children* want *to write: Donald Graves and the revolution in children's writing.* Portsmouth, NH: Heinemann.
* Writing Study Group of the National Council of Teachers of English Executive Committee. (2004). NCTE beliefs about teaching of writing. Retrieved from http://www.ncte.org/positions/statements/writingbeliefs

GO EVEN FURTHER WITH THIS TOPIC ON THE WORLD WIDE WEB

* www.nwp.org
* www.ncte.org
* www.ttms.org
* www.writingfix.com/index.htm
* www.readingrockets.org/article/teaching-elementary-school-students-be-effective-writers

THE Apps WE LOVE

* Apps Gone Free
* Primary Writer
* Write About This
* Apps for the Common Core

4

Successful Social Studies

Joyce H. Burstein and Greg Knotts
California State University, Northridge

WHAT REALLY WORKS IN SOCIAL STUDIES IN THE ELEMENTARY CLASSROOM

What Exactly Is Elementary Social Studies?

When teaching social studies to third graders, we asked students to explain the definition of social studies in their own words. One boy said, "It is the most boring subject in the world." Wow. Talk about a hard sell. After brainstorming some ideas and asking what they had learned in school so far, third graders decided it was the way we learned about people and how they live. The more technical definition of social studies is an integrated set of disciplines or themes; a combination of the social sciences and humanities that tells the story of humans in time and space. The social studies include history, geography, economics, political science, cultural anthropology, and philosophy—but how young students best understand these abstract concepts is through the teaching of cultural anthropology as the central focus of social studies. Cultural anthropologists study the ordinary experiences of contemporary people for the purposes of uncovering the patterns, meanings, and social relations that lie beneath them. These hidden *stories* illuminate how ordinary aspects of life are in fact extraordinary

(Scheld, 2011). In other words, they study how people live in everyday life to discover how people are similar and different. Even second graders do that with food and toys. So, maybe this is not so boring after all!

In sum, cultural anthropology provides a view of the world and a view of ourselves. It is a means to learn about others while learning about ourselves—the very focus of social studies.

Students have experiences in their home culture that they bring to school. By developing and naming those familiar concepts, young students can apply that learning to other situations. When you teach elementary school, especially in the primary grades, it is all about them anyway. Why not capitalize on that? In the primary grades, the study of culture might include learning how to interact with each other in the classroom and school environment. What are the norms and ways of being in that classroom? Second- and third-grade students might study how the community works and what it means to be a citizen. In the upper grades, students study the cultural aspects of the Native Americans, immigrants to early America, and how interactions with different cultures developed in the United States.

Anthropology is woven into 10 key themes developed by the National Council on Social Studies (NCSS) and includes lessons on culture, power, individual and group identities, the social dynamics of institutions, political and economic structures, and globalization and social change. In short, social studies and anthropology are aligned in the goal of pursuing cultural knowledge for the purposes of making the world a better place. That can certainly be an important topic for even a kindergartner.

The NCSS guidelines were designed to reflect changing trends in society. Today's guidelines speak of contemporary globalization reshaping the structures and social relations of American society. More than ever before, the guidelines suggest that K–6 students must develop a strong understanding of place and the past in order to navigate the present and prepare for the future. Students must command knowledge of geography and history and be able to explain their own relationship to political, economic, and social institutions, as well as to other communities in diverse regions of the world. Students must also be trained to see themselves as responsible members of a local community who possess the ability to problem-solve, assess, and make thoughtful value judgments (National Council for the Social Studies, 2010). This certainly connects with all we've heard about related to the new Common Core State Standards that encourage analysis, inquiry, and problem-solving, doesn't it?

No matter how we study human beings, three principles drive our engagement. One is the widening horizons concept that presents content starting from the child's perspective and then progresses to the larger world, requiring elementary students to connect content in various contexts: first the self, then family, school, and community, progressing to the larger environment of the nation-state and then the world. This helps answer the proverbial "What does this have to do with me?" question by helping students connect content to themselves and their own worlds, as well as the world in which the event/topic actually happened.

A second organizing principle is the spiral curriculum, in which content and curriculum are presented in age-appropriate and developmentally appropriate ways, while themes, concepts, and ideas repeat throughout the progression of the curriculum. While the widening or expanding horizons concept drives the content (smaller to wider environments), the spiral curriculum visits themes and ideas that repeat in that content and those varied contexts. For instance, a kindergarten student who tells her lunch buddy that she will give him her chips for his drink is just demonstrating what she eventually learns is called bartering. The spiral curriculum suggests that all concepts get taught over and over again through different content, with differing and varied levels of complexity, but that major concepts are introduced as early as kindergarten and just reappear in various guises throughout the curriculum. This emphasis on conceptual thinking should drive both your and your students' understanding of the discipline and its content.

The third component of the content is the content itself: What is actually being taught to students? The very nature of the discipline's name, social studies, suggests the plurality of this content area. The point of study of social studies in elementary school is to ensure students have been introduced to the complex world around them, to help them make sense of that world, and to aid them in discovering ways at making the world a better place in which to live. In addition, we are preparing future generations to be active citizens.

Students need to learn how the world works and how their actions can make a difference. From recycling to voting, being a citizen takes action. Social studies teaches those ideas. Our job, however, is to do more than present those ideas; we need to teach them in such a way that really works with students.

HOW SHOULD I TEACH SOCIAL STUDIES?

Since students often either dislike social studies or have no idea what it is, teaching social studies needs to be interactive and meaningful. It is the teacher's role to first understand what the subject is and how to make it make sense to students. Thematic units of study can help organize the subject so there is repetition in concepts but applied in different areas of study. The NCSS (2010) states that the primary goal of social studies education is "to help young people develop the ability to make informed and reasoned decisions for the public good as citizens of a culturally diverse, democratic society in an interdependent world" (p. 9). This definition of social studies is clearly very dull; but you can liven it up by creating engaging activities that you already do! Don't you teach how to be a citizen in your classroom? Let's start there to break down these heavy concepts. The goal is an informed citizenry; to reach the goal, we study human beings. First, elementary students must understand themselves through the study of cultural anthropology—to help them find their place in the world by studying their own culture and the culture that surrounds them. Many cultures express their cultural norms through the visual-performing and language arts, allowing a multifaceted view of inside that culture. Think about a time you went to a cultural event. What was the atmosphere? What were people doing? Most likely, there was food, music, dance, laughing, and sharing stories. This is cultural anthropology. Culture, especially visual culture, is shared in many ways through the arts. By integrating the arts, teachers tap into several strategies to help students make their own meaning of sociohistorical events. Using arts strategies can encourage open-ended thinking, "risk-taking, critical thinking, and diligence" (Gullat, 2008, p. 14). To encourage teachers to use the arts with social studies, the elementary curriculum should be taught with a multidisciplinary focus.

As part of a multidisciplinary approach, critical thinking skills are essential in helping students analyze open-ended problems and situations in the social studies curriculum. With the focus on Common Core Standards that ask students to use critical thinking skills such as synthesis and analysis, teaching social studies integrated with other subjects makes sense. The visual-performing and language arts help enhance critical thinking skills by providing visual and hands-on problems to consider from multiple perspectives. In the visual arts, several researchers promote the use of art inquiry to promote critical thinking (Burton, Horowitz, & Abeles, 2000; Housen, 2001; Lampert, 2006). Inquiry processes assist students in using multiple strategies to solve and evaluate open-ended problems, and using multiple perspectives gives kids an opportunity to learn empathy and how it feels to be in someone else's shoes. When examining the social studies curriculum, these strategies in the arts are aligned with strategies used in social studies. In fact, the use of observation, asking questions, drawing conclusions, analyzing themes, and using historical data are used in both artistic and historical inquiry (Burstein, 2014; Burstein & Knotts, 2011).

Even though there are variations on how arts integration is defined, researchers agree that there are benefits in how arts are integrated into the curriculum (Bresler, 1995; Burstein & Knotts, 2010, 2011, 2012). We will define and use arts integration as a way to teach concepts and skills from both the social studies and arts curriculum in a coequal manner. To further understand the constructs of integration with social studies, teachers must know the steps of how to integrate giving time for both social studies and the arts.

While we understand that time is limited to teach all subjects with no planning time, choosing to teach coequal integration actually saves time and provides students with several, differentiated ways to learn concepts. That's a worthwhile goal. The coequal approach to integration provides multiple entry points into content understanding and knowledge of the visual-performing and literary arts. One advantage is that students learn more abstract concepts more easily when the new knowledge is attached to previously learned knowledge. The use and practice of arts concepts and skills provide a different way for students to make sense of new ideas. Teaching the arts equally also taps into the various types of learners: visual arts for visual learners, music and drama for auditory learners, and drama and dance for kinesthetic learners. Another advantage is that many of the participation and social skills can be taught coequally in social studies and the arts. Students learn how to cooperate, take turns, and problem-solve in different situations. By practicing these skills, students are prepared to work in the real world (Mishook & Kornhaber, 2006). In a study of a Chicago arts program, researchers found that students who participated in coequal arts programs had positive learning outcomes such as under-standing the connections and big ideas more easily; coequal arts integra-tion helps reach content standards (Catterall & Waldorf, 1999). These listed benefits are worth the time and planning to make social studies more engaging, relevant, and contextual for young learners.

TEACHING SOCIAL STUDIES WITH ARTS FOR ENGAGEMENT

Making Connections

Check out Chapter 6 on Arts Integration

Although the primary objectives or goals will initially focus on social studies, the arts must also have equal importance to validate its inclusion (Bresler, 1995; Burstein & Knotts, 2010, 2011, 2012). Using the arts as a vehicle to understand only the social studies content is not integration. In fact, in Chapter 6, Mary Wolf and colleagues write about arts integration and caution against doing simple *crafts* and calling it arts integration; we concur! Depending on your students and the content you want to teach, the arts can be used to create projects or help students learn content better. The five steps in planning, below, are suggested to create a truly integrated use of the arts while teach-ing social studies content:

First, choose the social studies content standard that is the focus of the unit. It is important to have clear goals in planning for the social studies concepts, vocabulary, and skills the teacher wants to cover. Once these important areas are chosen, figure out which arts make the most sense and can be integrated in the unit.

Second, choose the arts content standard to complement the concept or skills you want to teach in social studies. For example, if the unit is on the American Revolution, the National History Standard is *Era 3: Revolution and the New Nation (1754–1820s)* or the National Council for the Social Studies

Standard is *Power, Authority, and Governance: Identify and describe factors that contribute to cooperation and cause disputes within and among groups and nations.* One example of a complementary standard is from music content standards: *Describe the influence of various cultures and historical events on musical forms and styles.* These standards examine period music, songs, and lyrics that exemplify that time period and support the context for the Revolution. Singing Yankee Doodle Dandy or learning to play easy rhythms on the drums can be engaging yet appropriate to the American Revolution unit.

Third, create social studies content and visual-performing arts objectives for the unit of study. The initial social studies objectives will guide how the teacher chooses the content and objectives in the arts. Then choose substantive arts goals that either teach content, a skill, or a combination of both so the arts have equal status with the social studies. Try to limit the amount of objectives so you don't feel overwhelmed but can teach the concepts in the way that makes sense to your students. Collaborating with art teachers can align both subjects. It is a 2 for 1 deal!

Fourth, teach academic content vocabulary in both subject areas. Students need to learn the vocabulary that defines the history-social science content, as well as vocabulary in the visual-performing and language arts. Students will benefit from treating both as content area vocabulary that conceptually support each other. This will help reinforce the vocabulary for both areas as well as provide more opportunities for English language learners and students with special needs.

And finally, create performance-based assessments with clear criteria in social studies and the arts. Using an equally integrated approach to teach, both social studies and arts concepts must be measured in real life tasks. Students who perform what they understand will use several skill sets across social studies and the arts. When you think of an assessment, make it fun. Try measuring how students learn concepts by having them perform a skit, sing a song, make an art project, or create a rap. They are still showing they understand the social studies ideas and content, but they are also using an interactive way to demonstrate that understanding.

Making Connections

Check out Chapters 11, 12, and 16 on UDL, Inclusion, Assessment, and English Language Learners

STOP TEACHING HOW YOU WERE TAUGHT!

Teachers

- ✗ **STOP teaching social studies content using your language arts text.** Your language arts textbooks are not aligned with the national or state history-social science content standards. These texts are not concept driven or developmentally appropriate for teaching social studies.

- ✘ **STOP teaching from textbooks (only).** A state-adopted textbook is typically aligned with content standards but currently not with the Common Core Standards. Many schools have antiquated texts that do not contain accurate or current information. Make social studies concepts relate to today's students' family, community, and daily lives.
- ✘ **STOP teaching through only lecture.** Social studies is teaching about the human experience, so let students interact with each other. Stop talking at students. Students need to talk and interact with each other. Use inquiry-based and hands-on learning to engage students and provide a foundation for their natural curiosity. Make it fun, engaging, and not boring!
- ✘ **STOP teaching with worksheets.** Fill-in-the-blank, multiple-choice, matching, and especially true/false responses all have their place in terms of front-loading content, perhaps, but an overreliance on worksheets creates students who are looking for only one answer. Social studies and history are about asking questions, analyzing multiple sources, and interpreting. Worksheets encourage convergent thinking rather than divergent thinking.
- ✘ **STOP teaching chronologically.** Students need to understand concepts and learn the skills to research, ask questions, and critically think about their world. History happens again and again so teach big concepts rather than rely on dates, facts, and famous people in chronology.
- ✘ **STOP having children sit in their seats during social studies.** Social studies is about the human condition, so encourage them to explore, interact with concrete items, and talk with each other about what they are observing and thinking. Let them be social. Sitting and listening to lectures, reading the text aloud, and doing worksheets lead to boredom. Boredom leads to disengagement and behavior issues, which leads to children surveyed saying things like, "social studies is their least favorite subject or it is boring and useless" (Burstein, Hutton, & Curtis, 2006; Zhao & Hoge, 2005, p. 218).

Administrators

- ✘ **STOP deemphasizing the discipline.** Although the recent accountability-driven assessments have prioritized language arts and mathematics, social studies must not be seen as a secondary citizen—by teachers or students.
- ✘ **STOP being driven by the system.** If the goal of all schooling is an informed citizenry, then elementary schools must be holistic places that encourage the development of the whole child. Social studies is in the state and national standards and by ignoring this content area, students are faced with lack of knowledge and understanding about themselves and their place in the world.

START TEACHING THE WAY YOU KNOW TO BE EFFECTIVE

Teachers, DO This

- ✓ **START teaching concepts over a fact-driven curriculum.** Conceptual understanding supported with context will help students understand the big ideas. These big ideas can be applied to various time periods, events, and people's lives. Concepts tied with other subjects such as the sciences, language arts, and the visual-performing arts will help children make connections with their community and the larger world (Burstein & Knotts, 2011). We do want to teach content, but in a way that makes sense to students.

- ✓ **START integrating with the arts.** Culture is an overarching theme in the elementary social studies curriculum. By integrating the visual-performing arts and the language arts, students tap into how culture is demonstrated by various societies (Burstein & Knotts, 2012; Eisner, 2000). Cultural norms and practices are shown by how we dance, play music, act, create visual images, and express ourselves through writing and oral language. Students need to see the connections between and among cultures to understand the global world.

- ✓ **START making the social studies relevant.** Too many students find little or no use for social studies nor can they even define what it is (Hutton & Burstein, 2008; Zhao & Hoge, 2005). Teachers often have them read about isolated facts in chronological order so they cannot apply it to their own lives. Instead, young students need to find personal meaning and relevance, so teachers must reposition themselves to focus on relevant connections. Have students study about their own family traditions before teaching about Native American family traditions. Then take those common concepts and experiences and have the students analyze similarities and differences. They will remember the facts but will now have developed skills of comparing multiple perspectives. That's the point!

- ✓ **START integrating by teaching in thematic units.** It is important to integrate content so that facts/topics/periods are not disconnected and seen in isolation. Concepts, themes, and facts are reiterated throughout a unit of study. Students need repetition, and by teaching concepts in several ways with several content areas, students can learn through multiple modalities and with multiple perspectives. In fourth grade, students learn about the impact of World War II, but you can provide experiences where students understand the lives of Japanese Americans in internment camps, how children viewed the war, and how everyday people like Rosie the Riveter had jobs in factories.

✓ **START teaching through directed inquiry.** Teachers need to demonstrate and guide students through the inquiry process. Inquiry starts with observations and questions from the students so you have to develop those skills in incremental steps. Getting students involved with primary sources—artifacts from their family, real maps, photographs, first-person journal accounts—will make history and culture alive and relevant. Using these sources will spark curiosity, which is the first step toward an inquiry-based social studies classroom.

✓ **USE primary sources along with textbook material.** Inquiry is supported by the use of real life objects that will make history concrete. Students will engage with a real arrowhead better than a picture of an arrowhead. Primary sources are now much easier to find on the Internet. (The Library of Congress is an excellent site to start your exploration: See the Plugged In box). Also consider going to local libraries, museum-lending centers, and even your own garage to find primary sources that would engage your students. Think about what is in your garage that children have never seen. Bring those objects to class and watch how excited they get!

Plugged In

www.loc.gov/

✓ **TEACH geography concepts and skills.** Students have no real sense of place or spatial concepts in elementary school. Teachers need to teach about space, location, movement, human interaction with their environment, and regions. These skills will help them in daily life so they do not have to depend on Google Maps or Siri to figure out where they are located. These concepts will build from kindergarten (knowing my address), to understanding how the explorers used various points of navigation to circle the globe.

✓ **OPEN your classroom to the outside world.** With limited funding for field trips, teachers need to bring outside experiences into their classroom. Search for guest speakers, family members, friends with expertise, and community members to speak and demonstrate in your classroom. Even have guests visit virtually via Skype or FaceTime.

✓ **TAKE advantage of the Internet by searching for primary sources, YouTube videos, lesson plans, and grants that would enhance your social studies curriculum.** For your mental health, collaborate to create units and lessons. Teachers often have a specialty area that can be shared with their grade level. Also, check out the Donors Choose website for ways to supplement materials that your school may not be able to purchase for you.

Plugged In

www.donorschoose.org/

✓ **START using authentic assessment along with tests.** Problem-based and project-based learning can be measured through authentic tasks; writing, plays, simulations, art projects, songs, musicals, and movements are some concrete ways to show understanding (Burstein & Knotts, 2011, 2012). Create and use criteria charts or rubrics to measure conceptual and skill-based learning rather than depending only on tests. Authentic measures pair nicely with an inquiry-based classroom where students are asking questions and solving problems. It just makes more sense to DO a task/project rather than asking questions about the process on a test. This also addresses the importance of differentiation for students with special needs.

Administrators, DO This

✓ **START scheduling professional development sessions for social studies instruction.** If language arts and mathematics, assessment, and compliance processes are the only areas of focus of professional development, teachers feel they must focus on these areas rather than creating well-rounded students and future citizens.

• With so many immigrant students entering our schools, it is necessary for teachers to teach about our democratic society and context. The Common Core State Standards (CCSS), project-based assessment, differentiation, Universal Design for Learning, and the use of technology in instruction might be easy places to begin this process. Arts integration is another area where teachers need professional development to enhance the role of the arts from a cultural perspective in the elementary social studies curriculum (Burstein, 2014; Burstein & Knotts, 2012). The inclusion of arts and social studies provides differentiated experiences with the content and, dare we say, adds fun and engagement!

✓ **START being an instructional leader at your site.** It is important to meet your accountability, assessment, and performance goals, but it is also important to create a school culture that privileges a clear and shared ideology, teacher voice, and has a focus on quality instruction. Provide time for teachers to collaborate and share ideas through grade-level meetings. Set aside part of the budget for arts supplies and materials to enhance the social studies curriculum. This will send the message that social studies instruction and teacher creativity are valued at your school site.

INQUIRY-BASED SOCIAL STUDIES ACTIVITIES

Some prompting questions that consider a variety of access strategies to help with inquiry are listed below. Consider this list of questions as a starting point for planning your instruction. The list of questions is not exhaustive or infinite, but provides a variety of techniques for you to consider as you begin the instructional planning process in inquiry.

A) What can students VIEW to gain access?

1) _____

2) _____

*Consider: primary sources, artifacts, DVDs, photos

B) What can students LISTEN TO in order to gain access?

1) _____

2) _____

*Consider: primary sources, CDs, read-alouds, guest speakers

C) What can students WRITE to gain access?

1) _____

2) _____

*Consider: creative responses, reflective or predictive writing

D) What can students READ to gain access?

1) _____

2) _____

* Consider: primary source materials, texts, Internet sites, and children's literature

E) What can students DISCUSS to gain access?

1) _____

2) _____

* Consider: Think-Pair-Share topics, debate

F)   What can students CONSTRUCT/INVESTIGATE to gain access?

  1) _____

  2) _____

    *Consider: primary sources, engagement with visual-performing arts

G)   What can students RESEARCH to gain access?

  1) _____

  2) _____

    *Consider: primary sources, teacher-chosen Internet sites, and library sources

H)   What can students COMPLETE to gain access?

  1) _____

  2) _____

  *Consider: teacher- or text-made worksheets, brainstorms, and graphic organizers

INTEGRATED SOCIAL STUDIES UNIT

INSTRUCTION PLANNING GUIDE

**Use This Planning Guide to Integrate
Concepts Across a Common Theme**

I.   ORGANIZING PRINCIPLES

Title/Topic/Central Theme: _____

Social Studies Standards: _____

Visual-Performing Arts Standard(s):_____

> **Rationale:** What is the value or significance of selecting this unit? Why do children need to learn about this unit? How does this unit relate to real life experiences? Explain how social studies and arts are integrated. What is the importance in combining this subject matter and concepts? Are there critical issues that arise from the content in this unit?
>
> - _____
> - _____
> - _____
> - _____
> - _____
>
> **Essential Questions/Big Ideas:** What are the three to five enduring questions you want children to understand as a result of this unit? (These are usually broad and conceptual.)
>
> - _____
> - _____
> - _____
> - _____
> - _____
>
> **Unit Goals:** What do you want children to learn as a result of this unit of study? What are the concepts that students will have that help concretize the big ideas and essential questions?

- _____
- _____
- _____

II. LESSON PLANS

Initiation: How will children be introduced to and interested in the unit? Be sure there is a concrete introduction to your unit that previews concepts or skills that will be taught in the unit.

_____

_____

LESSON CONTENT OUTLINE

Did I include: ___Technology ___ Literature ___ Primary Sources ___ Arts

CONCEPT 1: _(_____)_____

CONCEPT 2: _(_____)_____

CONCEPT 3: _(_____)_____

CONCEPT 4: _(_____)_____

CONCEPT 5: _(_____)_____

CONCEPT 6: _(_____)_____ _____

CONCEPT 7: _(_____)_____

CONCEPT 8: _(_____)_____

CONCEPT 9: _(_____)_____

Culminating Activities: How will children synthesize and put together the various learning they encountered during this unit of study?

- _____
- _____
- _____

III. LEARNING CENTER(s): to be used autonomously by students to supplement their learning of the objectives and content of the unit; what are the main concepts being delivered in the Learning Centers?

- _____
- _____
- _____
- _____

IV.   INSTRUCTIONAL MATERIALS: a bibliography of children and teacher books and resources for this unit with other visual and hands-on resources you will use. (This might include charts, maps, art prints, interdisciplinary materials, artifacts, posters, photographs, government documents, music CDs, films, etc.)

- _____
- _____
- _____
- _____

COEQUAL INTEGRATION TEMPLATE

Social Studies With Visual-Performing and Language Arts: Second Grade Example

Social Studies Concept/Skill(s):	Visual-Performing Arts Concept/Skill(s):
Culture, tradition, holiday, celebration	Visual—line, color, form, texture, cultural context
	Music—tempo, dynamics, cultural context
	Dance—pathways, locomotor movement, leveling, cultural context
	Drama—improvisation, character development
History-Social Science Content Standard(s):	**Visual-Performing Arts Content Standard(s):**
NCSS Theme: Culture	Identify and use line, color, form, and texture in a work of art.
Identify difference between primary/secondary sources.	Identify the tempo and dynamics in a piece of music.
Use family artifacts and interviews to learn about a family celebration.	Use different pathways and leveling to perform a cultural dance.
Identify and explain how cultural celebrations are the same or different.	Use improvisation to relay an idea.
Social Studies Academic Content Vocabulary:	**Visual-Performing Arts Academic Content Vocabulary:**
Holiday, tradition, cultural background, celebration, interview, artifact	Line, color, texture, form, tempo, dynamics, repetition, space, pathway, leveling, improvisation
Social Studies Goals (content knowledge, research skill, participation skill, critical thinking skill):	**Visual-Performing Arts Goals (content knowledge, art creation skill, participation skill, critical thinking):**
Use Venn diagrams to compare and contrast cultural celebrations.	Participate in a group dance.
Participate in cooperative groups by completing a task as a group.	Create a 3-D art piece.
	Compare and contrast two different forms of art.
Identify and explain the difference between the two calendar systems.	Participate in a 2-minute improvisation and use appropriate facial and body movements.

Identify common cultural traditions. Increase awareness of cross and multicultural celebrations in your community.	Compare and contrast the use of dynamics and tempo in music to the body movements created in dance (lion dance).
Social Studies Criteria for Assessment (What and how are you measuring your goals?): Venn diagram—compare and contrast holidays Rubric for paragraph explaining cultural celebration Checklist for completing interview Rubric for paragraph on calendar systems Checklist for group participation	**Visual-Performing Arts Criteria for Assessment (What and how are you measuring your goals?):** Rubric for puppet Rubric for music identification of tempo/dynamics (singing) Checklist for dance steps; Checklist for improv Checklist for group participation
Materials Needed (primary sources, books, photos, artifacts, realia): Films of lion dance, Chinese New Year Cut from TV footage of ball dropping Books on holidays Artifacts—noisemaker, funny hats, etc. Artifacts from Chinese New Year (red envelope, dumplings, music, puppet) "Auld Lang Syne" Photographs from both celebrations	**Materials Needed (paint or media, tools, books, sample art, paper):** Butcher paper Tempera paint—various colors + gold Red paper Props—masks, chop sticks, etc. CD player with CDs of Chinese music, "Auld Lang Syne" Streamers
Research (content knowledge and strategies): Use interview skills to interview a family member. Use photoanalysis with photos. Use descriptive sentences to explain an event.	Research (artists, biographies, techniques, strategies): Technique—use of various media: create a 3-D puppet Research commercial art of New Year

INTEGRATION TEMPLATE

Social Studies Concept/Skill(s):	Visual-Performing and Language Arts Concept/Skill(s):
History-Social Science Content Standard(s):	Visual-Performing and Language Arts Content Standard(s):
Social Studies Academic Content Vocabulary:	Visual-Performing and Language Arts Academic Content Vocabulary:
Social Studies Goals (content knowledge, research skill, participation skill, critical thinking skill):	Visual-Performing and Language Arts Goals (content knowledge, art creation skill, participation skill, critical thinking):
Social Studies Criteria for Assessment (What and how are you measuring your goals?):	Visual-Performing and Language Arts Criteria for Assessment (What and how are you measuring your goals?):
Materials Needed (primary sources, books, photos, artifacts, realia):	Materials Needed (paint or media, tools, books, sample art, paper):
Research (content knowledge and strategies):	Research (artists, biographies, techniques, strategies):

REFERENCES

Bresler, L. (1995). The subservient, co-equal, affective, and social integration styles and their implications for the arts. *Arts Education Policy Review, 96*(5), 31–37.

Burstein, J. H. (2014). Integrating arts: Cultural anthropology and expressive culture in the social studies curriculum. *Journal of Social Studies Research and Practice, 9*(2), 132–144.

Burstein, J. H., Hutton, L., & Curtis, R. (2006). Elementary social studies: To teach or not to teach. *Journal of Social Studies Research, 30*(1), 15–20.

Burstein, J. H., & Knotts, G. (2010). Creating connections: Integrating the visual arts with social studies. *Social Studies and the Young Learner, 23*(1), 20–23.

Burstein, J. H., & Knotts, G. (2011). *Reclaiming social studies for the elementary classroom: Integrating the arts through culture.* Dubuque, IA: Kendall/Hunt.

Burstein, J. H., & Knotts, G. (2012). Elementary teachers' strategies for integrating the arts into the social studies curriculum. *Journal of Social Science Research, 1*(1), 82–90.

Burton, J., Horowitz, R., & Abeles, H. (2000). Learning in and through the arts: The question of transfer. *Studies in Art Education, 41*(3), 228–257.

Catterall, J. S., & Waldorf, L. (1999). The Chicago Arts Partnerships in Education: Summary evaluation. In E. B. Fiske (Ed.), *Champions of change: The impact of arts on learning* (pp. 47–62). Washington, DC: Arts Education Partnership.

Eisner, E. (2000). Arts education policy? *Arts Education Policy Review, 101*(3), 4–6.

Gullat, D. (2008). Enhancing student learning through the arts integration: Implications for the profession. *High School Journal, 91*(4), 12–25.

Housen, A. (2001, April). *Methods for assessing transfer from an art-viewing program.* Paper presented at the annual meeting of the American Educational Research Association, Seattle, WA (ERIC Document Reproduction Service No. ED 457186).

Hutton, L., & Burstein, J. H. (2008). The teaching of history-social science: Left behind or behind closed doors? *Social Studies Research and Practice, 3*(1), 96–108.

Lampert, N. (2006). Critical thinking dispositions as an outcome of art education. *Studies in Art Education, 47*(3), 215–228.

Mishook, J. J., & Kornhaber, M. L. (2006). Arts integration in an era of accountability. *Arts Education Policy Review, 107*(4), 3–11.

National Council for the Social Studies. (2010). *National curriculum standards for social studies: A framework for teaching, learning, and assessment.* Washington, DC: Author.

Scheld, S. (2011). An anthropological lens for teaching social studies. In J. H. Burstein & G. Knotts (Eds.), *Reclaiming social studies for the elementary classroom* (pp. 23–36). Dubuque, IA: Kendall/Hunt.

Zhao, Y., & Hoge, J. (2005). What elementary students and teachers say about social studies. *Social Studies, 96*(5), 216–221.

RECOMMENDED READING

* Burstein, J. H., & Knotts, G. (2011). *Reclaiming social studies for the elementary classroom: Integrating the arts through culture.* Dubuque, IA: Kendall/Hunt.

GO EVEN FURTHER WITH THIS TOPIC ON THE WORLD WIDE WEB

- www.teacherspayteachers.com/Browse/PreK-12-Subject-Area/Social-Studies-History
- www.calisphere.universityofcalifornia.edu/
- www.webquest.org/index.php
- www.unitedstreaming.com
- www.memory.loc.gov/learn/lessons/primary.html
- www.getty.edu/
- www.whitney.org/jacoblawrence/
- www.artsedge.kennedy-center.org/

THE Apps WE LOVE

- Westward Expansion
- American Revolution Interactive Timeline
- Worldbook: This Day In History
- National Geographic Magazine

5

Stellar STE(A)M Strategies

Erica Rood

2014 Finalist for Presidential Award for
Excellence in Mathematics and Science Teaching

WHAT REALLY WORKS IN SCIENCE IN THE ELEMENTARY CLASSROOM

Full STE(A)M Ahead!

When was the last time your students were truly excited about learning? When their motivation and interest was so palpable that you were reminded why you chose teaching as a profession? Now what if I asked you when was the last time your students felt this way about math, science, or (gasp!) engineering? A methodology of teaching called STEM or STEAM has the potential to generate that wave of enthusiasm we so desperately hope for. For purposes of brevity, I continue by calling this movement STE(A)M.

Armed with new literacy and math standards and the upcoming rollout of the Next Generation Science Standards (NGSS), we teachers need to be ready to approach our students with a fresh perspective on academic disciplines. STE(A)M does just that, asking teachers to cater to the perspective that all kids are born investigators by putting a significant daily emphasis on mathematics, science, engineering, art, and technology disciplines.

WHAT IS STE(A)M AND WHY IS IT IMPORTANT?

STE(A)M is an acronym standing for science, technology, engineering, (arts), and mathematics. Sparked by the launch of the Russian satellite Sputnik in 1957 and fueled by a desire for innovation and a fear of falling behind other nations, Americans quickly charged into action, calling for an increase of science and engineering education among its citizens (Woodruff, 2013). Presidents Eisenhower and Kennedy began the difficult job of prioritizing these disciplines in our educational institutions. Did you know that until the 1960s, elementary education science instruction was simply teachers telling students "scientific things" out of books, if they chose to include it in the teaching day at all (Zuga, 2009)? Bob Karplus, a Nobel laureate in physics was justifiably unsatisfied with this. In 1959, he began engaging in scientific inquiry with elementary school students. At this time, a host of other curricula began to appear, including the *Unified Science and Mathematics for Elementary Schools* (1973). This curricula integrated math and science and helped students conduct investigations of everyday questions in their local environments (Zuga, 2009). By 1990, the National Science Foundation had begun to fund the creation of an integrated science, technology, engineering, and math curriculum. In the early 2000s, the National Science Foundation coined the acronym STEM (no integration of the arts yet) in response to the congressionally mandated advanced technological education program to help train experts for the new high-tech workforce (Zuga, 2009). So are we responding to the mandate? Well, the grim fact of the matter is that America will create nearly 800,000 jobs between 2008 and 2018 that require a graduate degree in a STEM field, but based on current trends, only 550,000 native-born Americans are on track to earn STEM graduate degrees during this timeframe (Tai, Liu, Maltese, & Fan, 2006). Without students fluent in STEM disciplines, our graduates will not be able to fulfill the need. Admittedly, it seems crazy that elementary teachers should be worried about this—but if we instill excitement early, more kids are likely to be eager to take on these STEM jobs! Can you imagine teaching the next Steve Jobs? Maybe they'll even remember their elementary STEM experiences when they are billionaires and gift us some cool educational technology for our classrooms.

Back to reality. Like many great educational initiatives, the understanding of the STE(A)M effort has conflicting interpretations. Some see it as an integration of the science, technology, engineering, (arts), and math disciplines, believing that by studying all areas of these academic subjects and looking at their overlap and connections, our students can become more scientifically literate. Others see STEM as four related disciplines that do not need to be taught as a cohesive interconnected curriculum (Barakos, Lujan, & Strang, 2012) but whose main goal is to create a broadly science-literate public capable of understanding the natural world. Both perspectives require students to make decisions, solve problems, and seek innovation that will improve the quality of our lives (Barakos et al., 2012). Whether you prefer to think of STE(A)M as integrated subjects or a collection of subjects, at least we can agree that the key purpose of STE(A)M is to prepare students for the 21st century workforce.

STEM educational initiatives have seen science and math instruction shift from rote memorization to a more inquiry-based practice, and now with the vital integration of the arts, we are encouraging more students than ever to participate in STEM activities. Art? What? How are the arts related to math and science, you ask? Glad you did! This is where the (A) comes in.

The STE(A)M movement adds art and design into the 21st century workforce equation. Savas Dimopoulos of Stanford University's Department of Physics says, "The thing that differentiates scientists is purely an artistic ability to discern what is a good idea and what is a beautiful idea" (Levinson & Kaplan, 2013). STE(A)M is "the interplay between left-brain convergent thinking and right-brain divergent thinking" (STEAMConnect, n.d.). It adds the constructs of imagination and play into STEM disciplines. Though scientific knowledge is empirically grounded, it must involve human imagination and creativity (Lederman & Lederman, 2004). Upon further reflection, the scientist asks, "How or what am I looking at?" The artist acknowledges its beauty, texture, and shadow. The scientist asks, "How can I document this discovery for the future?" while the artist strives to live in the present moment. We will need our students to wear both hats to discover and create true innovation for the future.

In 2011, a study conducted by Walker, Winner, Hetland, Simmons, and Goldsmith confirmed that students with formal art training had better geometric reasoning than those without. The study explains that formal visual arts training may help students by strengthening the visualization skills needed to be successful in geometric reasoning tasks. Additionally, it has been shown that arts integration helps students with retention of academic subjects (Burstein & Knotts, 2011; Hardiman, Rinne, & Yarmolinskaya, 2014) especially with those for whom reading achievement is especially difficult. Furthermore, think about how incorporating the arts into STEM disciplines engages students who might not have otherwise been engaged. In STE(A)M, the student who struggles in math but loves drawing is encouraged to

Making Connections

Check out Chapter 6 on Arts Integration

create a visual of how he solved the problem. The kid who thinks science is boring but loves to sing is asked to create a song that will serve as mnemonic (memory device) about a scientific principle. There are so many students who are typically left out of STEM opportunities by choice or by default, but including the arts may help play upon their strengths thereby creating an interest and motivation in a STEM-related field. These students may then choose a career choice they may otherwise have felt incapable of pursuing. As teachers, we need to take every opportunity to leverage these strengths into STE(A)M achievement.

FULL STE(A)M AHEAD: THINGS TO LEAVE AT THE STATION

- ✘ **STOP using science and STE(A)M as synonyms.** Just because you teach science, doesn't mean you teach STEM. Science is only a piece of the puzzle. The science component alone will not ready our students for the tasks they face in the coming years. Only the incorporation of all the STE(A)M pieces makes them critical thinkers and innovators who will be competitive in the workforce.
- ✘ **STOP relying on textbooks.** Our knowledge of STEM areas is always evolving, reflecting new research and developments. Thus, there is no way that a printed text book can remain relevant for long. Please use valid Internet resources and podcasts to keep you and your students current in the world of STEM. If your school requires a text, consider going digital. Apple has a wonderful free product that lets you create your own digital textbooks that can be updated at any time. For more information, check out the Plugged In box.

Plugged In

www.apple.com/ ibooks-author/

- ✘ **STOP using the traditional scientific method.** Let go of the traditional scientific method. Problem-solving is messy. It doesn't always conform to a particular set of structured questions and ordered steps ending with a neat conclusion. Stop thinking in terms of the old, linear model with its observations, questions, data, conclusions, and hypotheses. How often do problem-solving and inquiry follow a nice, neat straight path from Point A to Point B? Often, problem-solving takes us for a ride on a winding road rather than a linear path. As we teach our students to accept this, we encourage them to build stamina and creativity when solving problems. Why have a method at all? Well, it helps scientists (and students) understand why they do what they do and gives them a plan as to what to do next. Please consider it as a guide, not as structure intended to assess.

✘ **STOP using technology just for technology's sake.** Integrating technology into STE(A)M does not solely mean making Prezis and PowerPoints. Consider and challenge these formats to encourage higher levels of thinking. We know kids like using computers, so challenge them to use them in new and innovative ways! Consider Scratch.com, an innovative way of teaching computer programing, while enabling students to integrate other content areas. In the future, it isn't going to be enough for students to know how to use a computer. They are going to have to use computer technology to create and innovate. Learning the coding process can be challenging to both students and educators, but Scratch.com is a fun and interesting program that allows students to gather and build upon the basic coding foundations.

Making Connections

Check out Chapter 7 on Engaging With Technology

✘ **STOP relying on memorization and regurgitation to assess STEM areas.** The days of needing to memorize information are backsliding into our past. Need to know something? Any student will say, "Let me Google that for you." We have more information than we know what to do with. Students are going to need to know what to do with that information, so move your instruction and assessment toward concepts and inquiry-based activities that can help students synthesize and evaluate information instead of relying on memorization.

✘ **STOP teaching STEM disciplines without context.** Your students crave and deserve a real life connection between what they learn in class and how it directly applies to real life. Common Core has addressed this in its performance tasks in the math content area. We need to begin carrying it over to the other STEM disciplines as well. Challenge students to solve real problems affecting their own community instead of the hypothetical problems addressed in most textbooks. Now, when they ask, "Why do we have to learn this?" you'll actually have an answer!

✘ **STOP asking your students to prove things.** Renee Schwartz (2007) put it best: "Because we can never gather all the data for all time, we can never have 100% proof of any claim in science" (p. 31). Your elementary students are novices in the disciplines, and they are just beginning to scratch the surface. Common Core, though continuously asking us to support our thinking with evidence, does not ask us to *prove* anything. Supporting with evidence and proving things are not interchangeable concepts. Consider asking students to *support their thinking* or to *use evidence to validate* their arguments.

✘ **STOP confusing the words *investigation* and *experiment*.** Experiments are investigations that involve variables and establish a cause and effect relationship (Schwartz, 2007), but investigations are not experiments. A demonstration you do for your students at the front of your classroom is an investigation. While it is still a valid type of science, students need to leave your class understanding the difference. Ideally, a classroom would get to watch and participate in both types of activities, but it's important for you to know the difference, as you develop your curriculum.

✖ **STOP leaving art for the art teacher.** Our new science standards ask our students to plan, to model, and use graphical displays to evidence their learning. Dust off the crayons, and get drawing. Letting students visualize what they have learned not only leads to engagement but also to retention. Modeling, or making three-dimensional displays of concepts studied, is a fantastic way to incorporate aspects of STE(A)M into your required curriculum. Please note that high-quality art supplies are not necessary. My students love to use recycled materials whenever possible!

FULL STE(A)M AHEAD: THINGS TO TAKE WITH YOU ON YOUR ADVENTURE!

✓ **EMBRACE project-based learning.** Kids learn best by doing. Let your students do more than read a textbook and listen to you talk. It doesn't matter if you teach preK or fifth grade—kids need to *do*! Project-based learning (PBL) or problem-based learning is "action-based, hands-on learning at the core of STEM education" (Zuga, 2009, p. 14). By letting learners explore real-world problems, PBL uses collaborative groups that challenge students to use cross-curricular skills. PBL

Plugged In
www.pbl.uci.edu/wha-tispbl.html

encourages students to work together to solve problems posed by the teacher. It may be a design challenge or other problem that can only be solved by applying content knowledge using a hands-on approach. PBL can not only help your students retain information, but it encourages a deeper level of thinking by inspiring students to find the answers to questions for themselves (Zuga, 2009). More information can be found at www.pbl.uci.edu/whatispbl.html.

✓ **TEACH engineering!** Don't let the e-word scare you! The engineering design process provides students with a systematic approach to solving problems. Use the *Engineering Is Elementary* (Museum of Science, Boston, n.d.) design approach to help your students ask, imagine, plan, create, and improve their designs. The design process provides explicit problem-solving steps that give even the most creative kids the constraints that breed creative thinking.

Using the engineering process allows students a practical place to use math and science skills to create solutions and solve problems within authentic situations. This is the real-world application we desperately seek to make learning meaningful (Kelley, 2010). Resources like *Engineering Is Elementary* and *Teachengineering.com* offer students systematic instruction in predesigned lessons and activities. Consider using the *Engineering Is Elementary* or NASA design process templates at the end of this chapter.

✓ **HELP students gain interest in STE(A)M through knowledge about career opportunities.** Introduce careers that meld the STEM disciplines or that combine them with the arts. Begin locally by asking yourself, "Who are the parents in your class this year? What are their careers? Are they interested in sharing their experiences?" It may feel like you're being nosy, but a parent cartographer who mapped animal population migrations was one of my last year's most memorable science lessons! It doesn't have to be a formal presentation, just one that allows students to ask questions. Building knowledge about career opportunities helps kids develop an understanding for why they need to learn the STE(A)M disciplines.

✓ **USE socioscientific issues to pique student interest.** Did you have to read that three times? Don't worry. Socioscientific issues are just controversial social issues that relate to science (Zeidler & Keefer, 2003). They help students take topics of which they have prior anecdotal knowledge through popular media and engage them to answer questions in an objective fashion. It creates thinkers who can articulate their viewpoints through well-documented scientific evidence. Consider discussing global warming, its implications for the Earth, and possible solutions to its outcomes. Depending on where you live, you might talk about recycling or water issues, weather patterns, building collapses, or new construction built on wildlife. Connecting students' learning to issues that affect them is one of the most successful ways to involve your students in a meaningful scientific discussion.

✓ **USE good data!** STEM lessons often require using data. Whether student collected or teacher gathered, using good data allows students an authentic experience, a hallmark of STEM integration. What defines good data? Good data is accurate and comes from a reliable source. TMZ and Wikipedia might not be our best resources, but NASA has a variety of sources in its educator's resource section (including my favorite set in the Plugged In box. . . check it out!)

Plugged In

neo.sci.gsfc.nasa.gov/

✓ **TEACH your students the difference between** *data* **and** *evidence.* Data, or outcomes and observations gathered in science experimentation, are not evidence. Evidence is the interpretation of this data. Data sets are the information and results, but the evidence is the explanation and support that justifies our conclusion (Schwartz, 2007). Give your students practice synthesizing and analyzing others' data so they will be ready to interpret their own as they conduct experiments in your classroom. Yes, even first graders can do this!

✓ **KNOW the difference between using technology to enhance learning and teaching discrete technology skills.** STE(A)M encourages technological literacy for everyone. First, students and teachers need to know how to use technology. This means knowing successful operations of current technical systems and how the systems behave (Zuga, 2009). It is not okay for a teacher these days to say things like, "I don't believe in e-mail," "I don't use the computer," and "all that tech stuff is beyond me." You don't need to be a computer programmer, but you do need to have some basic technological knowledge. Next, students and teachers need to manage technology, making sure that it is both effective and suitable for its intended purpose. Finally, students and teachers need to understand technology, not just "facts and information, but the ability to synthesize the information into new insights" (Zuga, 2009, p. 12). Combining these skills will encourage students who are technologically literate and ready to innovate for the coming challenges of the next generations. Freaked out by this? Call in the cavalry! Talk to your tech support person or coteach with a colleague who is tech-savvy.

✓ **BEGIN lessons by identifying students' misconceptions.** One of my favorite, and most successful ways of beginning STE(A)M lessons is to poll the class about what they already know about a topic. Many teachers use a K-W-L chart (Ogle, 1986), asking students what they *know, want* to know, and what they have *learned.* They then use what the students want to know to drive instruction. In STE(A)M disciplines, what students believe prior to instruction is frequently incorrect. I suggest, however, using their misconceptions to drive the lesson. Have the students assume what they think is true. Then present them with text, data, and other tools and ask them to revisit their conceptions. With the given tools, can they support their personal perceptions with evidence? Do they have to change them? With this lesson structure, the "lightbulb" moments within your class will be visible from the moon.

NASA DESIGN PROCESS FLOW CHART

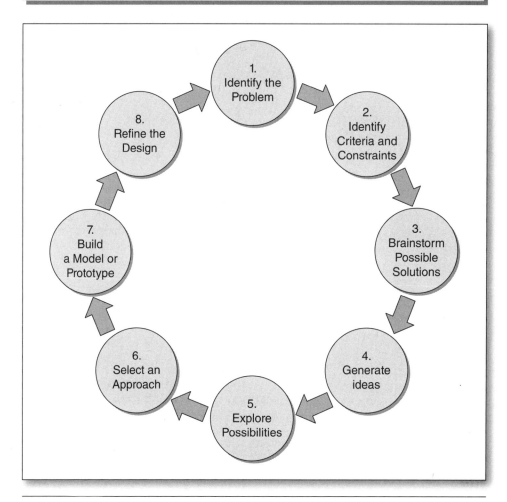

Source: Engineering is Elementry® Engineering Design Process (© Museum of Science, Boston, used with permission).

ENGINEERING IS ELEMENTARY
DESIGN PROCESS FLOW CHART

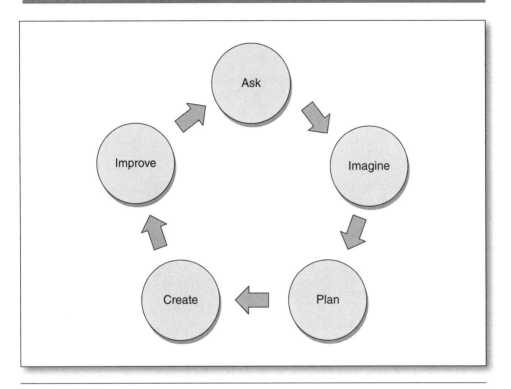

Source: www.eie.org/overview/engineering-design-process.

NASA'S 5-E MODEL LESSON TEMPLATE

Engage

- The purpose for the ENGAGE stage is to pique student interest and get them personally involved in the lesson, while pre-assessing prior understanding.

Explore

- The purpose for the EXPLORE stage is to get students involved in the topic, providing them with a chance to build their own understanding

Explain

- The purpose for the EXPLAIN stage is to provide students with an opportunity to communicate what they have learned so far and figure out what it means

Extend

- The purpose for the EXTEND stage is to allow students to use their new knowledge and continue to explore its implications

Evaluate

- The purpose for the EVALUATION stage is for both students and teachers to determine how much learning and understanding has taken place.

Source: www.nasa.gov/audience/foreducators/nasaeclips/5eteachingmodels/index_prt.htm.

NGSS STE(A)M IDEAS

A list of ideas and resources to support the implementation of NGSS. Consider using these ideas to integrate STE(A)M into your current curriculum.

	Science NGSS Topic	Technology	Engineering	Art	Math
Kinder	*Weather and Climate*	Have the students use NASA's NOAA webpage to look at real weather data. www.noaa.gov	Design and construct weather instruments.	Use dance and music to interpret weather conditions.	Chart temperatures and compare over the course of the week.
First Grade	*Space Systems*	Have the students use the Starwalk App to look at real time views of constellations.	Design lunar landers. rootengineering. weebly.com/first-grade.html	Listen to *The Planets* composed by Gustav Holst. Let students create models of the solar system.	Track the temperature on Mars with NASA's Curiosity Rover feed.
Second Grade	*Structure and Properties of Matter*	Have the students use The Elements App to look at how the elements interact with the real world. Use for visual pictures only.	Use the design process to solve a "properties of matter" problem. Can you design a way to keep your water cold while it's on your desk during the school day?	Use dance movements to demonstrate the atoms in different states of matter.	Calculate the time it takes an ice cube to melt and then refreeze.

	Science NGSS Topic	Technology	Engineering	Art	Math
Third Grade	*Interdependent Relationships in Eco-Systems*	Have the students use PowerPoint or Prezi to create presentations about how a chosen animal interacts with its ecosystem.	Design a solution to a problem in which humans interact with the local ecosystems.	Illustrate picture books about how animals interact within ecosystems.	Graph migration patterns of different local animals.
Fourth Grade	*Processes that Shape the Earth*	Have the students use Scratch to program simulations of processes that shape the Earth.	Design a solution to a problem in which humans can better prepare themselves against earthquakes.	Construct models of different processes that shape the Earth.	Chart and graph recent earthquakes.
Fifth Grade	*Earth's Systems*	Complete the NASA Summer of Innovation Challenge. Then blog about it. www.nasa.gov/pdf/635374main_Mission-to-Planet-Earth.pdf	Design ways that communities can protect the Earth's resources and environment.	Compose a song about the Earth's systems.	Graph levels of freshwater and saltwater in your local region.

Source: NGSS Lead States. 2013. Next Generation Science Standards: For States, By States. Washington, DC: The National Academies Press. The NGSS. 2013.

REFERENCES

Barakos, L., Lujan, V., & Strang, C. (2012). *Science, technology, engineering, mathematics (STEM): Catalyzing change amid the confusion.* Portsmouth, NH: RMC Research Corporation, Center on Instruction.

Burstein, J. H., & Knotts, G. (2011). *Reclaiming social studies for the elementary classroom: Integrating the arts through culture.* Dubuque, IA: Kendall/Hunt.

Hardiman, M., Rinne, L., & Yarmolinskaya, J. (2014). The effects of arts integration on long term retention of academic content. *Mind, Brain, and Education, 8*(3), 144–148.

Kelley, T. (2010). Staking the claim for the "T" in STEM. *Journal of Technology Studies, 36*(1), 2–11.

Lederman, N. G., & Lederman, J. S. (2004). Revising instruction to teach nature of science. *Science Teacher, 71*(9), 36–39.

Levinson, M., & Kaplan, D. (Producers), & Levinson, M. (Director). (2013). *Particle fever* [Motion picture – Documentary]. United States: Anthos Media.

Museum of Science, Boston. (n.d.). *Engineering is elementary: The EiE curriculum.* Retrieved from http://www.eie.org/eie-curriculum

Ogle, D. M. (1986). K-W-L: A teaching model that develops active reading of expository text. *Reading Teacher, 39,* 564–570.

Schwartz, R. (2007). What's in a word? How word choice can develop (mis)conceptions about the nature of science. *Science Scope, 31*(2), 42–47.

STEAMConnect. (n.d.). What is STE[+a]M? Retrieved from http://steamconnect.org/steam/

Tai, R. H., Liu, Q. C., Maltese, A. V., & Fan, X. (2006). Planning early for careers in science. *Science, 312,* 1143–1144.

Unified Sciences and Mathematics for Elementary Schools. (1973). *The USMES guide* (1st ed.). Newton, MA: Education Development Center.

Walker, C. M., Winner, E., Hetland, L., Simmons, S., & Goldsmith, L. (2011). Visual thinking: Art students have an advantage in geometric reasoning. *Creative Education, 2,* 22–26.

Woodruff, K. (2013, March 12). A history of STEM: Reigniting the challenge with NGSS and CCSS [Web log post]. Retrieved from http://us-satellite.net/stemblog/

Zeidler, D. L., & Keefer, M. (2003). The role of moral reasoning and the status of socioscientific issues in science education: Philosophical, psychological and pedagogical considerations. In D. L. Zeidler (Ed.), *The role of moral reasoning on socioscientific issues and discourse in science education* (pp. 7–38). Norwell, MA: Kluwer Academic.

Zuga, K. (2009). Background and history of the STEM movement. In K. de la Paz & K. Cluff (Eds.), *The overlooked STEM imperatives: Technology and engineering, K–12 education* (pp. 4–8). Reston, VA: International Technology Education Association.

RECOMMENDED READINGS

* Keeley, P., & Eberle, F. (2008). *Uncovering student ideas in science: Another 25 formative assessment probes.* Arlington, VA: NSTA Press.
* NGSS Lead States. (2013). *Next Generation Science Standards: For states, by states.* Washington, DC: National Academies Press.
* PBS Kids. (n.d.). Design squad nation: Parents, educators and engineers [Web log]. Retrieved from http://pbskids.org/designsquad/parentseducators/blog/index.html
* Pratt, H., & Bybee, R. W. (2012). The NSTA reader's guide to a framework for K–12 science education. Arlington, VA: NSTA Press.

GO EVEN FURTHER WITH THIS TOPIC ON THE WORLD WIDE WEB

* www.stemtosteam.org/
* www.teachengineering.org/
* www.zooniverse.org/
* www.nasa.gov/audience/foreducators/
* www.pbs.org/teachers/stem/

THE Apps WE LOVE

* Starwalk
* The Elements: A Visual Exploration
* STEM Mobile Labs
* NASA App

6

Awe-Inspiring Arts Integration

Mary Wolf

Daemen College

Ann Fontaine-Lewis

Seaford School District

Beth Thompson

Baltimore County Public Schools

WHAT REALLY WORKS IN ARTS INTEGRATION IN THE ELEMENTARY CLASSROOM

Arts Integration? But I Have NO Artistic Abilities!

Whether you realize it or not, the arts are a part of your everyday life. As educators, you design and decorate your classrooms in ways that are visually stimulating and help kids learn. You play music as students arrive in order to invigorate and set a positive tone for the day. Even when you aren't feeling well, you put on your teaching face, don a smile, and perform the "art" of teaching. You use your voice by changing the tone and volume when needed and use your hands and body to bring concepts, such as large and small, to life. You draw on the whiteboard and use visuals to help *all* learners envision what you are teaching. You make up or use songs to reinforce learning. The large majority of you probably do not consider yourselves artists, musicians, singers, dancers, or actors—and that's fine! But the reality is that as teachers you use many of the same tools that artists do to improve your teaching and student learning on a daily basis. Beyond the classroom, you, and everyone else in society, are surrounded by the arts in everyday life; they are and always have been a natural part of who we are.

So, if the arts are a natural part of teaching and learning and are embedded in life, why do we separate the arts in schools? Furthermore, why would a classroom teacher keep a student from going to an arts class because she did not finish her classwork? We've seen this happen far too many times. Some teachers do this because they know how much students enjoy arts classes and try to use it as motivation, saying things like, "If you get your classwork done, you won't have to miss art." Others do it because they don't understand the value of arts education in children's learning and lives. Life, learning, *and* art are about seeking and identifying connections with the world and worldly concepts, listening to and considering multiple perspectives, creating meaning, and sharing knowledge with others through words, numbers, images, notes, movements, and more.

Arts Integration (AI) is an effective way to help students seek, see, and make connections with worldly concepts relevant to all subjects; seek, hear, and consider multiple perspectives from a variety of people both in and out of the classroom; and not only make meaning but make that meaning visible in a myriad of ways. Students benefit when the arts are embedded in their learning because the arts are engaging and naturally motivate students. So what if, instead of punishing students by keeping them from what they enjoy, teachers integrate the arts into all subjects and lead them as they excitedly and actively engage in their learning and finish their work? Don't worry; you don't have to be an artist to integrate the arts. You don't even have to be able to draw a stick figure or carry a tune. You just need to be open to all that the arts have to offer your students. You can learn about the arts as you collaborate with those who are trained in the arts and co-create an arts integrated curriculum. Now that's a mouthful to say; but it's not that difficult to do. Start small, with just one arts teacher and one integrated lesson, and as you see the positive impact it has on your students and classroom, it will motivate you and your colleagues to do more. You will discover that it *really* works!

This chapter has culminated from the collaboration of three educators with an average of 33 years of experience in the profession. In our very different roles, we have experienced first-hand the impact of arts integration. Our perspectives include an art teacher who uses AI in her elementary school in Maryland, a K–12 curriculum specialist who provides staff development on AI in Delaware, and an art education professor who has taught AI units as a teacher and now teaches the theory and practice of AI in her college courses in New York. Together, we will provide you with the information and tools to get AI to *really* work for you!

WHAT IS ARTS INTEGRATION?

Arts Integration (AI) is an approach to curriculum planning and teaching that is often misinterpreted and misused. However, when understood and implemented effectively, AI really works. The confusion may come from the many visions and versions of integration that exist. Some of these versions include authentic arts integration (Smilan & Miraglia, 2009), substantive art integration (Marshall, 2005), interdisciplinary curriculum (Jacobs, 1989), interdisciplinary art education (Stokrocki, 2005), integrating arts across the elementary school curriculum (Gelineau, 2004), arts integration for classroom teachers (Cornett, in press), and more. (These are all included in the references section of this chapter so you can do your own research.)

Obviously, AI is not a new concept. Efland (2002) traces curriculum integration back to the progressive movement of the 1930s and to schools with similar philosophies such as the Waldorf Schools of the 1920s. The literature is overflowing with metaphors used to describe AI: opening doors, breaking down walls, crossing boundaries, building bridges, weaving, spinning, tying, collaging, and more. The metaphors all imply the joining of two separate entities. In this case, those entities are the arts and other content areas. We prefer Marshall's (2005) metaphor of weaving and spinning, which suggests an intertwining of the arts and other content areas that encourages students to *spin* or take their learning beyond the walls of the classroom and see how it relates to other subject areas and life. Whatever you call it, whatever acronym you use, or whatever metaphor you prefer, AI is historically and theoretically grounded, and it *really* works!

The main similarity among the numerous models of AI is that each integrates learning in the arts and core subjects with the intention of engaging students in deeper, more meaningful learning by engaging their hands, voices, minds, and bodies—aligning with Howard Gardner's (1983) theory of multiple intelligences. However, there are some AI models that integrate the arts in more meaningful ways, utilizing them to their full potential as ways of learning and communicating, while others take a more *arts and crafts* approach—making it an extra activity to support learning in *the core* subject. AI doesn't reach its full capacity when the arts are seen as *other than core*. Carpenter (2005) even refers to the arts as *core* and language arts, math, science, and social studies as the *other core*. Unfortunately, in most schools, the arts are literally referred to as the *specials* and are the first to go when there are budget cuts (Chapman, 2005). Such a devaluing of the arts by educational leaders and those classroom teachers who deprive students of arts classes because they didn't finish their classwork, promote the misunderstanding that the arts are not important—a grave misunderstanding.

Are you thinking, "But I don't understand; I'm not an expert in the arts!" That's okay. You are not alone! The arts teachers in your school will be excited to leave their isolated classrooms and collaborate because they often feel like outsiders as the only art, music, dance, or drama teacher in the school. You are not being asked to go back to school to become an art teacher. You're being asked to embrace the expertise of the arts teachers and reach out to collaborate with them to bring AI into your own elementary classroom—to weave, if you will, your expertise with that of the arts teachers. After all, these teachers were educated in *"the art of teaching art"* and should be responsible for the arts portion of the integration (Smilan & Miraglia, 2009, p. 39). Hopefully, that's a bit of a relief to you. If you do not have an arts teacher in your school, first advocate for one. Second, there are likely arts organizations and teaching artists in your local community that you can call for help. You can also contact local colleges and universities for professional development and even consider having arts education majors come in to collaborate with you. Additional resources are included at the end of this chapter, but first, let us give you some concrete examples of what this collaboration is and what it is not.

EXAMPLE 1: CRAFTY CATERPILLARS

Consider traditional misconceptions about AI as we illustrate them through a typical interdisciplinary unit theme of caterpillars becoming butterflies. In science class, the classroom teacher introduces students to this process and vocabulary terms such as egg, caterpillar, chrysalis, butterfly, and metamorphosis. Perhaps a few days later, the librarian reads *The Hungry Caterpillar* by Eric Carle to students. Then, weeks later, the art teacher helps kids turn egg cartons into caterpillars and clothespins and coffee filters into butterflies. Is this an example of well-planned, quality arts integration? No. Is it cute and engaging? Yes, but it is disjointed and doesn't ask students to think creatively. There is no requirement that students use divergent thinking to solve a problem. Instead, they simply follow step-by-step directions to complete a project that looks just like everyone else's. That is not to say that crafts cannot be part of a classroom activity; they most certainly can! However, we encourage you to go a step further and include the arts as well, making it a more meaningful and memorable experience for students. The "art" assignment in this unit lacks choice and voice and therefore should be considered an activity—not art. Don't worry, we will give you some suggestions for real arts connections and your arts teachers can give you even more once your collaboration begins!

EXAMPLE 2: CREATING CYCLES

Now consider a more effective implementation of arts integration, one that is truer to the intent of weaving the arts and other content areas in meaningful ways. The unit theme changes from a focus on caterpillars to the big idea of life cycles, which could be expanded to include or connect to life cycles of other animals, plants, and people, water cycles, cycles of time, song cycles, and more. Art teacher, Jamia Weir, works at a charter school in California that has an eco-literacy philosophy. She took a chance integrating art, music, movement, theater, and creative writing into a school project on *Cycles and Flows*. Originally, the fifth-grade science teacher was the primary teacher who tackled this theme. However, Jamia discussed cycles and flows with this teacher and ways to integrate the arts. In the AI unit designed by Weir, with input from her colleague, students further explored the cycles and flows that are inher-ent in artist Andy Goldsworthy's work. You can see Thomas Riedelsheimer's documen-tary *Rivers and Tides* in its entirety at the URL in our Plugged In box to learn more about this artist. In his art making, Goldsworthy's studio is outdoors in nature. He uses only

Plugged In

topdocumentaryfilms
.com/andy-golds
worthys-rivers-tides/

natural materials such as leaves, icicles, branches, and rocks. Most of his work is ephemeral, and only photographs and videos of the work remain, as the nature he uses to make his sculptures also destroys his work—an interesting cycle to observe. The tide may wash away one sculpture. The wind may cause another sculpture to tumble to the ground. The sun may melt an ice sculpture down to a puddle of water. After observing these cycles through videos and photos, students analyzed and discussed his work. The elementary school students used nouns, verbs, adjectives, and adverbs to create "pile" poems about cycles and flows. They read their poems using a song *cycle* approach where one student's reading followed and/or overlapped the next student's reading creating an aural rhythm, pattern, or dare we say—cycle. They created movements and enacted plays, which brought their understandings of cycles and flows to life through their bodies and voices. Students personally connected cycles and flows to their daily lives that flow one day to the next, one hour to the next, one meal to the next. Students collaborated to create a garden installation using discarded materials (litter) that disrupt nature's cycles and flows, all while learning about the importance of recycling and caring for their envi-ronment. Students themselves made connections to other subject areas, which were not formally included in the AI unit. One student referred to a book from social studies that discussed the ways that people depend on each other as a type of cycle. During this unit, students were actively engaged and motivated, as was their teacher, which led to a more dynamic learning environment. So what's your choice? Are you going to embrace a traditional unit of egg carton caterpillars with little academic reward, or will you take a chance with an AI unit about cycles that uses the arts in meaningful ways and really works for all students and teachers?

All in all, arts integration works for students, teachers, and administrators. Students naturally connect new information to prior life and educational experiences and use their mind and bodies to make sense of the new information. Intellectual experiences and sensory experiences are not separate entities (Irwin, Wilson Kind, Grauer, & de Cosson, 2005). When these experiences are seen as inseparable, as in AI, learning is enhanced. AI also helps prepare students to use thinking skills that will be required of them in middle school, high school, college, and in their personal and professional lives. Additionally, AI works for teachers because it reenergizes their commitment to exemplary planning and instruction. Teachers leave their isolated classrooms and collaborate to develop innovative units using progressive, collaborative teaching strategies. Through that collaboration, teachers learn more about the other disciplines as well. They become lifelong learners who rediscover their passion for learning *and* teaching. AI works for principals who are leading their schools to develop cultures of high-performance teaching and learning because, as it lessens the artificial fragmentation subjects in schools (Jacobs, 1989), it deepens learning for all students. AI develops motivated teachers, increases collaboration, and engages learners, which together lead to a more dynamic and successful learning environment. What more could an educator want?

ARTS INTEGRATION REALLY WORKS IF . . .

Teachers

- ✗ **STOP viewing the arts as nice but not necessary.** Crafts are nice activities. However, the arts encourage all students to engage in learning from a variety of perspectives using various thinking skills—creative, critical, divergent, and innovative. Also, the arts allow them to demonstrate their learning in various ways including art, music, movement, and drama. In fact, Howard Gardner's (1983) theory of multiple intelligences supports arts integration.
- ✗ **STOP viewing the arts as easy and mindless.** The arts are a way of learning, a form of inquiry, a method for gaining deeper knowledge, and a way of developing divergent thinkers. That's not mindless, nor is it all that easy to accomplish.
- ✗ **STOP looking at the arts as "specials" used only to provide planning time for classroom teachers.** The arts are often seen as the special activities students do so the *real* teacher can plan the *real* lessons. We know your time is limited, but take the extra 5 minutes to pick your class up early and ask your students questions about

what they are learning and doing. See firsthand the learning that occurs in *arts* lessons. You may be surprised to see the arts teachers are already making connections to your curriculum. So, why not collaborate?

✘ **STOP looking at the arts as just a way to support your content, and begin to understand the ways all disciplines can benefit from the integration of curriculum.** Yes, the arts can support learning of classroom content, but those same subjects could also support the arts. Don't let arts become the "side car" or "handmaiden" to other disciplines (Keifer-Boyd & Smith-Shank, 2006). Instead, balance the content from all subject areas involved for a stronger integrated curriculum.

Making Connections

Check out Chapter 4 on Social Studies

✘ **STOP being afraid of the arts.** So, you can't draw, sing, dance, or act? You can't look at a Picasso painting without really wanting to put the nose back where it belongs? That's okay! You don't have to be an art teacher to integrate the arts for your students. Art is also about how we observe the world and what our beliefs and experiences tell us (Keifer-Boyd & Smith-Shank, 2006). So go get coffee with the arts teacher, and talk about how you both can collaborate to ensure that arts integration becomes a vehicle for improved student learning. We can all demonstrate to students what it means to be open-minded, lifelong learners across an array of disciplines.

Administrators

✘ **STOP assuming that teachers intuitively know how to integrate curriculum.** AI requires in-depth training and sustained professional development for teachers of *all* content areas, which requires dedicated time and financial support (Chapman, 2005; Jacobs, 1989; Stokrocki, 2005). All school leaders and teachers will need professional development to understand arts integration and learn how to integrate the arts in their curricula.

✘ **STOP devaluing the arts.** Educate yourself on the ways the arts motivate, engage, and deepen learning for students. In a job interview, when asked about the art budget, a principal laughed and replied, "You don't need anything more than crayons, right?" It was obvious that this principal needed his own professional development on the value of arts education.

✘ **STOP eliminating arts teachers.** AI works because experts in a variety of disciplines, including the arts, collaborate to enhance lessons and promote deeper learning. Validate the contributions of the art and arts teachers by building opportunities into the schedule for them to collaborate with classroom teachers so that students can be more successful in all classes.

✗ **STOP using state testing and mandates as a reason to deprive students of quality arts instruction and arts integration.** The arts *are* core. Rabkin and Redmond (2006) describe scenarios of motivated students engaged in AI lessons. They share studies that reveal ways arts integration has helped improve test scores and higher order thinking and positively impacted teachers, students, and particularly disadvantaged students. The research is clear that the arts are an essential aspect of the learning process.

✗ **STOP referring to the arts as specials.** Language matters. The way you talk about something affects the way people think about it. It is especially powerful when it comes from someone of authority. Use the term *core arts,* and value the contribution of the arts and arts teachers to student learning.

🛑 GO SO NOW I KNOW WHAT NOT TO DO . . . BUT WHAT SHOULD I DO?

Teachers, DO This

✓ **REACH OUT to arts teachers in your building.** Invite the arts teachers to grade-level meetings. They can provide valuable arts resources to help support your lessons, which could lead to collaboration and arts integration. If you don't have an arts teacher in your building, consider that more attention is increasingly being paid to the idea of content teachers actually co-teaching with teaching artists (Murawski, 2013).

✓ **FIND a common understanding of Arts Integration.** Jacobs (1989) shares that one teacher's understanding of arts integration can be "180 degrees different from their colleague's down the hall" (p. 6). This can lead to misunderstanding and misuse of AI. Clearly, having a common understanding of what AI is, its purpose, and how it works is key to effective collaborative work in an arts integration school. We encourage you to develop your own definition, post it, and refer to it throughout the AI process. One simple definition could be that AI is a planning and teaching approach that relies on collaboration, includes divergent and critical thinking, requires connection-making among disciplines, and results in a wide variety of concrete examples of deep learning.

✓ **CHOOSE appropriate themes.** Collaborate with arts and other teachers to identify commonly investigated themes that have *meaningful* concepts *significant* to each discipline. Perkins (1989) uses the metaphor of *disciplinary lenses* to look at a theme and encourages teachers to ask the following of the lens chosen: (a) Can you apply the theme broadly and pervasively, (b) does it disclose fundamental patterns of the discipline, (c) does it lend itself for comparing and contrasting, and (d) does it fascinate? If it doesn't, then it's back to the drawing board to find a stronger theme. The theme of an arts integration unit must be a collaborative choice that promotes inquiry through the specific disciplines, highlights content from each content area, and illuminates the relationships among them and to life.

✓ **DO take risks and engage in the arts.** The arts teachers will be of great support helping you to better understand the arts and use them in your classroom. However, they should not be relied on to be the only ones using the arts. Don't just say to your kids, "I can't draw." Take the risk to draw yourself. Take the risk to sing and dance to model engaging with the arts. We'll let you in on a secret: not all kids are comfortable or confident with all arts forms. If they see you being vulnerable and taking risks, they are more likely to do the same. Who knows, maybe you'll be inspired to take an art, music, dance, or drama class on your own time to increase your own proficiency in the arts. Warning: The arts can be fun *and* relaxing, two things teachers desperately need and deserve!

✓ **ENGAGE in your own professional development.** Below are resources to help you learn more about arts integration. There are also numerous arts organizations, galleries, museums, theaters, and so on, in your community for you to engage with for your own development. We encourage you to seek them out. The arts can be fun *and* relaxing, two things teachers desperately need and deserve! (Yeah. That deserved a repeat.)

✓ **DO work with arts teachers to take field trips.** Many art museums and galleries have interdisciplinary focused field trip experiences available for your students that will support your in-school AI units.

✓ **FOCUS on the ways that arts integration can enhance 21st century skills.** AI integrates the 21st century "Cs" of communication, collaboration, critical thinking, and creativity naturally and seamlessly. AI enhances vital skills such as observing, analyzing, imagining, interpreting, designing, revising, creating, presenting, responding, and more. Arts integration provides the foundation for developing an array of 21st century skills.

✓ **REALIZE that the arts enhance dispositions vital in all classrooms.** Hetland, Winner, Veenema, and Sheridan (2013) argue that the thinking students are engaged in when creating art encourages students to engage and persist, envision, express, observe, reflect, and stretch and explore. Aren't these dispositions valuable in your classroom as well?

✓ **HELP students make meaningful connections between subject content and art content by using themes that relate to them personally and socially.** One simple way to connect both the arts' and various subjects' perspectives with students' personal and social characteristics and interests is to design units that explicitly provide those opportunities for connections at the elementary level (try themes like "Others & Me," "Nature & Me," "The Built Environment & Me," "Health & Me," or "Technology & Me"). Teachers collaborating in AI can strategically narrow down the specific concepts within these broader themes that are both common and significant to their various disciplines.

✓ **DO make learning memorable.** Gelineau (2004) argues that the arts make learning memorable. By engaging students' minds and bodies, by making themes relevant to students' lives and worlds, and by allowing students to learn, make personal connections, and express themselves in various ways, AI makes learning more powerful and memorable. Will they remember Andy Goldsworthy's name in 5 years? Probably not. . . . But will they remember that there was an artist who addressed cycles and flows and how that theme is relevant to many aspects of life? Probably so.

✓ **DO start small and make progress over time.** You likely won't be able to convince all teachers to integrate the arts immediately. So start by collaborating with one arts teacher and create one AI unit. Then share your success and see people come on board!

✓ **INTEGRATE a variety of subject areas with various arts forms.** There are simply too many potential connections among disciplines to explore in this chapter. We have already given you the example from the AI cycles and flows unit and will give a few more suggestions on page 98. But also, DO collaborate with your arts teachers to identify even more way to integrate curriculum.

✓ **DO value the arts as ways of thinking, making, and being.** The arts should be taught in ways that relate to the ways artists work today (Anderson & Milbrandt, 2005; Gude, 2004, 2007, 2013; Marshall, 2005). For visual arts teachers, if you take a Discipline Based Art Education (DBAE) approach to teaching art, read the texts just listed and look on page 101 for more contemporary perspectives on visual arts education.

Administrators, DO This

✓ **CONTACT arts integration experts, and provide sustained professional development for teachers so all team members are knowledgeable in the theory and practice of AI.** Professional development contributes to the success of AI. Stokrocki (2005) acknowledges that poor planning can lead to shallow learning experiences; so, without the necessary professional development, arts integration will not be successful. Schools and universities should collaborate to provide the professional development necessary for building the capacity to create and sustain AI over time.

✓ **DO provide time.** Provide classroom and arts teachers with consistent collaborative planning and assessment time. AI is more successful when common planning time is provided (Jacobs, 1989; Stokrocki, 2005). Arts integration requires both a front-loaded planning approach for teaching and learning and ongoing assessment in order to sustain arts integration over time.

✓ **CLARIFY the roles and expectations for teachers.** Involve teachers in the development of these roles and expectations after they have had the opportunity to build their understanding of AI through professional development.

✓ **USE staff development money to support work between the arts teachers and the other content teachers.** Cornett (in press) argues that AI is money well spent. If you want teachers to build engagement in their classes, encourage problem-solving and motivation, and ultimately increase test scores, get your teachers collaborating!

✓ **DO incorporate time in the year's schedule on a regular basis for arts teachers to meet with grade-level teachers.** This will show that you value them and the process of developing arts integrated curriculum.

✓ **DESIGN a system of rotating Professional Learning Communities (PLCs)** in which staff members who have designated planning at the same time meet across disciplines.

✓ **INVITE arts teachers to provide professional development to staff during after-school faculty meetings or on professional development days.** You will be pleasantly surprised to see teachers smiling at professional development. The same way the arts engage and motivate students, they will engage and motivate your teachers. Hands-on professional development that challenges teachers in new ways will offer exciting opportunities for professional learning.

✓ **INVITE interested staff members to voluntarily participate in after-school professional development sessions. Create an environment that values teachers' interests, experiences, and insights.** And offering food and treats will only enhance the experience!

START SMALL!

We already provided the example of cycles and flows. Below are some additional suggestions of themes that can be addressed across a few subject areas including at least the visual arts. As part of a professional development activity, try to brainstorm more of your own connections with teachers in your school or school district.

We'll start with a simple one. Consider the theme of patterns. Patterns are created through repetition and can be observed from a variety of subject area lenses and in life. Don't just ask students to draw and color patterns! Remember, if there is no choice or voice, it is an activity—not art. Instead, ask them to compare and contrast the patterns used in Chuck Close's 2-D paintings and Zac Freeman's 3-D assemblages of found, discarded objects. If you don't know about these artists, you will *love* learning about them and their life stories, which are very inspiring for students. Ask your art teacher for more information about each artist. Read Harvey's book, *Busy Bugs: A Book About Patterns.* Have them identify patterns in books, poems, nature, math, popular songs, or ever-famous *Macarena.* But don't *just* identify the patterns. Discuss *why* patterns are important in art, language arts, music, science, math, dance, and so on. The possibilities are endless!

Consider another theme—telling stories. Stories are universal and part of every culture and every time period. From a visual arts/social studies perspective, you can discuss the ways artists have told stories on walls including the early cave paintings of Lascaux, Mexican muralists such as Orozco and Rivera, and today's Mural Arts Program in Philadelphia. You can connect to language arts by reading Ancona's book *Murals: Walls That Sing*, which can inspire students to tell their own stories both visually and verbally. Consider how music, dance, and theater tell stories as well. Again, the possibilities are endless!

Finally, consider the theme "past heroes." Again, from a visual arts/social studies perspective, you can discuss ways artists have documented heroes from historical events such as the Underground Railroad and Great Migration. Jacob Lawrence not only created series of narrative paintings about each, he also created a children's book entitled *The Great Migration.* Clearly, we have another language arts connection! Students can recreate history visually or even act it out. Consider how heroes and heroism have been captured in patriotic songs, movies, or plays. Once again, the possibilities are endless!

Now consider some of your own and brainstorm ideas! Remember to start small!

Theme	Subject Area	Core Arts Area

WHAT IS THE STATUS OF ARTS INTEGRATION IN YOUR SCHOOL OR SCHOOL DISTRICT?

Use the Likert scale below to rate the current status in implementing an arts integration model for teaching and learning in your school or school district.

1—Not at All, 2—Just Beginning, 3—Developing, 4—Firmly in Place

	1	2	3	4
The arts are openly respected and valued by the administration in our school/district.				
The arts are openly respected and valued by the teaching staff in our school/district.				
The arts are openly respected and valued by the students in our school/district.				
There are arts experts in visual arts, dance, music, and dramatic arts among our teaching staff.				
The expertise of our arts teachers is utilized as a resource for enhancing the teaching and learning in our school/district.				
As a staff, we have considered what common themes across our disciplines are essential and relevant to our students' learning.				
Our school/district offers a variety of opportunities for teachers to collaborate on curriculum design and instructional planning.				
Students in our school/district have multiple meaning-making opportunities to understand content from a variety of perspectives.				
Our staff has a common understanding of what arts integration is and what it should look like in our classrooms.				
As a staff, we have clarified the roles and expectations for arts integration in our school/district.				
In-depth training and sustained professional development in arts integration is provided for teachers of all content areas in our school/district.				
There are regular and consistent opportunities for arts teachers and other content teachers to visit each other's classrooms.				
We have cross-discipline integration already happening in our school/district.				
We have models of effective arts integration in our school/district.				
Our students have multiple opportunities to construct meaning of concepts common to two or more disciplines, including one or more of the arts.				
Our students have multiple opportunities to engage in critical and divergent thinking strategies for deep learning across disciplines, including one or more of the arts.				

WHAT IS THE STATUS OF ARTS INTEGRATION IN YOUR CLASSROOM?

Use the Likert scale below to rate your classroom's current status in implementing an arts integration model for teaching and learning.

1—Not at All, 2—Just Beginning, 3—Developing, 4—Firmly in Place

	1	2	3	4
I see the arts as core and necessary.				
I see integrating the arts with other subjects as a way to enhance learning.				
I am open to learning and teaching about and through the arts, collaboratively.				
I recognize my role and the expectations for arts integration in my classroom.				
I have chosen to collaborate with other teachers to enhance teaching and learning in my classroom.				
My schedule provides specific times to meet with other teachers for collaborative planning and assessment and that time is being used accordingly.				
We have chosen specific themes that are meaningful and significant to each subject area, including the arts.				
Collaboratively, we are putting time and energy into finding meaningful content connections and comparisons.				
We are using the arts in meaningful ways rather than as extra activities.				
We are provided with in-depth training and sustained professional development in arts integration.				
Our students have multiple opportunities to engage in critical and divergent thinking strategies for deep learning across disciplines, including one or more of the arts.				
Our students have multiple opportunities to construct meaning of concepts common to two or more disciplines, including one or more of the arts.				
We are provided and take advantage of regular and consistent opportunities for arts teachers and other content teachers to visit each other's classrooms.				
We have models of effective arts integration in our school or school district.				
We have access to instructional coaching from professionals who know and understand arts integration.				
We have opportunities to receive feedback and are encouraged to reflect upon arts integration progress in our classrooms.				

TOP WEBSITES AND RESOURCES FOR ARTS INTEGRATION

Arts Integration

- artsedge.kennedy-center.org/educators/how-to/series/arts-integration/arts-integration
- www.artseveryday.org/Educators/detail.aspx?id=212
- education.jhu.edu/PD/newhorizons/strategies/topics/Arts%20in%20Education/The%20Center%20for%20Arts%20in%20the%20Basic%20Curriculum/oddleifson3.htm
- www.edutopia.org/stw-arts-integration-video
- www.edutopia.org/arts-integration-resources
- www.theedadvocate.org/happier-students-higher-scores-the-role-of-arts-integration/

Museums/Galleries

- teachers.phillipscollection.org/
- thewalters.org/integrating-the-arts/
- www.philamuseum.org/education/32–129–304.html

Visual Arts

- artsedge.kennedy-center.org/educators/how-to/arts-integration/arts-integration-in-practice/~/media/ArtsEdge/Images/Articles/Educators/how-tos/arts-integration/connections/ai-visual-arts-connections.pdf
- educationcloset.com/wp-content/uploads/2011/07/elements-of-visual-art.pdf

Music

- artsedge.kennedy-center.org/educators/how-to/arts-integration/arts-integration-in-practice/~/media/ArtsEdge/Images/Articles/Educators/how-tos/arts-integration/connections/ai-music-connections.pdf
- educationcloset.com/wp-content/uploads/2011/07/elements-of-music.pdf

Dance

- artsedge.kennedy-center.org/educators/how-to/arts-integration/ arts-integration-in-practice/~/media/ArtsEdge/Images/ Articles/Educators/how-tos/arts-integration/connections/ai-dance-connections.pdf
- educationcloset.com/wp-content/uploads/2011/07/elements-of-dance.pdf
- www.psychologytoday.com/files/attachments/1035/martha-graham-and-the-polymathic-imagination.pdf

Theater

- artsedge.kennedy-center.org/educators/how-to/arts-integration/ arts-integration-in-practice/~/media/ArtsEdge/Images/ Articles/Educators/how-tos/arts-integration/connections/ai-theater-connections.pdf
- www.edutopia.org/stw-arts-integration
- educationcloset.com/wp-content/uploads/2011/07/elements-of-drama.pdf

REFERENCES

Anderson, T., & Milbrandt, M. (2005). *Art for life: Authentic instruction in art*. New York, NY: McGraw-Hill.

Carpenter, B. S. (2005). Disciplines, boundaries, and bridges. *Art Education, 5*(4), 4.

Chapman, L. H. (2005). No child left behind in art? *Art Education, 58*(1), 6–16.

Cornett, C. E. (in press). *Creating meaning through literature and the arts: Arts integration for classroom teachers* (5th ed.). Boston, MA: Pearson.

Efland, A. D. (2002). *Art and cognition, integrating the visual arts curriculum*. New York, NY: Teachers College Press.

Gardner, H. (1983). *Frames of mind: The theory of multiple intelligences*. New York, NY: Basic Books.

Gelineau, R. P. (2004). *Integrating the arts across the elementary school curriculum*. Belmont, CA: Cengage Learning.

Gude, O. (2004). Postmodern principles: In search of a 21st-century art education. *Art Education, 57*(1), 6–14.

Gude, O. (2007). Principles of possibility: Considerations for a 21st century art and culture curriculum. *Art Education, 60*(1), 6–17.

Gude, O. (2013). New school art styles: The project of art education. *Art Education, 66*(1), 6–15.

Hetland, L., Winner, E., Veenema, S., & Sheridan, K. M. (2013). *Studio thinking 2: The real benefits of visual arts education*. New York, NY: Teachers College Press.

Irwin, R., Wilson Kind, S., Grauer, K., & de Cosson, A. (2005). Curriculum integration as embodied knowing. In M. Stokrocki (Ed.), *Interdisciplinary art education: Building bridges to connect disciplines and cultures* (pp. 44–59). Reston, VA: National Art Education Association.

Jacobs, H. H. (Ed.). (1989). *Interdisciplinary curriculum: Design and implementation*. Alexandria, VA: Association for Supervision and Curriculum Development.

Keifer-Boyd, K., & Smith-Shank, D. (2006). Speculative fiction's contribution to contemporary understanding: The handmaid art tale. *Studies in Art Education, 47*(2), 139–154.

Marshall, J. (2005). Connecting art, learning and creativity: A case for curriculum integration. *Studies in Art Education, 46*(3), 227–241.

Murawski, W. W. (2013, August). Co-teaching and partner building in the arts classrooms. Presentation at the 2013 Institute for Educators, The Music Center, Los Angeles, CA.

Perkins, D. N. (1989). Selecting fertile themes for integrated learning. In H. H. Jacobs (Ed.), *Interdisciplinary curriculum design and implementation* (pp. 67–76). Alexandria, VA: Association for Supervision and Curriculum Development.

Rabkin, N., & Redmond, R. (2006). The arts make a difference. *Educational Leadership, 63*(5), 60–64.

Smilan, C., & Miraglia, K. M. (2009). Art teachers as leaders of authentic art integration. *Art Education, 62*(6), 39–45.

Stokrocki, M. (2005). *Interdisciplinary art education: Building bridges to connect disciplines and cultures*. Reston, VA: National Art Educational Association.

GO EVEN FURTHER WITH THIS TOPIC ON THE WORLD WIDE WEB

- www.artsedge.kennedy-center.org/educators/how-to/series/arts-integra tion/arts-integration
- www.artseveryday.org/Educators/detail.aspx?id=212
- www.education.jhu.edu/PD/newhorizons/strategies/topics/ Arts%20in%20Education/The%20Center%20for%20Arts%20in%20 the%20Basic%20Curriculum/oddleifson3.htm
- www.edutopia.org/stw-arts-integration-video
- www.edutopia.org/arts-integration-resources

THE Apps WE LOVE

- MoMA Art Lab
- WordFoto
- PianoBall
- Book Creator
- Doink Express

SECTION II

What Really Works in Instruction

7

Tuning in With Technology

Lisa A. Dieker, Lauren Delisio, and Caitlyn A. Bukaty

University of Central Florida

WHAT REALLY WORKS IN ENGAGEMENT IN THE ELEMENTARY CLASSROOM

Enhancing Engagement via Technology

Your principal just called you into her office to let you know that she is going to give you a whole class set of iPads. She is excited to see how you'll use it and knows the school board will be looking forward to some incredible student outcomes. As you leave the office with a tentative smile on your lips, you think, "What do I do with iPads and a bunch of first graders?" None of your lessons are digital. None of your curriculum describes how to use tablets for instruction. But hey, you don't want to say no to such an amazing opportunity. . . do you?

Technology use has exploded across every facet of society and education. However, the increased use of technology in classrooms has boiled down to a basic question: Does technology simply increase student engagement because of its entertainment value, or are students actually learning content and social skills? The answer is yes. And no. Despite this tension, teachers need to be aware of emerging trends in technology, as well as the most recent research with regards to strategies for engaging learners through the use of technology. As new technology emerges almost daily, you need to understand the potential, and the pitfalls, in purchasing, adopting, and using a wide array of technologies that are innovative yet may only hold promise to impact practice and student engagement without producing real results.

In order to stay abreast of the near- and far-term technology that is emerging in our field, as well as the potential impact of these tools on students in the present day and in their future employment opportunities, we strongly suggest you read the New Media Consortium's (NMC, 2014) Horizon Report each February when it is released. We know that a report on technology sounds like it is way outside the realm of your elementary expertise, but trust us on this! Over the last decade, this report has been right on target in their pre-

Plugged In

www.nmc.org

dictions. More than 8 years ago, they predicted that everyone would be using tablet computers. The authors of the 2014 report remind the field that we have some challenges ahead of us associated with the adoption and rewards of these emerging advances in technology related to education. Page 116 shows information pulled from the Horizon Report that reminds the field that there is still work to be done and hurdles to overcome. There are so many incredible advancements that we can use in the elementary classroom—advancements that our kids will love. However, these advancements are pointless if they do not help students to master content more deeply or increase their ability to sustain their attention to learn more information. It is this blending of technology and engagement that is the focus for this chapter. We know that using technology as a tool for engagement, with an ultimate goal of increased and improved student learning, is something that can really work. That's a pretty good goal, right? If you agree, keep reading. If you don't. . . well, we're not sure how to help you.

Borrowing terms from the NMC, we know students are currently engaged with technology, and we know what is changing in their world technology-wise. This report also helps us realize that we need to consider the far-term horizon as it relates to education and technology as well. For now, page 116 also provides us with what is present and what is approaching. That's just not enough! Let's look at how we used to engage kids using the "old school" methods of paper-pencil and group work; now, let's apply these methods to new innovations in technology, both ones that are sustaining (meaning that they continue or evolve a technology we already know) or are disrupting (meaning that they are changing the field and maybe even displacing an older technology). The purpose of this approach is to help you think about what really works for the future of students who, born today, will be working in our society until approximately the year 2080. 2080! Scary, huh? So with that as our forecast for what really works, let's think about what we already know.

KEY RESEARCH YOU NEED TO KNOW ABOUT TECHNOLOGY AND ENGAGEMENT

The shift in standards is leading teachers to focus not on bell-to-bell teaching, but on bell-to-bell *engagement*; this shift is at the core of the College and Career Ready Standards. With this in mind, think about the impact and intertwining that technology can have. We encourage you to first think about who is disengaged in your class: Is it the student who loves technology, or the males, or the females, or the gifted, or the struggling learners? To do what really works, you must first have in mind which students to target in order to tackle the issue of engagement. The definition for disengagement, according to the Merriam-Webster Dictionary (2014), is "to stop being involved with a person or group." So as we think about integrating practices that increase engagement, we need to look first at the populations we most often disengage. There are some known populations in the literature that we are failing as a nation (minority males, students who are struggling with schoolwork; Jackson & Hilliard, 2013). However, each individual teacher needs to examine his or her own practices and classes of students (Smyth, McInerney, & Fish, 2013). What are we doing, or not doing, on a daily basis that might be causing these particular groups of students to disengage? Data-driven instruction is an effective way to address factors of disengagement (Datnow, Park, & Kennedy-Lewis, 2012). By spending time each day examining data, a teacher can determine which group or individual student did not meet the standard for learning or behavior and can then redirect the course of the next day's lesson to ensure engagement with those students; naturally, the ultimate goal remains a mastery of content and improved learning outcomes.

Want real engagement? Start with ensuring active learning. When you ask your students a question, do you always pick the few with their hands raised? Do you move on once one or two students have answered? Instead, we suggest that teachers encourage every student to answer every question asked throughout the day. How do you do that without losing all your time? Some simple examples (low- to high-tech) might include: (a) using clickers or a dry erase board, (b) asking students to stand or sit depending on the answer, or (c) using bring your own devices (BYOD) with socrative. com. Any of these formative assessment tools can change student behavior, as well as allow teachers to measure who does and who does not understand a concept. Oftentimes when we discuss classroom management, we talk about "managing" behavior. In the chapter on Classroom

Management in this book, authors Palomo Hare and Murawski clarify that classroom management involves both behavior and instructional management. We concur and suggest that teachers should be managing not just behavior but also the engagement of all learners. A student can be sitting quietly with absolutely no behavior issues, but she's

Making Connections

Check out Chapter 9 on Classroom Management

completely disengaged in the lesson; that's something we don't want to see anymore.

In fact, the shift toward College and Career Ready Standards and the push in education in general related to more inquiry-based instruction *requires* an increase in student discussions. (We know, many of us have spent years trying to get our kids to stop talking all the time. . . now we're asked to encourage it! But hang with us. There's a rationale here. And it's a good one.) Many students with or without disabilities may be shy to talk, find they need more time to share their opinion, or might need coaching or scaffolding to ensure they are successful. Providing safe and ongoing ways to participate ensures they are not dis-

Plugged In

www.teachthought .com/technology/26-teacher-tools-to-create-online-assessments/

engaged and provides for more robust assessment opportunities. A plethora of online assessment tools exist. Included in this article at teachthought. com is a summary of 26 great tools to try that really work. Try a few.

Why worry about engagement at all? Well, researchers involved in looking at student engagement found that disengaged behavior is directly linked to dropping out of school (Reschly & Christenson, 2006). The participation-identification model proposes that if students participate or are engaged in the school setting, regardless of whether it's in an academic or social context, the student will begin to identify with school, thus creating a positive cycle centered on school success (Finn, 1989). That doesn't surprise any of us, does it? To engage students in the academic setting, it is important to consider the individual needs of each student. Classrooms across the country are comprised of diverse learners who need to be catered to academically, socially, and behaviorally. Catering to students? If that idea bothers you, just think about it as differentiation; all you are doing is being a great teacher by figuring out what each student needs and then figuring out how to get it to him so he can be successful. If you are doing this proactively, we call it Universal Design for Learning. No catering apron required.

School engagement and self-advocacy also have the potential to affect long-term academic and social outcomes for all students (Errey & Wood, 2011). Previous researchers have reported that a strong, albeit negative, relationship exists between school engagement and school dropout (Reschly & Christenson, 2006). Kids are engaged? They tend not to drop out of school. It is as simple as that. So how do we engage them? We suggest that what really works are: (a) project-based learning (PBL), (b) peer support/collaborative structures, and (c) self-management strategies, all of which can involve some form of technology.

Project-based learning. Project-based learning is an instructional model whereby students learn by investigating and solving authentic problems and projects (Blumenfeld et al., 1991). Although PBL is a student-centered model of education, that does not mean that teachers no longer have a role in the classroom; in fact, their role is highly critical to the overall success of PBL. Successful implementation begins with a classroom climate of openness and inquiry, as well as effective social structures (Barron et al., 1998). Classroom teachers must create this climate of cooperative work by encouraging out-of-the-box thinking, questioning, and student discussions. Great social media tools and various components of the Google platform (e.g., Google Hangouts, Google Helpout, and Google Docs) can all help with PBL activities. Remember, all PBL models are created with problems and projects as the core outcome. Provide more of a Universal Design for Learning (UDL) approach and let students use an array of technologies within the PBL models. (Not sure what UDL is? Read the chapter by Dr. Tamarah Ashton and learn more!) Additionally, throughout the use of PBL, students must be provided with necessary scaffolds, multiple ways to express their learning, and opportunities to self-reflect, assess, and revise their work (Barron et al., 1998). What better way to help them shape the problem than by allowing students to work in cooperative groups to integrate technological tools in order to address the problem posed. Remember, this might be the perfect time for your students to introduce *you* to a useful technological device or app!

Making Connections

Check out Chapter 11 on UDL

Peer support. Students can address any lesson using various types of peer structures. The use of peer structures is clearly supported in the literature to increase engagement; it is so clearly supported that it made our top three as something that really works for engaging learners. Peer structures are also natural conduits to integrate an array of technologies. Consider how to use peer tutoring (same age or cross age) via Skype, or embrace the highly engaging role that cooperative learning can play in your classroom, with each student being given a different role for learning and using technology. Peer structures allow students to learn and teach each other as a means to better understand the content being covered (Hughes, Carter, Hughes, Bradford, & Copeland, 2002). You already know that your elementary students like to work together. How cool is it that you can validate the use of small groups because you know you're combining a rich, evidence-based practice with an array of technological tools to effectively engage kids?

Self-management strategies. Ever go onto the computer and spend more time on Facebook or checking e-mail than completing the task assigned? Welcome to the temptation students face between writing that paragraph or going off on a random search for the latest and greatest YouTube video. Clearly, with both technology and engagement, you need

Plugged In

www.intervention central.org/

to have synergy in both cases to attain some level of self-discipline. Self-management techniques do work and typically involve students using self-monitoring, self-evaluation, and self-instruction (Mooney, Ryan, Uhing, Reid, & Epstein, 2005). When using a self-management strategy, students monitor and record their own behavior, academically and socially, to increase academic outcomes (Mooney et al., 2005). Consider today how self-management tools could be electronic. A great discussion about tools, many of which involve technology and self-management, can be found at the Intervention Central website identified on our Plugged In box. We suggest you consider looking at ClassDojo or Goalbook and other personal time management apps, along with numerous other low-tech tools, such as behavioral rating sheets, to ensure time with technology is truly engaged time for learning.

Now, as you begin to think about technology, be sure to keep your thinking laser focused on *engaged* learning—not just on buying more stuff. Shiny objects can dazzle learners, but being dazzled may not produce the outcomes we all desire in this high stakes, learning outcome-driven environment. As we noted, technology is not the only answer, but if you want to do what works, stop fighting and start learning from your students about what works for them. What technological tools do they use? What keeps them engaged? Keep in mind, we will always continue to evolve as a society, and the jobs of the future will include higher and higher levels of technology competency, so think about how you might use some of the ideas provided to get kids ready for the year 2080 and beyond.

In the next sections, we funneled down what we feel are activities we see frequently that do not enhance engagement or technology use and those we wish teachers would do more of. Read on and take notes. . . on your tablet, smart phone, laptop, or even with a pen and paper.

IF YOU WANT AN ENGAGED CLASSROOM IN THE WORLD TODAY. . .

Teachers

- ✖ **STOP teaching to those who already learn the way you teach.** Look at your daily assessments, observe your students' behavior, and think about who is disengaged and how they learn. Then, change the way you teach to these students.
- ✖ **STOP using a one-size-fits-all strategy.** Whether it is technology, cooperative learning, or peer tutoring, consider a range of social,

technological, and engagement activities daily. Students learn differently but also engage differently, so broaden the menu of options.

✖ **STOP talking.** Kids are not engaged when the teacher is doing all of the talking. Make everything about students—let them do the talking, drawing, moving, and/or listening to each other! Make sure they know that these activities help them to learn.

✖ **STOP removing technology from kids as they move from one grade to another.** Let kids state what they need, and give it to them, from birth and on throughout their lives. Too many times, technology is teacher selected, instead of student driven. We have to stop allowing access or engagement in one grade or content area, but not another. We should allow students to learn the way they learn, whether that is with a paper and pencil or with a tablet computer.

✖ **STOP trying to micromanage all technology.** Let kids use what they want to use. Students have their own technologies, but schools and classrooms try to restrict the use of these technologies instead of embracing the billions of dollars of self-purchased tools. The movement to use Bring Your Own Device (BYOD) is an essential tool, but students must be provided with clear directives and class parameters to ensure proper use of their devices.

✖ **STOP making it about *stuff*.** Look at the verb instead of the noun; don't just buy an app—find an app that changes outcomes in math. Let the verb of what you want students to do be the driving force. Instead of thinking, "We need to buy more iPads," you should be thinking about what you want the iPad to *do*.

Administrators

✖ **STOP creating policies that work against the use of creative teachers.** BYOD can be used well and effectively, but many teachers will avoid figuring out its use if the school policy is "no cell phones, no iPads, no. . . no. . . no. . . . "

✖ **STOP thinking old school.** Technology moves more quickly than we can keep up. Try not to hold firm to how teachers used to teach and how curriculum used to be designed. Be open to a curriculum committee that eschews textbooks in favor of online research and virtual fieldtrips.

GO WANT TO UP YOUR ENGAGEMENT? THEN, YOU NEED TO

Teachers, DO This

✓ **ASSESS who is and is not *learning* and *engaged* on a daily basis.** As you reflect each day, do not just think about who learned the class objective, but also ask: How engaged were the students? Did your students who were gifted learn immediately and master the content but then quickly become disengaged? Did your student who struggles academically or socially fail to master the lesson due to a lack of engagement? Either way, ask students who are disengaged what you might change in your teaching to make them more active in their own learning. Even first graders can tell you what they'd like more or less of in their class. Consider using the form on page 117 to help you think about how you are meeting the needs of students. How will you help those students engage? Is technology warranted? Might it help? If so, what, how, and with whom?

✓ **ENSURE teacher talk is less than 50%.** Ever go to a lecture and make your grocery list? Remember, students are in school for 6 hours a day, and even 3 hours of listening is too much to ask of a student—especially 5 year olds! Remember, students who struggle often "think differently," so pause and ask students to share their thoughts with their peers. You will have increased engagement; you will be able to assess students understanding. Stand back and watch in awe. As your level of teacher talk decreases, student learning increases.

✓ **USE evidence-based practices**, like cooperative learning, peer tutoring, positive behavioral supports. Commit to learning something new, and then use technology to accomplish that learning goal. Beyond a Google search, what could you use to increase engagement? Some of our

Plugged In

www.edutopia
.org/technology-
integration-research-
evidence-based-programs

favorites are Edmodo, Puppet Pals, and Socrative, but remember, randomly selected technology may have the same outcome we had before. We like it, but students find what we selected boring. Want ideas related to evidence-based practices that use technology? Check out this helpful resource from Edutopia in the Plugged In box.

✓ **KEEP CURRENT with everything.** Find materials to read (like the NMC report), find information online (websites like Edutopia are helpful), or even just talk with knowledgeable colleagues to make sure that you are on the cutting edge.

✓ **LEARN and UNLEARN.** The most effective leaders today have to be ready to unlearn as much as they are to learn. Sure, we used to use a fax, but now we scan. We used to e-mail, but now we text or IM. Find shortcuts to do things that are critical. If you need help, use technology to help you. That's what your kids would do!

✓ **EMPOWER kids.** A great way to get kids engaged is to give them a role in technology adoption. Think of the school district that

bought all PCs for their computer lab, though most of the students at the school, when polled, preferred Macs. What a quick way to disengage the learners at the school! Want to know a real way to include kids in technology adoption? A great website for this is Genyes (www.genyes.org/). The leaders of this initiative believe that students should be leading school and district technology initiatives.

✓ **TEACH self-advocacy while keeping technology at the core.** Students need to know which tools will help them be engaged. When you make sure that students adopt technology that really works for them, you are helping to ensure they know how to advocate for themselves so that they are able to continue to use those tools in the future.

✓ **DO let kids give and receive with technology.** Consider having international pen pals (there are secure websites) or have your students Skype with older adults on a weekly basis about history questions or a variety of other topics. The point is that kids, especially those with disabilities, need to give as much as they receive, and technology provides an easy way to give back. Have you heard of the Free Rice website (freerice.com)? The beauty of this particular site is that it lets all students learn vocabulary across content areas, while giving food to kids who are hungry in other countries. Now you are teaching content, while using technology, while also helping out those in need—that sounds pretty engaging to us!

✓ **INVOLVE a range of service delivery providers to ensure students with disabilities have all of the supports they need to use technology.** For example, you could involve the Occupational Therapist who comes in once a week to help kids with the physical activity of being able to swipe on the glass pane to use an iPad. She may be there for just one particular student, but teaching this action could be helpful to many in your class. We've already mentioned tools such as Edmodo, Goalbook, and Google docs. Now consider using those same tools for sharing materials and resources for a specific student. Often, a quick 5-minute meeting via Skype or Google Hangouts between professionals can change the way you provide services to a student and is typically invaluable for engagement and learning.

✓ **DON'T BE INTIMIDATED to allow students to BYOD (bring your own device).** School policy and budgets often prevent the use of technology. Teachers frequently fear allowing students to use their own tools because they may get lost, stolen, broken, or be used inappropriately. However, research has found that the schools that allow these tools result in students who are more engaged, while teachers are able to use those same devices for content creation (Hartnell-Young & Vetere, 2008), student-centered learning, collaboration (Corbeil & Valdes-Corbeil, 2007), and differentiation of instruction (Kukulska-Hulme, 2007).

Administrators, DO This

✓ **ENGAGE your faculty.** If you can use technology with your faculty, they will see opportunities for how to do it with their own students. Consider flipping your faculty meetings, using Google Chat for a curriculum meeting, or having a school wiki for instructional ideas.

✓ **ASK the students and their families.** At the elementary level, students may or may not be able to articulate their ideas clearly, but they will most likely be able to tell you their teacher engages them—or doesn't! Go into the lunchroom and ask students about apps or software they use at home. Does Minecraft interest them? Then consider how you can help your teachers use the building and creating aspect of Minecraft in their instruction. Have parents found educational websites to reinforce learning that your teachers haven't had the time to find? Create a forum where they can share this information.

LEARNING FROM THE HIGHER EDUCATION HORIZON REPORT

Level of Challenge	Type of Challenge	What Does It Mean?
Solvable Challenges:		*Those that we understand and know how to solve*
	Low Digital Fluency of Faculty	How do we get teachers to adopt the technology in students' everyday lives?
	Relative Lack of Rewards for Teaching	What incentives will get teachers to adopt new technology?
Difficult Challenges:		*Those we understand but for which solutions are elusive*
	Competition From New Models of Education	How do educators have time to do one more thing with so many new initiatives (testing, standards, etc.)?
	Scaling Teaching Innovations	How do we take what works that is innovative and get it in the hands of all teachers?
Wicked Challenges:		*Those that are complex to even define, much less address*
	Expanding Access	How do we ensure everyone has access to the best in the easiest way possible?
	Keeping Education Relevant	How do we make teachers use technology for learning and make it not just about the technology?

Years to Adoption	Technology	What Is It?
One Year or Less	Flipped Classroom	Send home the low level tasks (watching a video, reading to find facts or Google it) and spend class time applying basic knowledge.
One Year or Less	Learning Analytics	Find ways to use what we already know about students' learning profiles instead of always creating new ones.
2–3 years	3-D Printing	Being able to print with materials and new products.
2–3 years	Games and Gamification	Using games for learning.
4–5 years	Quantified Self	Using data and storing data to have a more comprehensive view of a learner.
4–5 years	Virtual Assistants	OnStar in your car, Siri on your iPhone, and the Mayday button on the Kindle. The future will provide you with immediate assistance for many tasks that are all virtual.

Source: Adapted from New Media Consortium (2014).

ASSESSING ENGAGEMENT AND CHANGING YOUR BEHAVIOR

Assessment of Your Lesson Today

Student Engagement

Teacher Behaviors

☐ What population of students were disengaged?

☐ Were students engaged through all types of intelligence?

☐ Were all students equally involved?

☐ Were boys as equally involved as girls?

☐ Did I have all students answer all questions?

☐ Did students talk with each other on topic the majority of class time?

☐ Did I focus on very specific target skills and assess the target?

☐ Were my examples boy and girl friendly?

Three things I will do differently to increase student engagement that reflects changes in my behavior.

_____

_____

_____

HOW DID YOU ADDRESS EACH TYPE OF MULTIPLE INTELLIGENCE IN YOUR CLASSROOM TODAY?

Use this checklist daily as you plan your instruction. If you co-teach, a great role for your partner would be to use this form throughout the lesson to ensure you both are addressing the range of learners in your classroom.

Multiple Intelligence Checklist	✔	Ideas for Each
Kinesthetic (body smart)		
Musical (musical smart)		
Naturalistic (nature smart)		
Spatial (picture thinker)		
Linguistic (word smart)		
Interpersonal (people smart)		
Intrapersonal (self-smart)		
Existential (deep thinking smart)		
Logical-Mathematical (numbers/ reasoning smart)		

SAMPLE LESSON

Essential Question
What is a bird and why is it important to the ecosystem?

Learning Goal(s):
Students will be able to orally state the characteristics of a bird, create a representation of the characteristics of a bird through a variety of options (e.g., crayons and paper, Wikkistix, sculpture, WordArt, cartoon, etc.), and give two or more reasons why this animal is important to our ecosystem.

Formative Assessments	**Identify in writing, orally, or by drawing these characteristics:** • All birds have feathers. • Birds have a backbone. • All birds are warm-blooded. • Female birds lay eggs. • Birds have wings, but not all birds use them to fly. • Identify birds' contribution to our ecosystem (pollination).
Ensuring types of intelligence	Allow students to make a short song about birds. (Musical) Ask students at the middle of lesson to pause for a 1-minute break, close their eyes, and state any characteristics of a bird that they can recall. Then, open their eyes and share with a neighbor or jot it in a personal journal. (Interpersonal and Intrapersonal) As an exit ticket, have students share with a peer if they were a bird what type would they be and where would they want to migrate to each year. Students are allowed to Google types of birds or different habitats for migration. (Interpersonal and Naturalist)
Lesson activity	Jigsaw activity: Students will be placed into cooperative groups. Each group will be assigned a different type of bird to become an expert on. Students can use Internet resources and hard copy or digital books to learn about their bird. Books on tape are available. After 10 minutes, students will regroup and share what they learned with their new group. Use cooperative learning strategies.
Technology integration options	Use blabberize.com or oddcast.com to sing their song. Allow students to watch Youtube videos of birds to reinforce concepts. Allow students to use iPad to draw images or to share ideas. BrainPOP video on bird migration to end the lesson.

Academic Vocabulary
Ecosystem **Backbone (vertebrae)** **Pollination** **Migration** **Mimicry** **Habitat** **Predator**

REFERENCES

Barron, B. S., Schwartz, D. L., Vye, N. J., Moore, A., Petrosino, A., Zech, L., & Bransford, J. D. (1998). Doing with understanding: Lessons from research on problem- and project-based learning. *Journal of the Learning Sciences*, 7(3–4), 271–311.

Blumenfeld, P. C., Soloway, E., Marx, R. W., Krajcik, J. S., Guzdial, M., & Palincsar, A. (1991). Motivating project-based learning: Sustaining the doing, supporting the learning. *Educational Psychologist*, 26(3–4), 369–398.

Corbeil, J. R., & Valdes-Corbeil, M. E. (2007). Are you ready for mobile learning? *EDUCAUSE Quarterly*, 30(2), 51–58.

Datnow, A., Park, V., & Kennedy-Lewis, B. (2012). High school teachers' use of data to inform instruction. *Journal of Education for Students Placed at Risk*, 17(4), 247–265.

Errey, R., & Wood, G. (2011). Lessons from a student engagement pilot study: Benefits for students and academics. *Australian Universities' Review*, 53(1), 21–34.

Finn, C. E. (1989). A nation still at risk. *Commentary*, 87(5), 17–23.

Hartnell-Young, E., & Vetere, F. (2008). A means of personalizing learning: Incorporating old and new literacies in the curriculum with mobile phones. *Curriculum Journal*, 19, 283–292.

Hughes, C., Carter, E. W., Hughes, T., Bradford, E., & Copeland, S. R. (2002). Effects of instructional versus non-instructional roles on the social interactions of high school students. *Education and Training in Mental Retardation and Developmental Disabilities*, 37(2), 146–162.

Jackson, B. T., & Hilliard, A. (2013). Too many boys are failing in American schools: What can we do about it? *Contemporary Issues in Education Research*, 6(3), 311–316.

Kukulska-Hulme, A. (2007). Mobile usability in educational contexts: What have we learnt? *International Review of Research in Open and Distance Learning*, 8(2), 1–16.

Merriam-Webster Dictionary. (2014). Disengagement. Retrieved from http://www.merriam-webster.com/dictionary/disengagement

Mooney, P., Ryan, J. B., Uhing, B. M., Reid, R., & Epstein, M. H. (2005). A review of self-management interventions targeting academic outcomes for students with emotional and behavioral disorders. *Journal of Behavioral Education*, 14(3), 203–221.

New Media Consortium. (2014). *NMC horizon report: 2014 higher education edition*. Austin, TX: Author.

Reschly, A., & Christenson, S. (2006). Prediction of dropout among students with mild disabilities: A case for the inclusion of student engagement variables. *Remedial and Special Education*, 27(5), 276–292.

Smyth, J., McInerney, P., & Fish, T. (2013). Blurring the boundaries: From relational learning towards a critical pedagogy of engagement for disengaged disadvantaged young people. *Pedagogy, Culture, and Society*, 21(2), 299–320.

GO EVEN FURTHER WITH THIS TOPIC ON THE WORLD WIDE WEB

- www.edmodo.com
- www.classroom20.com
- www.edupln.ning.com
- www.masteryconnect.com
- www.co-operation.org/
- www.interventioncentral.org/
- www.teachthought.com/technology/

THE Apps WE LOVE

- Puppet Pals
- Flashcards
- Bitsboard
- Educreations Interactive

8

Perfectly Positive Behavior

Brittany Hott and Laura Isbell

Texas A&M University-Commerce

Jennifer Walker

University of Mary Washington

WHAT REALLY WORKS IN PBS IN THE ELEMENTARY CLASSROOM

Positive Behaviors Schoolwide!

Do you find classroom management challenging? Wish sometimes that you could duct tape those lil' rascals to their chairs (but you know that is frowned upon)? If so, welcome to the club. . . . It turns out that you're not at all alone! Teachers report that their number one challenge is classroom management (Anhorn, 2008; Merrett & Wheldall, 1993), and student behavior is a common reason teachers identify for leaving the profession (Ingersoll & Smith, 2004; Smith & Ingersoll, 2004). Furthermore, approximately 59% of primary and elementary teachers report at least one of their students is suspended each year (Gilliam & Shahar, 2006). Seriously? We're suspending kindergarteners? Challenging behaviors adversely impact students, families, teachers, and the community. Therefore, quality interventions are needed to maximize student potential and minimize disruptions to the school environment. Here's where PBS comes in!

Positive Behavior Supports (PBSs) is an empirically validated approach for managing student behavior and promoting positive social growth (Horner, Sugai, & Anderson, 2010). The primary premise of PBS consists of rules, routines, and physical arrangements developed and taught by school staff to prevent initial occurrences of problematic behaviors (Office of Special Education Programs, 2014). For effective implementation to occur, educators must use practices that represent students' best chance for success (Scott & Eber, 2003).

PBS models focus on (a) teaching social skills and positive behaviors, (b) maximizing the physiological, environmental, and curricular factors that contribute to student success, (c) emphasizing quality universal prevention measures, and (d) early identification of students needing additional support (Lewis, Barrett, Sugai, & Horner, 2010). At the school level, common rules and procedures are collaboratively designed, implemented, and revised. The team uses data (e.g., office referrals, observations, surveys) to reach consensus and promote buy in. At the classroom level, effective PBS implementation involves (a) designing effective classroom environments, (b) reviewing research-validated behavior management strategies, (c) incorporating instructional strategies, and (d) understanding comprehensive school systems to support grade-level, team, and/or individual classroom procedures. This might seem overwhelming, but it will be well worth it when you're no longer faced with the chaos that is a poorly managed school or classroom.

PBS RESEARCH OVERVIEW

PBS emphasizes tiered procedures and supports for maintaining a safe and productive learning environment for all students (Lane, Oakes, & Menzies, 2014). Every student is provided with preventative measures. Yep, every student. We don't wait for problems to arise before procedures are put in place. As data indicate the need for additional supports for some students, the level of intervention increases until all student needs are met (Sailor, Dunlap, Sugai, & Horner, 2009).

Effective PBS models include systematic schoolwide prevention measures. Behavioral expectations are clearly defined, systematically taught, and universally implemented throughout the school (Bradshaw, Koth, Bevans, Ialongo, & Leaf, 2008). At the classroom level, school rules are consistently reinforced and procedures align with schoolwide expectations. The emphasis is on prevention and teaching (Sugai & Horner, 2002).

Students are rewarded for following school rules and demonstrating social skills. That sounds nice and positive, doesn't it? And that's the goal of PBS. Conversely, a consistent continuum of consequences for maladaptive behaviors is also in place.

One of the most effective preventative measures involves creating an effective classroom environment (Strout, 2005). It is important to carefully consider the placement of both student and teacher materials as well as the physical layout of the classroom to maximize both social and academic success. Emmer, Everston, and Worsham (2003) offer the following suggestions related to physical environment: (a) avoid unnecessary materials and items in high-traffic areas, (b) ensure the teacher is able to monitor all students in all areas of the classroom, (c) keep common teaching and student materials in accessible locations, and (d) ensure students and teachers can view instructional materials. Paying careful attention to each area before the school year begins increases student learning time and decreases the amount of instructional time needed to address and correct undesired behaviors (Strout, 2005).

Making Connections

Check out Chapter 9 on Classroom Management

After determining physical environment, creating a schedule and plan for addressing changes is important. All students experience some level of anxiety and frustration when presented with new tasks or environments; however, these feelings are often more pronounced in students with learning, emotional, and behavioral difficulties (Mercer, Mercer, & Pullen, 2011). Therefore, the security of a predictable, consistent schedule is helpful. A daily, routine schedule is most beneficial at the elementary level (Scheuermann & Hall, 2012). Teachers should create a schedule that balances tasks that are more difficult with preferred activities. For example, if the goal is to provide 2 hours of reading instruction daily, consider several shorter reading segments throughout the day rather than completing reading entirely in the morning. Another option is to vary reading instruction tasks within the 2-hour block. Once a schedule is established, post the schedule prominently in a central location in the classroom and provide visual cues to support student understanding (Mercer et al., 2011).

Another classroom level prevention and intervention method involves implementing research-based behavior management strategies. These strategies include teacher-directed activities, such as opportunity to respond (Blood, 2010; George, 2010), technology integration (Hott & Walker, 2012), and praise (Sutherland, Wehby, & Yoder, 2002), as well as student-directed strategies, such as self-monitoring (Hott, Walker, & Brigham, 2014; Hott & Weiser, 2013) and peer tutoring (Hott, Walker, & Sahni, 2012). These low-cost, no-cost interventions aim to not only foster engagement but also improve academic progress and behavioral compliance. That certainly works as a win-win, doesn't it?

STOP: SUGGESTIONS TO OPTIMIZE PBS

When schoolwide PBS models are implemented with fidelity (that means, we actually do them in the way they were intended to be done), academic achievement is likely to increase and behavioral infractions decrease (e.g., Gresham, Lane, MacMillan, & Bocian, 1999; Horner et al., 2010; Lewis, Hudson, Richter, & Johnson, 2004). Putting a STOP to these common pitfalls will help to avoid PBS implementation barriers. By the way, did you see how we did that cool acronym? STOP: Strategies To Optimize PBS. Aren't we clever? Aw, thanks.

- ✖ **STOP confusing** *positive behavioral supports* **with** *schoolwide discipline.* They are not the same thing. PBS includes preventative measures and tiered interventions to promote learning and social skills acquisition. Schoolwide discipline involves reactionary measures focusing on punishment *after* behaviors have occurred. A rich body of research supports PBS, while schoolwide discipline lacks a credible research base.
- ✖ **STOP creating numerous, confusing, and/or complicated rules.** PBS requires clearly stated universal school rules and classroom procedures. Simple is better. Focus on creating two or three rules that work. For example, "Follow Directions" and "Keep Hands, Feet, and Objects to Self" covers most common behavioral infractions. Yep, even glue in the hair.
- ✖ **STOP focusing on the negative.** Explain the positive behavior that you want to see, provide step-by-step instructions, and offer students plenty of opportunities for success. Refer to the classroom rule (e.g., follow directions), state what the behavior looks like (e.g., following directions during circle time means you are sitting quietly), and offer practice opportunities (e.g., daily circle time). Focus on progress by offering praise when a student demonstrates the desirable behavior.
- ✖ **STOP waiting for the students to arrive to create physical classroom structures.** Creating a welcoming environment comforts parents and helps children to quickly settle into classroom routines. More time is devoted to instruction and less time to explaining how to navigate new areas of the classroom.
- ✖ **STOP placing all of the high-traffic areas in the classroom together.** Too much space encourages running, while too little space causes congestion, increasing the probability of hitting or pushing. Create a space where the teacher is able to see all students at all times.
- ✖ **STOP making decisions based on personal opinions and unstructured observations.** Focus on data collection and analysis. Data collection can seem daunting given the myriad of instructional

responsibilities. A few easy-to-use data collection tools and strategies are provided on page 134 of this chapter.

✘ **STOP gossiping about a child's behavior with other teachers, students, or community members.** Discussing the child's behavior with others who are not directly involved with the child is inappropriate and unprofessional. Only discuss the child with members who are directly involved to help the child reach his or her behavioral goals. Focus on stating the behavior in measurable, objective terms. For example, "During the 30-minute lunch block, John is out of his seat eight to ten times. He walks around the lunch room or visits other classes without permission." Then share a plan to help the student comply with rules. Don't forget to think about, and talk about, the student's strengths!

✘ **STOP beginning a conversation with negatives.** Beginning a conversation negatively could make parents feel defensive, upset, or angry. Try starting the conversation with a positive, and then address your concerns about the child. Finish the conversation with a strategy to correct behavior or develop appropriate behavior and social skills.

✘ **STOP blaming families for a child's behavior.** Let parents know that you want to work with them to help the child. That way everyone works together to reach the same goal. Try to contact parents for positives first. A phone call or chat during Back to School night goes a long way. When a behavioral infraction does occur, you are more likely to receive support.

Making Connections

Check out Chapter 20 on Family Involvement

✘ **STOP prescribing or diagnosing a child's symptoms.** Use data to support statements. Checkout the *Tips for Tackling Data* resource for easy data collection ideas. Focus on the behavior; don't waste time trying to label it.

✘ **STOP suggesting medication to resolve or minimize the child's behavior.** Focus on understanding what the family and child share about his or her medication. Remember medication management is a family decision and outside of the purview of school personnel. Refer families to the school nurse or social worker if families have questions.

PBS: RECOMMENDATIONS FOR ELEMENTARY SETTINGS

While there are some barriers that must STOP, there are many supports and interventions that can improve outcomes for the entire school community.

Teachers, DO This

- ✓ **KNOW the schoolwide PBS model.** Make sure you have developed classroom procedures that align with the schoolwide rules, and don't contradict them. Consistency will be your friend. We promise.

- ✓ **FOLLOW THROUGH.** Say what you mean and mean what you say. If the classroom procedure requires a student to raise his hand to ask a question, make sure that questions are only answered after students raise their hands and are recognized by the teacher. If Timmy is experiencing difficulty remembering to raise his hand, immediately call on him when he does remember to raise his hand and wait to be recognized.

- ✓ **COMMUNICATE with families and students.** Frequent communication and absolute collaboration with students and their families encourages successful outcomes for PBS implementation. Communication with students allows them to understand and follow classroom rules and expectations accordingly. A quick phone call or personal note goes a long way in fostering positive relationships and promoting positive behaviors.

- ✓ **ENGAGE in schoolwide collaboration.** Working as a unified, collaborative team can help outline objectives, responsibilities, and goals for members to achieve. Seek out specialists who can help. School counselors, psychologists, and social workers can provide a wealth of knowledge. When students reach their objectives, then the team achieves their objectives. Check out the simple ABC chart provided on page 132 to assist with determining the function of behaviors and a basis for teams to brainstorm possible interventions.

- ✓ **DETERMINE a reward system.** Teachers and students should determine a reward system that works for their classrooms. Token economy systems and cost-response systems can work well. Either system rewards students who follow the procedures, rules, routines, and expectations of the classroom; for that reason, they should receive recognition and positive reinforcement from their teachers.

- ✓ **SPEND TIME designing and organizing the classroom.** Organize desks to accommodate student learning. Some students may benefit from sitting closer to the front, by the teacher, or in the back of the classroom. Ensure that each area of the classroom has a purpose and that a procedure for transitioning between areas is in place. For additional guidance about classroom set up, check out the additional resources in this chapter.

- ✓ **MAXIMIZE student opportunities to respond (OTR).** An OTR is defined as any means of student responding to a teacher prompt (Scheuermann & Hall, 2012). During the guided practice portion of a lesson, students need four to six opportunities to respond per minute (Gunter, Coutinho, & Cade, 2002) and at least nine opportunities to respond during the independent practice portion of the lesson (Scheuermann & Hall, 2012). The use of preprinted cards (Haydon, Maheady, & Hunter, 2010), flashcards (Hott, Evmenova, & Brigham, in press), write boards (George, 2010), and Clickers® (Blood, 2010) are just a few ways to incorporate more OTR in the classroom. Start with one tool and then expand to incorporate additional tools to keep students engaged.

✓ **USE positive supports and praise.** Teachers should address desirable behaviors with rewards and reinforce disruptive behaviors with consequences. Allowing the student to participate in a rewards program decreases classroom disruptions and inappropriate behaviors. Remember, even the most challenging students respond to praise. Try to catch students demonstrating desirable behaviors and then provide immediate, specific praise. For example, Beth remains seated after the bell rings, dismissing students for lunch. Not sure what an effective praise statement looks like? Try something like this, "Beth, great job waiting for me to dismiss the class. Waiting ensures that everyone is prepared for dismissal. . . . Super work!" If a student continues to struggle after praise and encouragement, try implementing a self-monitoring chart. Samples are provided on page 133.

✓ **CELEBRATE the successes.** Some examples include "high fives" which acknowledge students demonstrating correct behavior with a simple hand motion with students, and "Gotcha" which acknowledge students following the rules. A "Gotcha" card can be created by adding stickers to an index card or providing a sticky note with "Gotcha" recorded in a bright color. Always pair the Gotcha card with praise, "Gotcha for [behavior], awesome work!"

Administrators, DO This

✓ **FOSTER schoolwide collaboration.** Working as a unified, collaborative team outlines objectives, responsibilities, and goals for members to achieve. Provide time for teachers to meet. Help teachers with data analysis and offer suggestions to meet identified needs.

✓ **PROVIDE ongoing staff development for all personnel.** All school staff members who work with students must understand their roles and responsibilities during PBS implementation. Developing a PBS committee, identifying training needs, and providing ongoing objective evaluation of progress will help the team to refine PBS implementation.

✓ **PROVIDE necessary resources for teachers.** Provide opportunities for peer observation, means of accessing service providers, and tools to implement the PBS plan with fidelity.

✓ **ALLOW enough time for PBS implementation.** According to Neresian, Todd, Lehmann, & Watson (2000), schools require 2 to 3 years of district-level support to establish schoolwide discipline systems. Make sure teachers know this isn't going away!

✓ **IMPLEMENT effective leadership skills.** Some leadership skills include demonstrating confidence in what you propose, portraying knowledge of the material, answering questions effectively, planning for budget commitments, and remaining open to comments and feedback (Sadler, 2000). Individuals need to demonstrate these forms of leadership skills to convey the message intended for the recipients.

✓ **FOCUS on the data!** Help teachers and staff learn to collect classroom level data. Review data with teachers and offer support resources to assist. Consider assisting with observations. The ABC chart provided is a great way to objectively share data. Present schoolwide data and involve stakeholders in adjusting the PBS model based on data collection

✓ **ASK for help and seek advice when experiencing difficulty.** Communicate! Collaborate!

CLASSROOM PROCEDURES AND PROCEDURES PLANNING FORM

The chart below can be used to plan classroom procedures that align with school rules. Sample rules and morning routine expectations are provided. For additional information, check out the additional resources and recommended websites.

Class	School Rule: Follow Directions	School Rule: Hands, Feet, Objects to Self	School Rule: Inside Voice
Morning Routine	Arrive to class by 7:15, hang backpack, report to seat, begin morning work.	Remain in assigned seat.	Say good morning, and then silently begin morning work until the announcements begin.
Reading	Select book from reading cart, complete reading log, report to assigned reading center.	Move to and from seat, reading cart, and centers while keeping hands and book to self.	Select book from reading cart and finish reading log without talking, use whisper voice when talking at your center, only talk to others at your center and not other centers.
Mathematics	Pick up math notebook from the math basket, place pencil and eraser on desk, wait until called upon to go to the manipulative center.	Move to and from seat and manipulative center while keeping hands at your side.	Move to and from the manipulative center quietly, during partner work use a whisper voice with your elbow partner.
Lunch	Walk to the lunch line, enter from the left if you are buying lunch, stay in your seat, raise your hand if you need anything, wait until you are dismissed and throw your trash in the bins.	In the lunch line and at the lunch tables, keep hands to self and keep feet under the table below the seat, on the floor.	Use a whisper voice to talk to those on either side of you or in front of you, conversations should only take place with those sitting in your immediate area.

Class	School Rule: Follow Directions	School Rule: Hands, Feet, Objects to Self	School Rule: Inside Voice
Physical Education	Walk into the gym following the red line on the floor, sit criss-cross on the blue line facing the basketball hoops, quietly wait for directions.	On the blue line sit criss-cross with hands in lap, keep hands and feet to self unless given specific directions for games or exercises.	Sit quietly while waiting on the blue line, use inside voices or "alert calls" when playing in the gym.
Science	Pick up science folder from the science basket, place pencil and eraser on desk, wait until called upon to pick up science materials.	Move to and from seat and science center while keeping hands at your side.	Move to and from the science center quietly, during partner work use a whisper voice with your elbow partner.
Social Studies	Pick up social studies folder from the social studies basket, place pencil and eraser on desk.	Remain in assigned seat.	Sit quietly during instruction, during partner work use a whisper voice with your elbow partner.

Source: Adapted from Hott & Weiser (2013).

SAMPLE ABC CHART

Directions: A designated observer systematically completes this form during a class or observation period that a student has experienced difficulty. Behaviors are recorded in objective terms and are free from opinions.

Antecedents-Behaviors-Consequences (ABC) Chart			
Date:_____ Name:_____ Grade: ____ Age: ____ Data Collected by: _____Campus: _____			
	Antecedents (Describe what happens before the behavior)	Behaviors (Describe the behavior)	Consequences (Describe what happens after the behavior)
Time			

Source: Adapted from www.pbis.org/resource/446/problem-behavior-pathway-%E2%80%93-analysis-of-the-problem-behavior.

SAMPLE SELF-MONITORING CHARTS

Directions: The following charts are designed to be used AFTER instruction is provided. Each chart should be individually created to match student needs. The student should be able to demonstrate the skill, or set of skills, independently but may inconsistently demonstrate the skill or skills, across settings. Students use the charts to record their behaviors.

SAMPLE PRIMARY CHART (GRADES K–2)

Student Name: Maci Anne   **Date:** Tuesday

Good Choice	Not Such a Good Choice	Poor Choice	Activity	Teacher Comments
😁	😮 (crossed out)	🙁	7:50–8:30 Morning Routine	Kicking bookbag across floor
😁 (crossed out)	😮	🙁	8:30–9:00 Calendar/ Math	Earned ☺ on math practice
😁 (crossed out)	😮	🙁	9:00–9:30 Guided Reading	Sat quietly during circle time

SAMPLE PRIMARY CHART (GRADES K–2)

Student: Sara Grace   **Activity:** Writing

✓	✓	✓	✓

SAMPLE ELEMENTARY CHART (GRADES 3–5)

Student Goal: Each class, Maci will ask two questions and answer two questions posed by the teacher.

Subject	Questions Asked	Questions Answered	Goal Met Yes/No
Reading	/ /	/	No
Math	/ / /	/ /	Yes
Science	/	/ / /	No
Social Studies	/ /	/ /	Yes
Writing	/ /	/ /	Yes

SAMPLE ELEMENTARY CHART (GRADES 3–5)

Goal: Sara will complete her mathematics assignments with at least 80% accuracy.

Day	Total # Correct	Total # Complete	Accuracy (total correct/ total complete)	Fluency (total correct/time)	Did I meet my goal?
Monday	5	8	63%	50%	No
Tuesday	6	8	75%	75%	No
Wednesday	8	8	100%	100%	Yes
Thursday	7	8	88%	90%	Yes
Friday	8	8	100%	100%	Yes

Adapted from: Hott & Weiser, 2013; Hott & Walker, 2012.

DATA COLLECTION MADE EASY

Autism Lite

Behaviors and measures can be changed and recorded through a calendar format. Options include "non/mild/moderate" as well as "yes" or "no." The application also includes a timer and an anecdotal feature. An at-a-glance report feature allows for quick comparisons.

E Cove SpEd

This application provides continuous data collection. The timer remains running while data on several behaviors can be easily collected by clicking between students and behaviors. Data collection can be supplemented with anecdotal notes.

Super Duper Data Tracker

Multiple goals and response types (tally, correct responses, approximations, etc.) can be created for each student. Students can be organized by groups and anecdotal notes recorded. Data can be e-mailed once recorded and compiled.

ClassDojo

Customizable and user-friendly, ClassDojo provides immediate feedback on student behavior. Data can be analyzed, and reports can be generated and e-mailed. The application can be accessed on the computer or through an application.

Information Sharing

- Dropbox
- Zoho
- ThinkFree
- Google Docs and Google Tools

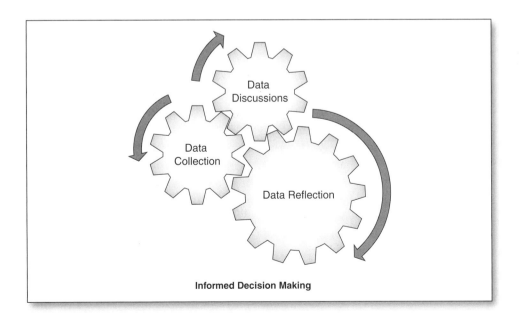

Websites

- OSEP's PBIS Resources—www.pbis.org
- PBIS World Data Tracking—www.pbisworld.com/data-tracking
- RtI Intervention Network Checklists—www.rtinetwork.org
- Intervention Central Warehouse—www.interventioncentral.org
- TeachwithyouriPad—teachwithyouripad.com
- Online Observation Tools—www.onlineobservationtools.com

Teaching About Data

Make learning about data collection fun! A good way to do this is to find enjoyable and amusing short videos on YouTube and similar programming. For example:

Teaching frequency counts: Throwing objects at peers (define *throwing*, define *peers*) using The Three Stooges in a Pie Fight

Teaching duration: Making disruptive noises using Cody the Howling Dog

Teaching latency and time sampling: Laughing at peer behavior using Baby Hiccups

Source: Adapted from Walker & Hott, 2014.

REFERENCES

Anhorn, R. (2008). The profession that eats its young. *Delta Kappa Gamma Bulletin*, 74(3), 15.

Blood, E. (2010). Effects of student response systems on participation and learning of students with emotional and behavioral disorders. *Behavioral Disorders*, 35(3), 214–228.

Bradshaw, C. P., Koth, C. W., Bevans, K. B., Ialongo, N., & Leaf, P. J. (2008). The impact of school-wide Positive Behavioral Interventions and Supports (PBIS) on the organizational health of elementary schools. *School Psychology Quarterly*, 23(4), 462.

Emmer, E., Everston, C. M., & Worsham, M. E. (2003). *Classroom management for secondary teachers*. Boston, MA: Allyn & Bacon.

George, C. L. (2010). Effects of response cards on performance and participation in social studies for middle school students with emotional and behavioral disorders. *Behavioral Disorders*, 35(3), 200–211.

Gilliam, W. S., & Shahar, G. (2006). Preschool and child care expulsion and suspension: Rates and predictors in one state. *Infants and Young Children, 19*(3), 228–245.

Gresham, F. M., Lane, K. L., MacMillan, D. L., & Bocian, K. M. (1999). Social and academic profiles of externalizing and internalizing groups: Risk factors for emotional and behavioral disorders. *Behavioral Disorders*, 24(3), 231–245.

Gunter, P. L., Coutinho, M. J., & Cade, T. (2002). Classroom factors linked with academic gains among students with emotional and behavioral problems. *Preventing School Failure, 46*(3), 126–132.

Haydon, T., Maheady, L., & Hunter, W. (2010). Effects of numbered heads together on the daily quiz scores and on-task behavior of students with disabilities. *Journal of Behavioral Education, 19*(3), 222–238.

Horner, R. H., Sugai, G., & Anderson, C. M. (2010). Examining the evidence base for school-wide Positive Behavior Support. *Focus on Exceptional Children*, 42(8), 1–15.

Hott, B. L., Evmenova, A., & Brigham, F. J. (in press). Effects of peer-tutoring on the mathematics vocabulary performance of middle school students with emotional or behavioral disorders. *Journal of the American Academy of Special Education Professionals*.

Hott, B. L., & Walker, J. D. (2012). Five tips to increase student participation in the secondary classroom. *Learning Disabilities Forum*. Retrieved from http://www.cldinternational.org/Publications/LdForum.asp

Hott, B. L., Walker, J. D., & Brigham, F. J. (2014). Implementing self-management strategies in the secondary classroom. In A. Honigsfeld & A. Cohan (Eds.), *Breaking the mold of classroom management: What educators should know and do to enable student success* (pp. 19–26). Lanham, MD: R & L Education.

Hott, B. L., Walker, J. D., & Sahni, J. (2012). Peer tutoring. Retrieved from https://www.cldinternational.org/InfoSheets/PeerTutoring.asp

Hott, B. L., & Weiser, B. L. (2013). *Implementing self-management techniques to support content area learning* [webinar]. International Council for Learning Disabilities. Retrieved from http://members.cldinternational.org/civicrm/event/info?reset=1&id=3

Ingersoll, R. M., & Smith, T. M. (2004). Do teacher induction and mentoring matter? *NASSP Bulletin, 88*(638), 28–40.

Lane, K. L., Oakes, W. P., & Menzies, H. (2014). Comprehensive, integrated, three-tiered models of prevention: Why does my school—and district—need an integrated approach to meet students' academic, social, and behavioral needs. *Preventing School Failure, 58*(3), 121–128.

Lewis, T. J., Barrett, S., Sugai, G., & Horner, R. H. (2010). *Blueprint for school-wide positive behavior support training and professional development.* Retrieved from www.pbis.org

Lewis, T. J., Hudson, S., Richter, M., & Johnson, N. (2004). Scientifically supported practices in emotional and behavioral disorders: A proposed approach and brief review of current practices. *Behavioral Disorders, 29,* 247–259.

Mercer, C. D., Mercer, A. R., & Pullen, P. C. (2011). *Teaching students with learning problems* (8th ed.). Upper Saddle River, NJ: Pearson Education.

Merrett, F., & Wheldall, K. (1993). How do teachers learn to manage classroom behaviour? A study of teachers' opinions about their initial training with special reference to classroom behaviour management. *Educational Studies, 19*(1), 91–106.

Neresian, M., Todd., A. W., Lehmann, J., & Watson, J. (2000). School-wide behavior support through district level system change. *Journal of Positive Behavior Interventions, 2*(4), 244–247.

Office of Special Education Programs Technical Assistance Center on Positive Behavior Interventions. (2014). Retrieved from http://www.pbis.org

Sadler, C. (2000). Effective behavior support implementation at the district level: Tigard-Tualtin School District. *Journal of Positive Behavior Interventions, 2*(4), 241–243.

Sailor, W., Dunlap, G., Sugai, G., & Horner, R. (2009). (Eds.). *Handbook of positive behavior support.* New York, NY: Springer.

Scheuermann, B. K., & Hall, J. A. (2012). *Positive Behavioral Supports for the classroom* (2nd ed.). Upper Saddle River, NJ: Pearson.

Scott, T. M., & Eber, L. (2003). Functional assessment and wraparound as systemic school processes primary, secondary, and tertiary systems examples. *Journal of Positive Behavior Interventions, 5*(3), 131–143.

Smith, T. M., & Ingersoll, R. M. (2004). What are the effects of induction and mentoring on beginning teacher turnover? *American Educational Research Journal, 41*(3), 681–714.

Strout, M. (2005). Positive Behavioral Support at the classroom level: Considerations and strategies. *Beyond Behavior, 27*(1), 3–8.

Sugai, G., & Horner, R. (2002). The evolution of discipline practices: School-wide positive behavior supports. *Child and Family Behavior Therapy, 24*(1–2), 23–50.

Sutherland, K. S., Wehby, J. H., & Yoder, P. J. (2002). Examination of the relationship between teacher praise and opportunities for students with EBD to respond to academic requests. *Journal of Emotional and Behavioral Disorders, 10*(1), 5–13.

Walker, J. D., & Hott, B. L. (2014, April). *Tips for tackling data.* Paper presented at the Council for Exceptional Children Conference, Philadelphia, PA.

RECOMMENDED READINGS

* Honigsfeld, A., & Cohan, A. (2014). *Breaking the mold of classroom management.* Lanham, MD: Rowman & Littlefield Education.
* Kauffman, J. M., & Brigham, F. J. (2009). *Working with troubled children.* Verona, WI: Attainment.
* Lane, K. L., & Beebe-Frankenberger, M. (2004). *School-based interventions: The tools you need to succeed.* Boston, MA: Allyn & Bacon.
* Wright, J. (2008). *The power of RTI: Classroom management strategies (K–6)* [DVD]. Port Chester, NY: National Professional Resources.

GO EVEN FURTHER WITH THIS TOPIC ON THE WORLD WIDE WEB

* www.pbis.org/school
* www.swis.org
* www.iris.peabody.vanderbilt.edu/iris-resource-locator
* www.modelprogram.com/
* www.rtinetwork.org/learn/behavior-supports/schoolwidebehavior
* www.interventioncentral.org/behavioral-intervention-modification

THE Apps WE LOVE

* Interval Minder
* Behavior Tracker Pro (BTP)
* Behavior Assessment Pro (BAP)
* Tallymander
* D.A.T.A

9

Classy Classroom Management

Luisa Palomo Hare

Nebraska 2012 Teacher of the Year

Wendy W. Murawski

California State University, Northridge

WHAT REALLY WORKS IN CLASSROOM MANAGEMENT IN THE ELEMENTARY CLASSROOM

Teaching the Seven Dwarfs

It's the day before school starts, and you've got a bunch of information in your box about new incoming students. It turns out that Steve has allergies, Sondra is on medication that zones her out at times, Kiernan is gifted, Sam is super shy, D'mitra has narcolepsy, Kathie has a behavioral disability, and Timmy has bipolar disorder but appears to be in the manic phase right now, according to his mom. And of course you have at least 20 other students with their own strengths, personalities, and issues! Right after you page through all this information, you get the flyer from your principal reminding all teachers that she expects excellent classroom management techniques in place from all of you. Really? Classroom management, when it seems like you'll have to teach the seven dwarfs?! How are you supposed to get Sneezy, Dopey, Doc, Bashful, Sleepy, Grumpy, and Happy to sit on the carpet, follow directions, get out their materials and start work, all while also teaching to the new Common Core State Standards? Wait—don't despair! This chapter is for you. We will take these kids and show you how, with the right strategies in place, anyone (yes, even Snow White or the Evil Queen) could be a successful, and well-organized, teacher.

First of all, let's get something straight. Classroom management isn't the same thing as discipline (Wong, Wong, Rogers, & Brooks, 2012). That's a common misconception. Classroom management includes behavior management (which may involve discipline), but even more importantly it involves instructional management (Martin & Sass, 2010; Rytivaara, 2012). It should involve both proactive strategies (such as establishing rules and procedures, as well as a positive environment and community) and reactive strategies (such as the way you address conflict) (Alber, n.d.). In fact, early research found that having a strong, well-managed classroom is more directly related to the *teacher's* behavior than the *students.'* Yes. It's on you. Have you ever watched a teacher who just seems to be "with-it?" Believe it or not, that was an actual factor identified by Kounin, back in 1970, when he characterized strong teachers: those who had "with-it-ness" and those who did not! Which will you be?

Let's start with why classroom management is so critical. Classroom management is actually one of the top concerns of all teachers (Evertson & Weinstein, 2006) and is often considered one of the most difficult aspects of an elementary teacher's job (Prior, 2014). Kids simply won't be able to learn if there is a chaotic mess around them. This doesn't mean that we are advocating for the days of old when students (supposedly) sat quietly and did their worksheets at their desks. A room full of children learning may be loud and messy, but it is an organized chaos that is well controlled, structured, and has a plan in place. Organization and management go hand-in-hand, but our goal is not merely to have an organized atmosphere. Far more than that, "the fundamental task of classroom management is to create an inclusive, supportive, and caring environment" (Weinstein, 2003, p. 267).

Our colleagues Hott, Isbell, and Walker wrote the chapter on what really works in Perfectly Positive Behavior, and we strongly recommend you read that chapter prior to reading this. Why? Because Positive Behavior Support (PBS) promotes schoolwide positive behaviors, and having a great schoolwide PBS

Making Connections

Check out Chapter 8 on Positive Behavior Supports

plan makes classroom management so much more effective—for kids and their teachers! We know you may not be in a school that employs a school-wide PBS model, but regardless, we want you to know about it. Also, you *are* in charge of your classroom. Thus, this chapter focuses not on the schoolwide level but rather solely on the classroom level, though classroom management certainly addresses more than just behavior. By the way, we are fairly comfortable in saying these are things that *really* work. Luisa was the Nebraska Teacher of the Year, and Wendy was California's Teacher Educator of the Year, so we've had some pretty great successes with our own practices!

THERE'S ACTUALLY RESEARCH ON CLASSROOM MANAGEMENT? SURE IS!

What exactly is involved in classroom management? Since well-managed classrooms may have students laughing, talking, and moving about, we know it no longer entails just sitting quietly at one's desk, waiting patiently for the teacher to provide the next tidbit of information to learn and regurgitate. Classroom management involves (a) organizing the physical arrangement of the class, including supplies management, (b) choosing rules and procedures, (c) managing student work, (d) planning and conducting instruction, (e) managing cooperative learning groups, (f) maintaining appropriate student behavior, (g) communicating effectively, (h) addressing problem behaviors, and (i) differentiating for special groups (Evertson, Emmer, & Worsham, 2003). So . . . yeah. That's a lot.

Fortunately for us, there is a ton of research on each one of these areas! We actually do know research-validated best practices in each of them. We also know that teachers are different, kids are different, and nothing works with everyone. That doesn't mean we should wing it though. Quite the opposite. As Wong and colleagues (2012) remind us, "Just as a pilot has a flight plan, a coach has a game plan, and a wedding coordinator has a wedding plan, effective teachers have a classroom management plan" (p. 63). Teachers who want to be successful need to get their hands on as much research as possible in each area. Or read this chapter and call it a day. Either one.

While there is certainly a plethora of research and strategies on the specifics of classroom management available online or in books, we are here to provide you with the basics in a nutshell. Prior (2014) writes that her recipe to successful classroom management involves love, engagement, support, and consistency. While these seem pretty basic, consider each of them.

Love involves establishing a caring relationship between your students and you. This type of relationship is actually supported in the research as key to creating the type of environment where students feel comfortable sharing and trusting (Klem & Connell, 2004; Marzano & Marzano, 2003). Having an inclusive environment where differences are accepted and strengths are emphasized moves us away from the punitive classrooms of old. Students need to know that you care about them, that they are safe, and that there is a classroom community that promotes learning, positive behavior, and appropriate social interactions (Alber, n.d.).

Making Connections

Check out Chapter 12 on Inclusion

Engagement has started to replace the previous term *on-task*. Researchers realized that students can be on-task just sitting passively and not actively learning, though not causing any behavioral issues either. Instead, academic engagement is a term that indicates that the students are actively responding and engaged in the academic task assigned to them (Gettinger & Ball, 2008). In fact, the three variables that most strongly impact positive academic engaged time are (a) classroom management, (b) instructional variables, and (c) student-mediated strategies (like self-monitoring). When teachers create activities and assignments that engage their learners academically, inappropriate behaviors are reduced (Prior, 2014). Simple as that.

Support for students involves teaching them the way things should be done, rather than punishing them for doing things incorrectly after the fact. There is much research telling us that we need to have strong rules and procedures in place if we want to be effective managers of our classroom (e.g., Marzano & Marzano, 2003; Sanford, 1984; Wong & Wong, 2009). That said, how we create and establish those rules and procedures can vary. Garrett (2008) compared elementary teachers who used more student-centered approaches, wherein the students co-created the rules, rewards were often intrinsic, and consequences were individualized, versus more teacher-centered traditional approaches, wherein the teacher posted the rules, often used extrinsic rewards for behavior, and maintained the same consequences for rule infractions for all students. Garrett found that, while the teacher-centered approach appeared to save time, the student-centered approach appeared to better equip students to self-regulate their own behavior and solve their own problems. Are you using the new Common Core Standards? If so, and you realize that means your students are going to need to seriously up their skills in critical analysis and problem-solving, you may want to consider an argument made by Brophy (2006). He stated, "A management system that orients students toward passivity and compliance with rigid rules undercuts the potential effects of an instructional system that is designed to emphasize active learning, higher order thinking, and the social construction of knowledge" (p. 40). Well then. Huh. Maybe we need to make sure our kids are part of our design of our classroom management strategies—within reason, of course!

Finally, *consistency*. It's important. 'Nuff said.

Okay, we lied. That wasn't enough. It is so difficult to be consistent with our kids, especially when the concepts of *individualization* and *differentiation* have been pounded in our heads as teachers. So, think about it like this. Consistency with flexibility. We need to have procedures and rules in place that we maintain consistently (Marzano, 2011; Wong & Wong, 2009). However, we also need to know that if Sondra's mom calls and says they are trying a new medication this morning, we may be willing to repeat a direction for her that we typically would not. If putting one's head down in class is not an acceptable behavior, instead of constantly disciplining D'mitra who has narcolepsy, we might proactively assign her two seatmates who are willing to lightly touch her arm or remind her before her head goes down. In his amazing video called *F.A.T. City* (Frustration, Anxiety, Tension), Rick Lavoie (2004) reminded us that "Fair doesn't mean equal. Fair means that everyone gets what he or she needs." This is one of our favorites! We can be very consistent teachers, without forgetting our humanity.

So, what do love, engagement, support, and consistency look like in the elementary classroom? Unfortunately, we have to first tell you what they do not look like.

"OH, NO THANK YOU!" THINGS TO STOP DOING IN ELEMENTARY CLASSROOM MANAGEMENT

Teachers

- ✗ **STOP focusing on the behaviors you don't want to see.** Frame everything you do and everything you say in a positive way. Instead of saying, "No shouting during learning centers," train yourself to say, "We will use quiet voices at learning centers today." When something happens that you do not want, simply say, "Oh, no thank you."

- ✗ **STOP waiting until the last minute to figure out your routines and procedures.** Before school even starts, you need to think about how you will set up your classroom. What will expectations be? How will you follow through? What configurations can desks be in? What will be the procedures for the class? A very important question to reflect on is, "*Why* am I putting these routines and procedures into place?" All classroom management should be focused on doing what is best for children and maximizing student academic engaged time.

- ✗ **STOP relying on others to be the "bad guy."** Setting up classroom expectations is half of the equation, but following through on those expectations is the other half. Remember when we talked about consistency? It is important that children see their teacher follow through. Do not expect someone else to be the "bad guy" or the one who enforces your classroom management. Your students will still love you, even when you need to follow through. In fact, they may grow to love you more. . . . Okay, we won't push that one.

✖ **STOP reinventing the classroom management wheel.** Do not feel the need to create something new and earth shattering for your classroom management systems. Strong teachers love to share their ideas, so take advantage of this and talk to teachers you respect about their classroom management. Use your time to focus on students and content—not on finding a new way to spin classroom management.

✖ **STOP trying to be cutesy in your classroom management.** In a world of Pinterest and online sharing, one would get the idea that everything elementary needs to be cutesy and clever. Do not fall into this trap. Classroom management should be easy to implement and have visuals, but cutesy themes/visuals/phrases are not the main selling point of a strong system.

✖ **STOP creating your classroom management plan in isolation.** Please remember that the time of one-room school houses is long gone. You do not teach in a bubble. Check in with your grade level and school administrators to see what classroom management expectations are in place throughout the building.

✖ **STOP waiting until problems arise before involving parents.** All parents—regardless of language or socioeconomic barriers— want to be involved with their child's education. The important part is to figure out the best way to make this happen. Communication with parents should be early and often. Having a consistent communication history with parents will help when tough conversations come up.

✖ **STOP compromising a student's dignity (and your own) when discipline issues come up.** An important part of classroom management is following through on expectations. When the need to discipline a student comes up, remember to keep the child's dignity intact. Not only is this the right thing to do for children, but how you handle discipline issues speaks volumes about who you are as a teacher. There is never a need to belittle or humiliate.

✖ **STOP rewarding children with extrinsic things.** Children love stickers, candy treats, and visiting the magical treasure box or other variations of these rewards. However, while they are easy to use, they are not always what is best for children. Use them sparingly, and instead, focus on teaching children to be motivated intrinsically to do well in school.

✖ **STOP treating all students the same way "to be fair."** You've read time and time again in this book that we need to treat students differently. In addition to different strengths, abilities and disabilities, languages, and interests, also consider students' culture. Behavior and learning are both impacted by whether a student comes from a collectivistic culture or one that is individualistic (Rothstein-Fisch & Trumbull, 2008). Learn more about them.

✘ **STOP being inconsistent—in your teaching, in your expectations, and in your follow-through.** All children thrive on consistency. Don't change up your way of doing things out of the blue. If you need to make a change to something that you are doing, take a moment to acknowledge the change, quickly implement it, and then stick to it. Always follow through on routines and procedures. This will help the children to do the same.

✘ **STOP getting worked up about circumstances out of your control.** Teachers cannot control what our children come to school knowing (academically and socially), nor can we control what our children do when they are not in school. Teachers need to focus on what do with students during the short amount of time that they are in our classrooms.

Administrators

✘ **STOP expecting each teacher to come in ready to manage his or her class.** Set up schoolwide Positive Behavior Support systems, but also facilitate mentorships between new and veteran teachers. Consider having teachers with strong class management skills share some of their instructional or behavioral strategies at a faculty meeting.

✘ **STOP encouraging teachers to send their difficult students to you.** Teachers who use the principal's office as their main line of defense never learn the skills to manage their own class. Students who are sent out of the room are no longer learning. If you notice a teacher who frequently sends students out of the room, make an appointment to go in and observe and then work with that teacher to come up with more productive strategies.

IN OUR PERFECTLY MANAGED WORLD, TEACHERS WOULD DO THESE THINGS

✓ **BUILD relationships.** As important as content knowledge is, building relationships is more important! Be genuine and be open. Share parts of yourself to get your students to open up to you. Nurture student relationships always—even after students have left your classroom. Have a fun lunch with former students so that you can continue your relationship. Let students know they are loved and valued and everything else will follow.

✓ **REMEMBER that parent and family involvement is key!** Teachers with successful classroom management take the initiative to involve families early and often. Start the year off by writing a short letter to introduce yourself, your expectations, your excitement to work with them to educate their child, and the best way to contact you. Keep these letters brief—all families are busy and shorter letters can be better absorbed. Consider using an assignment notebook to maintain daily communication with all parents in your classroom, not just the ones who are frequently in trouble or those kids with special needs. The important part of this tool is that parents sign the book and return it each night.

✓ **KEEP it positive.** With every situation, teachers can choose to react positively or negatively. Always choose to stay positive. If your kids appear to be having an exceptional, difficult day, that's when you need to make even more of an effort to be positive. Greet them at the door with caring and optimism. Upset children already feel bad, so react kindly and positively. Remember that sending children out of the room when they are upset sends the message that we don't want to deal with them.

✓ **BE consistent!** As fun as it can be to act impulsively, it is best for students that teachers stay consistent. Teachable moments are great, as long as they remain consistent with your teaching. As you transition from one activity to the next, look at your daily schedule and say, "Team, we just finished art class and we ate lunch. Our schedule tells us that math is next." This helps relieve anxiety, which can lead to difficult behavior and a lack of academic engaged time.

✓ **DO have plans for transitions.** Transitions are the number one issue in classroom management, so plan for them! In Luisa's class, students know that when the lights are turned off and Louis Armstrong's "What a Wonderful World" comes on, that they should begin to clean up. This is a perfect opportunity to continue her small group lesson without trying to manage the whole class. Her children have been taught that by the end of the song (just over 2 minutes), they should be sitting on the carpet ready to learn. Use timers during group transitions: kitchen timers, sand timers, PowerPoint timers, digital timers. Whatever you choose, timers help teachers track the appropriate time to devote to each group and provide a soft reminder to the kids when it is time to start work or wrap up. To get their attention, use chimes, a clapping technique, or a small bell. Remember that as weird as it sounds, the louder the students get, the quieter the teacher should get.

✓ **TEACH with a sense of urgency.** Teachers have so much to do in such a brief amount of time. Plan so that every moment—down to every single minute—is accounted for. Read Eric Jensen's (2009) *Teaching With Poverty in Mind*, mentioned in our Recommended Readings section at the end of the chapter, for more about employing a sense of urgency in your teaching. Make sure there are never any moments where you are searching for things to do with the kids. Check out the "Daily Tutoring Schedule (page 152)," which shows indirect instruction times and how you can utilize each moment to work with individual student goals.

✓ **DO collaborate and co-teach.** Ask your colleagues for ideas, and be willing to share your own and get feedback. Take advantage of lunchtime and dismissal to chat with other teachers. Co-teaching is a great way to improve your classroom management (Murawski, 2010). During co-planning, you are able to share ideas, while during co-instruction, you are offering students twice the support (while also having twice as many eyes and ears on the kids!).

✓ **CONSIDER the *why* in classroom management!** When setting up any routine or procedure, ask yourself *why* you are setting it up. Likewise, when students struggle with routines or procedures, again ask yourself *why*. Many times, when students are struggling, it shows a need for reteaching of the expectations. Not punishment, reteaching.

✓ **PLAN your room based on the students.** Many teachers plan their classroom layout based on what works best for them, rather than what the children will need. Kids need space to move around and space to collaborate with their peers. Plan your room so that they get both of these. Think carefully about your instruction and where the students will be.

✓ **LABEL, label, label.** Be very specific in your expectations of how things will run and where things should go, including the kids. For example, at the beginning of the year, take a picture of your class sitting in their rug area and post it to help them remember where they sit and what sitting on the rug the right way looks like. Labeling other aspects of the room will save your sanity, especially if you do it when the kids are watching! This is a good way to introduce procedures and routines at the start of the year. As you introduce an area (e.g., their seats, the pencil sharpener, the reading corner), label it and make a quick anchor chart of expectations. Not only is this helpful for the students, but it saves you time as well.

✓ **DO be very clear in your delivery of expectations!** Whenever possible, post the expectation or learning goals, preferably in student-friendly language. Review these often. This can be as simple as reminding what hallway expectations are or as complex as teaching children the learning goal for each content area. During the first few weeks of school, practice the right way to do things (snap a photo of it) and the wrong way (snap another photo). Post those photos! The kids get a kick out of trying to be over-the-top for the wrong way, which makes doing it the right way seem so much more realistic. Sometimes, for schoolwide expectations (e.g., walking in the hall), it is fun to get *teachers* to model the right and wrong way!

✓ **PUBLICIZE the possible consequences—for positives also.** All teachers are familiar with classroom rules and likely know they are supposed to keep them brief (three to five rules), to the point, and positive. Most teachers also have consequences posted with their rules. Take a look at yours. Are they all negative? What about when students follow the rules? What then? Consider posting your consequences as "If you break the rules, these things might happen: warning, call home, removal from activity, parent visit, office visit, suspension. If you follow the rules, these things might happen: praise, positive call home, happy teacher, more friends, positive note home, improved grades, recognition on the 'On a Roll' board, college."

✓ **GET anchored!** Anchor charts are an important tool, for both content and behavior. Create them with students, and they will help reinforce expectations (see page 151). You might connect these with a visual, like a stoplight. When students make mistakes, they change their color from green to yellow or yellow to red. In kindergarten, you might use small individual photos, whereas in older grades, students can use numbers in lieu of their names. This strategy is powerful for two key reasons: All adults in the classroom are included on the visual (because really, teachers make mistakes too), and students are encouraged to fix their mistake and return to green. It is simple and positive, and it teaches kids to

Plugged In

www.2teachllc.com/ self-determination%20 article.pdf

maximize their engaged time while also empowering them to be in control of their choices. Another idea is the use of driver's dashboard. Check out Murawski and Wilshinsky (2005) in the Plugged In box to learn how to make them and use them!

✓ **PLAN ahead!** Great teachers are prepared for anything because they have taken time to plan ahead. Create a "busy bag," put it by your front door, and bring it with you everywhere. Stock it with a first-aid kit, a photo roster of your students, the most current contact information, a few books, snacks, and water. When planning for class, preplan your content, as well as your student learning groups and materials, so that no student time is wasted.

✓ **PREPARE for unexpected absences.** Create a separate binder for your sub to get through the day. Include your daily schedule, a narrative explaining the day, label nametags, a photo roster, pages that students can complete (with enough copies for the class), a cd with familiar classroom songs, as well as information about who in your building can help out. If you co-teach, be sure to mention who your co-teacher is, when she arrives, and that she will take lead upon arrival (Murawski, 2010).

✔ **LET students do the talking!** As much as teachers want to be in control, it is important to let students have control of their learning. A great way to do this is to have students state the learning goal or behavioral expectation. It is so powerful for students to hear expectations from each other. This will take modeling and coaching on the teacher's end, but within the first month of school, students can take over this routine. This is especially powerful for children who have behavioral/emotional struggles. When they are allowed the opportunity to voice classroom expectations, it empowers them to do the right thing. Conversely, when they struggle, they understand that it is a class expectation and not a teacher rule, which students sometimes view negatively.

✔ **DIFFERENTIATE.** Consistency is critical, but don't forget the flexibility within that structure. Kids have bad days, just like we do. Also, if you have a student with an identified emotional or behavioral disability, you will need to do things differently for him than you might do with other students. That's okay. You may also recognize that students from more collectivistic cultures may do better working in small groups, whereas some students from more individualistic cultures prefer to work alone (Rothstein-Fisch & Trumbull, 2008). Be willing to mix it up. If teaching were easy, anyone could do it. They can't. You, however, can.

✔ **REFLECT on your teaching—often!** Incorporate reflection into your daily routine as a teacher. As you are preparing for the following day, take a moment to reflect on what worked and what you could improve, and make a quick note of it. Allow your teaching to evolve. Buy a small planner each year and take a minute or two to jot down anything that stood out to you that day. Keep the past year's planner with you as you create lessons for the current year. It will save you from repeating silly mistakes and help you remember lessons that went extremely well.

✔ **DO roll with it.** Classroom management is about having strong instructional and behavioral strategies in place to help your day run smoothly. Even with the most engaging lesson and well-thought-out rules and procedures, things can happen. When something unexpected happens, do your best. If it was a bad day, reflect on it, think about what you could change for the future, make a mental note, then give yourself a break—or a bubble bath, or a glass of wine, or a guilty pleasure. These days happen. Start tomorrow with a positive attitude, a new commitment to your structures, and a smile and welcome to your students.

VISUALS, VISUALS, VISUALS!

Stoplight as Study Skill Visual

Daily Schedule for Children

Center Chart

TUTORING SCHEDULE: AN EXAMPLE OF PLANNING FOR EVERY MINUTE OF TIME WITH STUDENTS

2nd Quarter Daily Tutoring	
Mrs. Maxwell 9:00–9:20 Morning Opening (6 minutes each × 3 kids = 18 min.)	
Nicolas (Tu-Th)	-See individual goals below to see what each child specifically needs to work on.
Domingo (Tu-Th)	
Emma (Tu-Th)	
Henry (M-W-F)	
Keron (M-W-F)	
Cayden (M-W-F)	
Mrs. Palomo 9:00–9:20 Morning Opening (6 minutes each × 3 kids = 18 minutes)	
Emma (M-W-F)	-See individual goals below to see what each child specifically needs to work on.
Kimbertyn (Tu-Th)	
Christopher (M-W-F)	
Fabiana (M-W-F)	
Shanteria (Th-Tu)	
Palomo 9:25–9:45 Morning Centers (5–6 minutes each)	
Aaliyahnah (Tu-Th)	# writing (11-20), sight words (whole 75 list), blending/segmenting *42
Gabriel	# writing (11-20), sight words (ours taught + all of first 25 list). blending/segmenting *17
Tristan	blending/segmenting/c-v-c- words, sight words (ours taught + all of first 25 1ist), # 11-20 *16

Mrs. Maxwell 9:25–9:45 Morning Centers	
Henry	blending/segmenting/c-v-c words, sight words (ours taught + all of first 25 list),* 11-20 *14
Shanteria	7 capital, 7 lowercase, 7 sounds, sight words (ours taught only), #s 1-10, *9
Danielle	letter, sounds, sight words (ours taught only), #s 1-10, *7
Ms. Burns 9:25–9:45 Morning Centers	
Anthony (Tu-Th)	# writing (11-20), sight words (ours taught + all of first 25 list), blending/segmenting *27
Christopher	0 capital, 0 lowercase, 0 sounds, sight words (ours taught only), #s 1-10, *0
Javier (Tu-Th)	# writing (11-20), sight words (ours taught + all of first 25 list) blending/segmenting *23

- There is so much asked of teachers that we really need to micromanage each minute we have students with us.
- This schedule is great to organize adults to be most efficient and focused on individual learning goals.
- A quick summary (30 seconds or less) is recorded in a class data binder so that student time is not compromised while teachers discuss the current day's tutoring sessions.
- I use my data binder often to track student successes or areas students still need to improve on.

EXCELLENT APPS TO HELP WITH CLASSROOM MANAGEMENT

To Help With Management/ Participation	To Help With Noise	To Help With Timing	To Help Teachers
ClassDojo	Too Noisy	Timer for YouTube	NetSupport News
Socrative	Too Loud?	Best Sand Timer	Instant classroom
Nearpod	Stop go!	Screen time	Smart seat
Faronic Insight	Stop light!	Screen time/Media manager	Teacher Kit
		Thyme	Class Act

Source: www.teachthought.com. Used with permission from Chris Beyerle.

GREAT CLASSROOM RULES

Our Classroom Rules

- *I will treat you with respect, so you will know how to treat me.*
- *Feel free to do anything that doesn't cause a problem for anyone else.*
- *If you cause a problem, I will ask you to solve it.*
- *If you can't solve the problem, or choose not to, I will do something.*
- *What I do will depend on the special person and the special situation.*
- *If you feel something is unfair, whisper to me, "I'm not sure that's fair," and we will talk.*

Source: www.loveandlogic.com.

REFERENCES

Alber, R. (n.d.) Ten tips for classroom management. Retrieved from http://www .edutopia.org/classroom-management-resource-guide

Brophy, J. (2006). History of research. In C. M. Evertson & C. S. Weinstein (Eds.), *Handbook of classroom management: Research, practice, and contemporary issues* (pp. 17–43). Mahwah, NJ: Lawrence Erlbaum.

Evertson, C. M., Emmer, E. T., & Worsham, M. E. (2003). *Classroom management for elementary teachers* (6th ed). San Francisco, CA: Allyn & Bacon.

Evertson, C. M., & Weinstein, C. S. (2006). Classroom management as a field of inquiry. In Evertson & Weinstein (Eds.), *Handbook of classroom management: Research, practice, and contemporary issues* (pp. 3–15). Mahwah, NJ: Lawrence Erlbaum.

Garrett, T. (2008). Student-centered and teacher-centered classroom management: A case study of three elementary teachers. *Journal of Classroom Interaction, 43*(1), 34–47.

Gettinger, M., & Ball, C. (2008). Best practices in increasing academic engaged time. In A. Thomas & J. Grimes (Eds.), *Best practice in school psychology V* (pp. 1043–1058). Bethesda, MD: National Association of School Psychologists.

Klem, A. M., & Connell, J. P. (2004). Relationships matter: Linking teacher support to student engagement and achievement. *Journal of School Health, 74*(7), 262–273.

Kounin, J. S. (1970). *Discipline and group management in classrooms.* New York, NY: Holt, Rinehart & Winston.

Lavoie, R. (2004). *How difficult can this be? The F.A.T. City Workshop: Understanding learning disabilities* [DVD]. United States: PBS Videos.

Martin, N. K., & Sass, D. A. (2010). Construct validation of the behavior and instructional management scale. *Teaching and Teacher Education, 26*(5), 1124–1135.

Marzano, R. J. (2011). Classroom management: Whose job is it? *Educational Leadership, 69*(2), 85–86.

Marzano, R. J., & Marzano. J. S. (2003). The key to classroom management. *Educational Leadership, 61*(1), 6–13.

Murawski, W. W. (2010). *Collaborative teaching in elementary schools: Making the co-teaching marriage work!* Thousand Oaks, CA: Corwin.

Murawski, W. W., & Wilshinsky, N. (2005). Teaching self-determination to early education students: Six-year-olds at the wheel. *Teaching Exceptional Children Plus, 1*(5), Article 3. Retrieved from www.2teachllc.com/self-determination%20 article.pdf

Prior, J. (2014). Love, engagement, support, and consistency: A recipe for classroom management. *Childhood Education, 90*(1), 68–70.

Rothstein-Fisch, C., & Trumbull, E. (2008). *Managing diverse classrooms: How to build on students' cultural strengths.* Alexandria, VA: Association for Supervision and Curriculum Development.

Rytivaara, A. (2012). Collaborative classroom management in a co-taught primary school classroom. *International Journal of Educational Research, 53,* 182–191.

Sanford, J. P. (1984). Management and organization in science classrooms. *Journal of Research in Science Teaching, 21*(6), 575–587.

Weinstein, C. S. (2003). Classroom management in a diverse society. *Theory Into Practice, 42*(4), 266–268.

Wong, H. K., & Wong, R. T. (2009). *The first days of school: How to be an effective teacher.* Mountain View, CA: Harry K. Wong.

Wong, H., Wong, R., Rogers, K., & Brooks, A. (2012). Managing your classroom for success. *Science and Children, 49*(9) 60–64.

RECOMMENDED READINGS

* Jensen, E. (2009). *Teaching with poverty in mind.* Alexandria, VA: Association for Supervision and Curriculum Development.

* Marzano, R. J. (2003). *Classroom management that works: Research-based strategies for every teacher.* Alexandria, VA: Association for Supervision and Curriculum Development.

* Wheeler, J. J., & Richey, D. D. (2014). *Behavior management: Principles and practices of Positive Behavior Supports* (3rd ed). San Francisco, CA: Pearson.

GO EVEN FURTHER WITH THIS TOPIC ON THE WORLD WIDE WEB

- www.behavioradvisor.com
- www.pbis.org
- www.theteacherscorner.net/management/
- www.teachnet.com
- www.glencoe.com/sec/teachingtoday/tiparchive.phtml/4
- www.disciplinehelp.com

THE Apps WE LOVE

- Class DoJo
- Too Noisy
- Teacher Kit
- Behavior Pro
- Random Student
- Thyme

10

Cool Cooperative Learning

Scott Mandel

Los Angeles Unified School District

WHAT REALLY WORKS IN COOPERATIVE LEARNING IN THE ELEMENTARY CLASSROOM

Including Cooperative Learning Into Your Common Core Class

Elementary students like to work together. Whoa! No surprises there. But did you know this is actually a practice based in research? Seriously! In fact, a major aspect of the new Common Core State Standards (CCSS) initiative is the implementation of *inquiry-learning* or *project-based learning*. The basic concept is that students will delve deeply into curricular material and subsequently incorporate higher order critical thinking into their discussions—a primary tenet of the Common Core (Burris & Garrity, 2012). Right . . . this type of teaching is nothing new. In fact, before the onset of No Child Left Behind (NCLB) in 2002, this methodology had a different name and was highly popular and widely successful. It was called *Cooperative Learning,* and pre-NCLB, its implementation could be found in most classrooms in some form or another. So why are we spending a whole chapter on it?

Unfortunately, with the advent of No Child Left Behind and the new nationwide focus on teaching primarily to pass an end-of-the-year test, Cooperative Learning virtually vanished in many classrooms. Whereas thousands of publications were written on the subject in the late 1980s and 1990s, from 2002 to 2014, scarcely a book or article focused on cooperative learning, and fewer and fewer teachers incorporated it into their classrooms. However, with the teacher freedom promoted by the Common Core, Cooperative Learning has the opportunity to flourish once more. Call it *inquiry-learning* or *project-based learning,* in its essence, it is all Cooperative Learning. More important, you will find that your students will flourish, whether they are gifted, special education, English language learners, or simply the "typical" student.

So what is cooperative learning, if it's not just throwing a bunch of kids together in a group? In its most basic form, it involves two or more students working with curricular material in a way that their discussion provides them with new insights into the material. It may indeed be as simple as pairs of students working together for 20 minutes on a worksheet. It may also be as complex as a group of students working together over a 2- to 3-week period on a special project. Whenever learning happens between two or more students, rather than directed by the teacher, you have a form of Cooperative Learning. Anyone who has worked with kids before knows that it takes more than throwing them together though; this chapter will help you know what really works in making Cooperative Learning activities successful.

This chapter will focus on the more extensive forms of Cooperative Learning. The type that we will be looking at is an adaptation of the Group Investigation Model developed by the Sharans in the 1980s and 1990s at the height of the Cooperative Learning movement (Sharan, 1994; Sharan & Sharan, 1992). In this version, students are normally placed into groups for 3 or more days as they work to solve an academic problem presented by the teacher. This is the type of activity that you will find yourself implementing in your classrooms as your school adopts the Common Core State Standards.

RESEARCH ON COOPERATIVE LEARNING

Cooperative Learning was extensively researched from its popular origins in the mid-1980s through 2002. The research demonstrated that using this teaching method significantly raised students' levels of higher order critical thinking skills across the board, regardless of intellectual level, race, ethnicity, or special needs (Slavin, 1995). That's good for us all, right? Letting kids work in cooperative learning groups was actually shown to help students think divergently, work together to generate and test hypotheses, reason causally, master complex bodies of information, analyze social situations, and develop flexible social skills (Joyce, Calhoun, & Hopkins, 2002). In addition, this has also been found to be highly successful in including special education students (Slavin, 1995). You can't argue against those kind of results, can you?

Cooperative Learning is project based by its very nature and, more importantly, prepares students for the real working world as adults. Today's businesses increasingly want workers who function successfully and productively with others on projects (Carnevale, 1996, 2002). Cooperative Learning provides students with the basic skills necessary to succeed in this type of environment—one that is very different from the "traditional" sit-and-take-notes classroom.

Cooperative Learning is also based on inquiry-based learning. As stated above, these two are often synonymous. Since this type of learning is the basis of the CCSS (Dana, Burns, & Wolkenhauer, 2013; Wolk, 2008), Cooperative Learning is expected to be regularly implemented into the Common Core classroom. Kids will actually be taught to think, question, problem-solve, and not just regurgitate facts; in today's Google society, it's easy enough to find those facts online in seconds. Most kindergarteners can use Google quicker than their grandparents can!

Unfortunately, most published models of Cooperative Learning require teachers to drastically change their teaching styles to fit a particular model. We all know that is not reality. Each of us has a particular style based on our experiences, personalities, and classroom. Luckily, extensive classroom research has identified a number of key concepts central to Cooperative Learning success that can be easily transferred and implemented into the everyday teacher's classroom situation and teaching style—without requiring wholesale changes to a teacher's repertoire (Mandel, 2003). It's those basic core concepts of Cooperative Learning implementation that will be the focus of this chapter—hence, what really works.

As stated earlier, the type of Cooperative Learning that will be the primary focus is the Group Investigation Model. Based on the work of educational pioneer H. A. Thelen (1954, 1960), the Sharans further developed this specific practice years later. This methodology allows students to delve into greater detail, where they can spend more time using higher order critical thinking skills than they would in short, one-day Cooperative Learning experiences (as found in most of the other models). Therefore, this model is the most appropriate for reaching the goals of the Common Core State Standards.

 WHAT YOU NEED TO AVOID AT ALL COSTS!

Teachers

✗ **STOP using Cooperative Learning lessons as a substitute for frontal teaching.** Cooperative Learning is meant to replace seatwork, not directed lessons. There is still a need for students to learn the content from qualified teachers. This doesn't mean that students can't learn new information during their Cooperative Learning group time, but that teachers shouldn't completely abdicate their role as instructional leader.

✘ **STOP feeling that you have to adapt your classroom to a specific Cooperative Learning methodology or model in order to be successful.** You have your own personal style and your unique group of students. An "expert" across the country can't determine what's best for your classroom. Nor can an out-of-classroom district person. Use the basic concepts of group formation, teacher questioning, group leadership, and so forth, and apply them to your individual style and situation (see Mandel, 2003). A few basic tips have been provided for you at the end of this chapter, including a cooperative learning lesson planning template on page 165.

✘ **STOP refusing to try Cooperative Learning because you have special education students or English language learners in your class.** Cooperative Learning has been demonstrated to be extremely successful with students of diverse populations (Slavin, 1995). In fact, the research on these groups emphasizes the positive outcomes when they are able to work collaboratively with heterogeneous groups (Murawski & Spencer, 2011).

✘ **STOP making groups of three students.** When students are in a group of three, most decisions come as a result of social relationship reasons. Four or six are actually the best size, because all decisions have to decided by a sizable majority of the group, rather than a one-person margin.

✘ **STOP assigning students randomly to long-term group projects (those lasting more than a day).** Groups require certain skills and abilities of their members to ensure success in whatever project you have assigned. Random grouping equals random success. See the Group Formation Chart on page 167 for assistance with this.

✘ **STOP letting classroom setup determine whether or not you use Cooperative Learning.** If your classroom set-up (desks, tables, open space) leads to barriers to group work, create a solution within the room or some other workspace. Move around desks, chairs—let students use open floor spaces if necessary.

✘ **STOP rotating jobs among the group members.** Research has shown that students with leadership skills will always take leadership—and will unknowingly sabotage the group if they are not allowed to lead (Mandel, 1991). Don't worry; I'll give you the key to doing this in the next "DO THIS" section.

✘ **STOP assuming that higher order critical thinking will automatically happen in the group discussions.** Research has shown that the critical thinking level of the teacher's questioning or assignment of task is the primary determinant of the level of thinking that the group will incorporate into their discussions (Mandel, 1991). That means, you need to model what you are looking for!

✖ **STOP having the students conduct all of their research.** Elementary students do not have experienced research skills. When forced to find materials from scratch, they will inevitably spend over 90% of their time on locating material and less than 10% of their time discussing and using the data. More time spent analyzing is preferable to more time spent searching.

Administrators

✖ **STOP thinking that teaching isn't happening or standards aren't being covered during a Cooperative Learning lesson.** When entering a classroom, it is important not to make any decisions on the level of teaching or learning that is occurring without listening to the discussions taking place and asking the teacher about how the Cooperative Learning project fits in within the overall curricular unit.

✖ **STOP worrying about noise during a Cooperative Learning lesson.** If you observe a Cooperative Learning session, the more talking you hear, the more students are actively engaged in the lesson. Spend some time and listen to the students' talk.

GO STRATEGIES FOR SUCCESS WITH COOPERATIVE LEARNING

Teachers, DO This

✓ **USE Cooperative Learning to eliminate seatwork, not directed teaching.** Cooperative Learning projects should always begin with the teacher giving some form of directed lesson to provide the students with the background needed and context for their project. Core material from the standards should be presented during this time in order to ensure that all students cover it, rather than hoping that groups will touch on the subjects.

✓ **MAKE groups of four to seven students.** Groups of three have social issues as the primary determinant of decisions (two to one). Groups of more than seven become a committee and lose effectiveness. As stated above, the best groups are four or six because decisions have to be by general consensus versus a one-vote majority.

✓ **DETERMINE the skills necessary for each group's success.** It is critical that groups are not put together randomly. You need to match skills and traits of students to the requirements of that particular group's work. For example, if there is higher level reading required for the group, ensure that at least one member of the group can read at that level. If art is required, ensure that a student with a high Spatial Multiple Intelligence is a member (see Mandel, 2003, for a discussion on group formation and how to use Multiple Intelligences for determining student traits). Want ways to get kids in groups that seem heterogeneous but are still thoughtful and teacher designed? Check out "Tips for Creating Cooperative Learning Groups" on page 166.

✓ **LET the groups develop their own leaders.** Studies have demonstrated that students with strong leadership personalities will naturally take over the leadership of the group (Mandel, 1991). What's worse, a student with a strong leadership personality who is not able to take a "positive" leadership role will inevitably take on a "negative" leadership role and disrupt the group. Similarly, a student who does not have a strong leadership personality who is put in that position will either be highly uncomfortable with the role and not do the job or will allow someone else to take over. Instead of you giving out the jobs, provide a list of the jobs that you require of each group (such as a recorder, presenter, and materials getter) and let the group determine how best to hand out roles (Mandel, 2003). Turn to page 167 for a list of potential jobs.

✓ **PREPARE higher order critical thinking questions to use with students.** Studies have shown that the critical thinking level you leave the students with at the end of your directed lesson is the level in which they will work for the remainder of the lesson. Likewise, if you talk to an individual group while they are working, whatever critical thinking level you last use will be the level in which they operate after you leave (Mandel, 1991). For example, if you ask kids a low-level critical thinking question such as, "How did the Native Americans live in the Great Plains?" they will simply find examples of teepees and wigwams. However, if you ask them a higher order critical thinking question such as, "Determine why the Plains Native Americans chose the housing they chose," students will investigate available local raw materials, geographic factors, transportation needs, and other relevant variables (see Mandel, 2003). Also, be aware of asking too many questions as students work or hanging around groups for too long; they will tend to want to defer to the teacher as opposed to listening and communicating with one another.

✓ **READILY INTEGRATE special education students into your groups.** Special education students often have a discrepancy in particular learning areas. You need to always predetermine those discrepancies when planning your Cooperative Learning experience and then ascertain if any adaptations are needed. For example, if the student has a discrepancy in

Making Connections

Check out Chapter 12 on Inclusion

reading comprehension, make sure that he is in a group where reading at a level above his ability is not a requirement for all members of that group. If the student has behavioral problems due to her disability, ensure that she is in a group with other students with whom she has positive relationships, and avoid those who may pose a problem. Being proactive is a major component of universally designing strong differentiated and successful lessons (Murawski & Spencer, 2011).

✓ **READILY INTEGRATE English language learners into your groups.** English language learners have difficulty with the use of the English language; that does not mean they have cognitive problems. Therefore, many can fully integrate the use of higher order thinking skills once you account for their language barrier. This can be accomplished in a myriad of ways: You can partner an ELL student with another fluent in the primary language, and they can serve as a translator in the discussion back and forth. Group investigative materials taken from the Internet can easily be translated using the facilities of Google Translate (translate.google.com). Just type in the web address (URL), select your language, and print out the material for the students to read in their primary language. Finally, if you have enough students who speak the same language, you can create a group of them and let them discuss the material and work with it in their primary tongue, using their higher order thinking skills. If the goals of your lesson are content based versus English language based, this is a perfectly acceptable accommodation. Also consider collaborating with an ELL coach or teacher to come up with more helpful adaptations.

Making Connections

Check out Chapter 16 on English Language Learners

✓ **PROVIDE students with packets of materials to investigate.** For Cooperative Learning to be successful, students need sufficient material to investigate. Simply using textbooks and/or encyclopedias is not enough. In addition, elementary students will spend 90% of their time looking for material when asked to do their own research. Therefore, it is imperative that you acquire material that you can put into file folders and hand to the appropriate groups. The students can then concentrate the vast majority of their time on discussing and manipulating the material rather than on a search for the data. The Internet is the ultimate resource center (see Mandel, 2003)! Even though this is time consuming for the teacher, once it is completed, you can save the material for Cooperative Learning sessions in the future. A list of some of the best curricular sites for materials is listed later in this chapter.

✓ **USE an Adapted Group Grade system if you are giving grades for group work.** Too often one student does not get credit for doing more work than the others, and another student gets the credit for doing less than the average. If you give a group grade, use that as a basis—but then adapt it. For example, you determined that a group should receive a B for their work. Then determine—by observation throughout the work sessions and by questioning the students as a whole—who did work above and beyond. You raise that student's grade to an A. At the same time, you determine someone did little. You give that student a new grade of a C. The students immediately see that you are being fair in your grading and that all are held responsible for their work.

Administrators, DO This

✓ **ENCOURAGE creativity with your teachers.** Promote Cooperative Learning methodologies with your staff, especially with your more experienced teachers. After a dozen years of the limitations of No Child Left Behind (scripted curricula, strict timelines), teachers may need encouragement to try something as different as Cooperative Learning. This will also assist your school with the upcoming Common Core exams, as they are largely based on higher order critical thinking and often will have a group inquiry work component.

✓ **SET UP a Cooperative Learning Materials Center for your teachers.** Set aside a couple of file cabinets in a convenient location and encourage your teachers to deposit copies of their Cooperative Learning materials. This way, teachers can share with each other and not have to recreate group materials every time they have a Cooperative Learning session.

A COOPERATIVE LEARNING LESSON PLANNING TEMPLATE

TITLE OF LESSON:

COMMON CORE STANDARDS ADDRESSED:

1.

2.

3.

WHERE DOES THIS LESSON OCCUR IN THE OVERALL UNIT (How does it relate to the directed lesson):

MATERIALS NEEDED FOR THE GROUPS:

INTERNET SITES TO USE TO ACQUIRE MATERIAL:

TITLE:
URL:
Content Description:

TITLE:
URL:
Content Description:

TIPS FOR CREATING COOPERATIVE LEARNING GROUPS

Cooperative Learning projects, which are fairly short (under 5–6 hours of work) do not require a lot of group determination.

- Look in your gradebook at the last major test/project in the subject matter of the Cooperative Learning lesson you're about to begin. Then assign every group an equal number of students at the various ability and achievement levels. Be flexible and make slight adjustments for students who do not work well together or students with specific special needs.
- Use your roster and knowledge of students to create groups in advance that will serve different purposes. For example, for large heterogeneous groups, create color groups (e.g., Red, Blue, Green, Yellow), number groups (1–6), and shape groups (e.g., Circle, Square, Triangle). Be thoughtful about who is in each group and why, but create them proactively. Now, whenever you want students to get in groups of four to six for shorter projects, you can ask them to get in their number, color, or shape groups.

    For long-term Cooperative Learning projects, it's much more important to construct groups that you know will work and achieve your desired long-term goals. For more complex or longer tasks, take the following steps in creating your groups:

1. <u>Determine the basic traits and skills you need students in each particular group to possess.</u> For example, you may determine that "high-level reading" is important for one particular group; "art/drawing skill" may be critical for another group.

2. <u>Go through your roll book, and start to place students in the groups based on what you know of their personal abilities.</u> Important—not every group member must possess every skill! They will help each other with the tasks. For example, if there is high-level reading required, you simply must have at least one or two high-level readers in that group. The rest will still participate in the group discussions and other tasks. Using the students' Multiple Intelligence levels is an excellent tool here. (For easy tests for determining Multiple Intelligence level, you can copy the appendices in *Cooperative Work Groups*, Mandel, 2003).

3. <u>Fill out the Group Formation Chart (included here) and adjust membership in each based on social considerations.</u> For example, pay extra attention to students who should not be with each other and the abilities and areas of concern or strength of students with disabilities, special needs, language differences, or giftedness.

The following chart will help you in listing the requirements of your groups and creating them.

GROUP FORMATION CHART

Group 1	Group 2	Group 3	Group 4	Group 5
Traits and Skills Required for Each Group				
1- 2- 3-	1- 2- 3-	1- 2- 3-	1- 2- 3-	1- 2- 3-
Group Members				

GROUP GOALS

Group 1—*Their Main Task:*   *Extra Tasks:*

Group 2—*Their Main Task:*   *Extra Tasks:*

Group 3—*Their Main Task:*   *Extra Tasks:*

Group 4—*Their Main Task:*   *Extra Tasks:*

Group 5—*Their Main Task:*   *Extra Tasks:*

Teacher Notes

POSSIBLE GROUP MEMBER ROLES

Facilitator: Your job is to keep the process moving.

Recorder: Your job is to keep notes on what you are doing and who is doing what.

Reporter: Your job is to report out what your group did.

Timer: Your job is to help with time management for the group.

Member: Your job is to help complete the tasks given.

Cheerleader: Your job is to keep up the motivation and morale of the group.

Materials Manager: Your job is to get and disseminate any materials necessary for the task.

Tech Consultant: Your job is to help with any technological needs of the group.

Consultant: Your job is to help the group solve the task, without giving them the answers.

Housekeeper: Your job is to ensure all materials get put away and that group members have cleaned up after the task.

Questions Asker: Your job is to be a liaison with the teacher if the group has any questions about the process or task.

Source: Adapted from Murawski (2003) with permission from author.

MORE COOPERATIVE LEARNING TIPS!

Here are a number of extras for you to consider as you start to use cooperative learning strategies listed above:

How Do You Determine Students
With a Strong Leadership Personality?

The easiest way to determine those with strong leadership personalities is by observation. Who do the students gravitate to in the class or outside after school or during lunch? In the classroom, who are the students who are the first to raise their hands in a discussion? This is whether or not they know the correct answers! Leadership and academic achievement are not connected.

What Happens if Someone Refuses to Work?

After a number of warnings and discussion as to the reason for their actions, students who refuse to work should be given an alternate assignment that covers the same material. Usually, this comes in the form of a written assignment/report. Be very careful, however, to determine the function of their behavior. If their purpose is to avoid working in groups, they may choose to continue their negative behavior. For most students, however, they will often soon determine that group work is preferential to this boring paper-pencil type of alternative!

How Do I Assess the Lesson?

What are your original goals for the lesson? If students are supposed to be learning core material for the unit, then test them on the content to be learned. If you want to grade group work and process, then use the Adjusted Group Grade mentioned earlier. Above all—you know your curriculum and you know your students. Assess them in whatever way you feel is most appropriate and fair!

REFERENCES

Burris, C. C., & Garrity, D. T. (2012). *Opening the common core: How to bring all students to college and career readiness.* Thousand Oaks, CA: Corwin.

Carnevale, A. P. (1996). Liberal education and the new economy. *Liberal Education, 82*(2), 4–11.

Carnevale, A. P. (2002). Preparing for the future. *American School Board Journal, 189*(7), 26–29, 47.

Dana, N. F., Burns, J. B., & Wolkenhauer, R. (2013). *Inquiring into the common core.* Thousand Oaks, CA: Corwin.

Joyce, B., Calhoun, E., & Hopkins, D. (2002). *Models of learning: Tools for teaching* (2nd ed.). Buckingham, England: Open University.

Mandel, S. (1991). *Responses to cooperative learning processes among elementary-age students.* ERIC Clearinghouse on Elementary and Early Childhood Education, ED 332808.

Mandel, S. (2003). *Cooperative work groups: Preparing students for the real world.* Thousand Oaks, CA: Corwin.

Murawski, W. W. (2003). *Co-teaching in the inclusive classroom: Working together to help all your students find success.* Medina, WA: Institute for Educational Development.

Murawski, W. W., & Spencer, S. (2011). *Collaborate, communicate, and differentiate! How to increase student learning in today's diverse schools.* Thousand Oaks, CA: Corwin.

Sharan, S. (1994). *Handbook of cooperative learning methods.* Westport, CT: Greenwood Press.

Sharan, Y., & Sharan, S. (1992). *Expanding cooperative learning through group investigation.* New York, NY: Teachers College Press.

Slavin, R. E. (1995). *Cooperative learning: Theory, research, and practice* (2nd ed.). Englewood Cliffs, NJ: Prentice Hall.

Thelen, H. A. (1954). *Dynamics of groups at work.* Chicago, IL: University of Chicago Press.

Thelen, H. A. (1960). *Education and the human quest.* New York, NY: Harper & Row.

Wolk, S. (2008). School as inquiry. *Kappan, 90*(2), 115–122.

RECOMMENDED READINGS

* Armstrong, T. (2009). *Multiple intelligences in the classroom* (3rd ed.). Alexandria, VA: Association for Supervision and Curriculum Development.

* Johnson, D. W., & Johnson, R. T. (1986). *Learning together and alone* (2nd ed.). Englewood Cliffs, NJ: Prentice Hall.

* Kagan, S. (1990). The structural approach to cooperative learning. *Educational Leadership, 47*(4), 12–15.

* Mandel, S. (2003). *Cooperative work groups: Preparing students for the real world.* Thousand Oaks, CA: Corwin.

GO EVEN FURTHER WITH THIS TOPIC ON THE WORLD WIDE WEB

- www.teachershelpingteachers.info
- www.people.ucalgary.ca/~dkbrown/index.html
- www.mathforum.org
- www.besthistorysites.net
- www.eduq.com/Sites/Codys-Science-Education-Zone.aspx

THE Apps WE LOVE

- Corkboard Me
- Sync.In.
- Mixed Ink
- Live Binders
- Edmodo
- Collaborate

11

Unique Universal Design for Learning

Tamarah M. Ashton

California State University, Northridge

WHAT REALLY WORKS IN UDL IN THE ELEMENTARY CLASSROOM

Adopting the UDL Frame-of-Mind

Walk into any elementary classroom in the country and what do you see? Different genders, different colors, different heights, different abilities, different clothes, and different, well, everything. Elementary school teachers today are working with the most diverse set of students our country has ever experienced (National Center for Education Statistics, 2009). These are exciting educational times. As a citizenry, we have made the choice to teach everyone—no matter what (e.g., Individuals with Disabilities Education Improvement Act, 2004). Diversity, of course, includes not just ethnicity.

Consider all the students with disabilities who are now included in general education classrooms; they have special needs in learning, cognition, physicality, emotions, health, and more. What about those with gender identification issues or those in need of second language skills? Socioeconomic issues, sexual orientation, homelessness—the list goes on and on. Additionally, in some places, physical classrooms are a thing of the past and are rapidly becoming virtual educational experiences (see Connections Academy, 2014). How do educators even begin to address all of these situational elements in the daily design of their class instruction?

Incorporating Universal Design for Learning (UDL) into their planning, instruction, and assessment can make all the difference in the world for an elementary teacher. Adopting a UDL frame-of-mind means recognizing that we all learn differently (Chiasson, 2005) and that we can use those differences to enhance instruction, rather than hinder it.

> Universal Design for Learning (UDL) is a set of principles and techniques for creating inclusive classroom instruction and accessible course materials. At its core is the assertion that *all* students benefit when they are given multiples ways to take in new information, express their comprehension, and become engaged in learning. (Access Project, 2012, para. 1)

Therefore, UDL minimizes barriers and maximizes learning for all students (Center for Applied Special Technology, 2010). That certainly sounds like a good plan, doesn't it?

UDL: WHAT THE RESEARCH SAYS

> The intent of universal design is to simplify life for everyone by making products, communications, and the built environment more usable by as many people as possible at little or no extra cost. Universal design benefits people of all ages and abilities. (Center for Universal Design, 2008, para. 2)

Universal Design (UD) was first conceived to address the barriers created in the original development of architectural elements, methods of communication, and many everyday products (Rose & Meyer, 2002). For example, using curb cuts to ease our shopping cart out of the market and into the parking lot has become routine. Most of us probably do not even think about why those indentations in the pavement were originally put there (i.e., smoother mobility for those who use walkers or wheelchairs). And what about television remote controls? It seems everyone, even the youngest of us, now knows that the CC button stands for closed captioning used primarily by those who are deaf or hard of hearing. Instead, kids can turn it on to indicate that their parents are talking too loudly on the phone while they are watching an important reality TV show.

It is not surprising that soon after UD was recognized as an important contribution to our society, the need for a broader access to learning became a point of focus with educators. The term UDL was developed in the 1990s by the Center for Applied Special Technology (CAST) (Ashton, 2005). It was defined as "the practice of embedding *flexible* [italics added] strategies into the curriculum during the *planning* process so *all* students can access a variety of learning solutions" (DeCoste, n.d., p. 3).

Flexible planning for all. Those are the words italicized in the previous quote, and if you walk away from this chapter with nothing else, let it be the notion that UDL equates with flexible planning for all. We must continue to emphasize that there is no one kind of learning! Learning differs across tasks, development, and individuals (Rose, 2014).

Thus were born CAST's UDL Guidelines. The three guiding principles of UDL are more fully described on page 178: (a) Provide multiple means of representation, (b) provide multiple means of action and expression, and (c) provide multiple means of engagement. This may sound daunting, but hang in there. I'll explain this so you'll see how to do it easily. After you've finished reading this chapter, take a look at the sample UDL lesson plan. The items that fall under representation, action and expression, and engagement are highlighted so you can see the thought processes that go into creating a good UDL lesson.

Plugged In
www.cast.org

Proactive Nature of UDL. UDL means making things accessible before they occur (Rose & Meyer, 2002), rather than adapting them afterward. In other words, if you think about how to reach all of your learners *after* teaching a lesson, you will only be reacting to the problems created by not thoroughly thinking them through before you began. For example, a third-grade general education teacher must take into account that his or her class of 30 students with mixed ethnicities, several of whom have disabilities, as well as a variety of levels of English learning, is not going to require the identical planning as his colleague's class across the country with 22 students of all one ethnicity and one language background. Planning proactively is a necessity.

When physical structures were the main target of UD, architects and other designers focused on avoiding the retrofit (Rose & Meyer, 2002). They front-loaded their planning as much as possible to save time, money, and other resources. So why is this early planning important in Universal Design for *Learning?* Researchers and practitioners alike say it is more efficient (e.g., Basham, Israel, Graden, Poth, & Winston, 2010), it benefits more students (e.g., Basham & Marino, 2013), and it is more acceptable to students (e.g., Chita-Tegmark, Gravel, Serpa, Domings, & Rose, 2012). Great. So UDL is good. "Got it," you think, "but how exactly does that look in my class and my planning?" In these next sections, I provide you with concrete actions to avoid and those actions you should engage in instead.

AVOID THESE UDL BLUNDERS IN ELEMENTARY EDUCATION

- ✘ **STOP dismissing UDL as a viable option for your instructional design because you already know a lot about modalities and multiple intelligences.** Learning modalities (visual, kinesthetic, tactile) and multiple intelligences (spatial, linguistic/verbal, musical, etc.) have been introduced to teachers for years. These are interesting constructs to think about regarding your students, but UDL is much more than just adding pictures to your lessons or having kids listen to recorded books. UDL is about design—instructional design. A lot of thought and many elements go into really well designed lessons. Modality preference and intelligence strengths might come into play in informing your design, but it is not the design itself.

- ✘ **STOP confusing UDL with differentiation.** Differentiation allows teachers to design instruction to meet the broadest range of students possible. It is simply one piece of UDL. For example, you may plan to start the lesson with a warm-up activity, followed by 5 to 10 minutes of direct instruction through lecture, then move to a few stations for application of the new content. For UDL, you are proactively planning to mix up your representation of the material and the way the kids engage with it; well done! However, just because you have stations doesn't mean you have differentiated for the kids with special needs. You may still need to incorporate some additional accommodations or modifications.

Making Connections

Check out Chapter 12 on Inclusion

- ✘ **STOP trying to fix problems you have created *after* it is too late.** Remember that UDL's origins are based in architecture. Addressing possible problem areas *before* instruction saves everyone a lot of time and heartache.

- ✘ **STOP "teaching to the middle."** No teacher wants to leave students who process more slowly in the dust or punish the ones who pick up quickly by boring them to tears. Yes, the majority of your class probably will be in "the middle." Consider *all* students in your flexible planning!

- ✘ **STOP buying into the idea that there is one true, effective, and proven way to teach something.** No one would ever discover anything new if we all felt that way. Let yourself think out-of-the-box and have fun with teaching. Engaging your kids is the hardest part of any lesson.

- • **STOP pointing out to the whole class that you have created something in a special way so Jimmy can participate.** This kind of behavior defeats the purpose of UDL. UDL values diversity. Remember that old adage many of us have attributed to Rick Lavoie's video of F.A.T. City (1989): "If you want to give students equal opportunity, you must treat them all differently."

Making Connections

Check out Chapter 12 on Inclusion and Chapter 15 on Gifted Education

- **STOP defining UDL as "just good teaching."** UDL is good teaching, but good teaching is not necessarily UDL. Do not forget the three basic components: (a) provide multiple means of representation, (b) provide multiple means of action and expression, and (c) provide multiple means of engagement. Still not sure what that means? Look at page 178.

- **STOP thinking that UDL is a "special ed thing."** UDL is about providing access to the curriculum for *everyone.* If you keep in mind that all students are *your* students, you will start thinking of them all as special. Aw . . . isn't that sweet?

STEPS TO UDL SUCCESS IN ELEMENTARY EDUCATION

- ✓ **EXPLAIN to your students what UDL is and why you are doing it.** Remember that those little minds are much more clever than we give them credit for. Use *all* your resources. Students have great ideas, too! This helps them to see diversity in a positive light. Ask them for ideas . . . and then be open to them.

- ✓ **REMEMBER that it is acceptable to go deep with differentiation for a few while planning instruction for the needs of many.** Consider making yourself a copy of the magnifying glass on page 179. Post it near your workstation to continually remind yourself of this concept. Here's an example: Imagine you are teaching a class of first graders and you're working on single-digit addition. Some students might be just fine practicing the way we were all taught (i.e., complete all the odd numbered problems by themselves while the teacher circulates and assists as needed). But what about those who just aren't getting it? If you could find a way to have them access the content in a variety of ways, it just might help their magnifying glasses hone in on the way single-digit addition makes most sense to them. Try setting up areas in your classrooms so students can rotate through centers. One could focus on word problems with single-digit addition scenarios, one could have some manipulatives available for hands-on practice, and one could have them explain the process through journal writing.

✓ **TELL students that we all learn differently and that it is okay.** Give them an example of someone who does one thing well but really struggles with another. Short-term memory versus long-term memory is a good way to introduce this topic. Maybe you can recall a student who memorized information quickly and got perfect scores on every test. But you also remember he or she had difficulty remembering that information for very long. You might actually want to use yourself as an example; students love learning the strengths and weaknesses of their teacher. Okay, so you have no weaknesses, make one up.

✓ **OFFER options for students to show they understand the concept or can do the task.** Whenever possible, ask kids to work in their preferred modes (e.g., acting, singing, dancing, puppetry, multimedia). You will feel better knowing they understand the topic, and they will feel more successful for having demonstrated it *their* way. Don't worry about the fact that they'll have to demonstrate their learning on standardized tests; they'll have plenty of opportunity to practice traditional test taking. If your goal is to see if they've learned the material, then let them show you they have!

✓ **MAKE learning fun and engaging.** Promise right now that you will never stand in front of your class again and simply lecture in a dry monotone. Even adult students enjoy humor, variety, and an appealing presenter. Younger students deserve even MORE of that!

Making Connections

Check out Chapter 6 on Arts Integration

✓ **THINK back on your own educational experiences in elementary school.** Who were your favorite teachers? Why? Consider using some of their "magic." Mine was Mrs. Fahrenbach. She taught second grade and told us to call her Mrs. Farmbox. She was the original Miss Frizzle (look up the Magic School Bus if this reference eludes you)!

✓ **ASK, "What are the *essential* elements of your standards? How could you teach something in a different way?"** Teaching in the same format, using essentially the same words, day in and day out, cannot be very much fun for teachers. Just assume the kids do not like it either. Feeling brain dead? Ask a colleague for some ideas. Collaborate, communicate, share—these are encouraged words in today's schools!

Plugged In

https:// daretodifferentiate .wikispaces.com/ Tiering

✓ **USE tiered lessons and menus to proactively provide options.** Go online and look up tiered lessons and lesson plan menus. There is so much out there! Teachers can give a Tic-Tac-Toe board with nine options and ask students to choose three (that, of course, need to go either horizontally, vertically, or diagonally). Or give different points to different activities and allow students to choose. For example, if they need to do 10 points worth for a book in Language Arts, they could choose to write an essay (10 points), *or* write a poem (5 points) *and* draw a new cover to the book (5 points), *or* draw 3 characters (2 points each) *and* create a song about the book (4 points), and so on. You could also create lessons that have MUST DO sections that the whole class needs to complete, with a variety of options for MAY DO sections. Let the class know they need to select at least one MAY DO in addition to the MUST DO.

✓ **INSERT variety and choice without too much work.** A simple example of this is to stop telling your class WHAT they have to write about. A little autonomy goes a long way. When the content isn't the point of your lesson, allow students choice whenever possible. You create the guidelines for those choices, but ultimately, they've chosen themselves.

✓ **FOCUS on the idea that UDL is based in design elements.** Educators call that *planning*. FLEXIBLE PLANNING for ALL!

UNIVERSAL DESIGN FOR LEARNING GUIDELINES

I. Provide Multiple Means of Representation

1: Provide options for perception
1.1 Offer ways of customizing the display of information
1.2 Offer alternatives for auditory information
1.3 Offer alternatives for visual information

2: Provide options for language, mathematical expressions, and symbols
2.1 Clarify vocabulary and symbols
2.2 Clarify syntax and structure
2.3 Support decoding of text, mathematical notation, and symbols
2.4 Promote understanding across languages
2.5 Illustrate through multiple media

3: Provide options for comprehension
3.1 Activate or supply background knowledge
3.2 Highlight patterns, critical features, big ideas, and relationships
3.3 Guide information processing, visualization, and manipulation
3.4 Maximize transfer and generalization

Resourceful, knowledgeable learners

II. Provide Multiple Means of Action and Expression

4: Provide options for physical action
4.1 Vary the methods for response and navigation
4.2 Optimize access to tools and assistive technologies

5: Provide options for expression and communication
5.1 Use multiple media for communication
5.2 Use multiple tools for construction and composition
5.3 Build fluencies with graduated levels of support for practice and performance

6: Provide options for executive functions
6.1 Guide appropriate goal-setting
6.2 Support planning and strategy development
6.3 Facilitate managing information and resources
6.4 Enhance capacity for monitoring progress

Strategic, goal-directed learners

III. Provide Multiple Means of Engagement

7: Provide options for recruiting interest
7.1 Optimize individual choice and autonomy
7.2 Optimize relevance, value, and authenticity
7.3 Minimize threats and distractions

8: Provide options for sustaining effort and persistence
8.1 Heighten salience of goals and objectives
8.2 Vary demands and resources to optimize challenge
8.3 Foster collaboration and community
8.4 Increase mastery-oriented feedback

9: Provide options for self-regulation
9.1 Promote expectations and beliefs that optimize motivation
9.2 Facilitate personal coping skills and strategies
9.3 Develop self-assessment and reflection

Purposeful, motivated learners

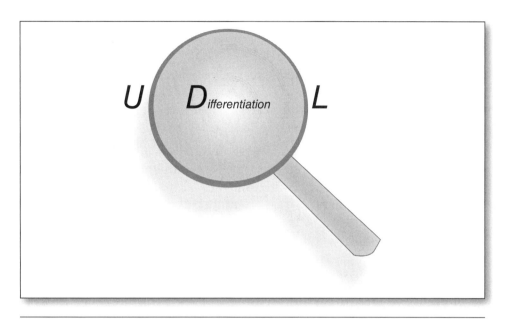

Source: Phillip Bell (2014), San Pedro High School, CA. Used with permission.

UDL LESSON PLAN EXAMPLE

Let's Build a Pond

Elementary Science

UDL components of this lesson have been highlighted.

Essential Question: What factors are necessary to support an ecosystem?

- Students will use scientific skills and processes to explain the dynamic nature of living things, their interactions, and the results from the interactions that occur over time.
- Students will use scientific skills and processes to explain the interactions of environmental factors (living and nonliving) and analyze their impact from local to global perspectives.

Overview: Student pairs brainstorm materials needed to build a pond and share their ideas with the class. The teacher will record materials using the interactive whiteboard and Inspiration software, creating a graphic organizer for the students to use to sort biotic and abiotic factors. Students will then work together as a group to build a habitat in a classroom environment that has the biotic and abiotic factors necessary to support a population of fish. Following this hands-on, kinesthetic experience, students will write a letter from the viewpoint of a goldfish on the new home that was just built, taking into account the biotic and abiotic impact factors, as well as human activity, on the ecosystem.

Engage: Think/Pair/Share—Whole Class (5 minutes)

Place an empty aquarium on a table at the front of the room. Tell students that today you will build a pond! Have students think about what is needed to turn the empty aquarium into a small ecosystem that will support goldfish. Students share their thoughts with a partner, then groups share answers with the class. Record responses with Inspiration software in the *Build a Pond* organizer, using the interactive whiteboard system.

Explore: Build a Pond Demo—Whole Class (20 minutes)

Discuss with the students what needs to be added to the aquarium, in what amounts, and in what order. Add this information to the list of materials on the interactive whiteboard. As students help add materials in the amounts and order that has been determined by the class, using the *Build a Pond* graphic organizer, have them take turns going to the whiteboard and sorting the materials into abiotic and biotic factors.

Explain: Supporting Ideas—Individual (20 minutes)

Move to the computer lab. Have students write a letter as the goldfish, with the prompt below. In the Class Shared Folder on the school network, provide a file in Word and Kurzweil with the writing prompt, and a file with the prompt and a template of a friendly letter. The saved *Build a Pond* graphic organizer with the materials sorted should also be available in the shared folder for reference by the students. Allow students to choose the amount of scaffolding for the lesson that they prefer, reminding those with text to speech accommodations on their IEPs that Kurzweil is available. Remind students with word prediction accommodations to open Co:Writer or Word Cue when they begin writing.

Prompt: Imagine that YOU are the goldfish! Write a letter to your friend in which you describe your new home. Does it have everything you need? Will you be happy there? Explain your answers. Be sure to refer to the Goldfish Letter rubric as you write.

Peer Editing: (5 minutes)

Students swap computers and read a peer's letter. Have them enable **Track Changes** from the **Tools Menu** (for letters written in Word) or use the **Notes** feature (for letters written in Kurzweil) and record comments and feedback based on the Goldfish Letter rubric.

Assessment: Students are assessed using the following rubric, which has been provided prior to beginning their writing:

GOLDFISH LETTER SCORING RUBRIC

Criteria	Unsatisfactory	Satisfactory	Exemplary
Letter format	Letter is not written according to the guidelines for a friendly letter.	Letter is written adhering to most of the guidelines for a friendly letter.	Letter is written adhering to the guidelines for a friendly letter.
Abiotic/biotic factors	Few or no abiotic and biotic factors that make up the home (less than 3) are listed and the effect of these is not described.	Some examples of abiotic and biotic factors that make up the home are listed (between 3–5), and some of the ways these factors affect the home positively or negatively are described.	A variety of examples of abiotic and biotic factors (at least 6) that make up the home are listed and the ways these factors affect the home positively or negatively are described with supporting details.
Impact of human activities	The impact of human activities on the ecosystem is not described.	The impact of human activities on the ecosystem is described.	The impact of human activities on the ecosystem is described in detail.

Source: Adapted from a lesson presented on the Maryland Assistive Technology Network website: matnonline.pbworks.com/f/Build+a+Pond+UDL+Lesson.doc.

REFERENCES

Access Project. (2010). *Universal design for learning.* Colorado State University. Retrieved from http://accessproject.colostate.edu/udl/

Ashton, T. M. (2005). Students with learning disabilities using assistive technology in the inclusive classroom. In D. Edyburn, K. Higgins, & R. Boone (Eds.), *The handbook of special education technology research and practice* (pp. 229–238). Whitefish Bay, WI: Knowledge by Design.

Basham, J. D., Israel, M., Graden, J., Poth, R., & Winston, M. (2010). A comprehensive approach to RTI: Embedding universal design for learning and technology. *Learning Disability Quarterly, 33,* 243–255.

Basham, J. D., & Marino, M. T. (2013). Understanding STEM education and supporting students through universal design for learning. *Teaching Exceptional Children, 45*(4), 8–15.

Center for Applied Special Technology (CAST). (2010). *UDL at a glance.* Retrieved from http://www.youtube.com/watch?v=bDvKnY0g6e4

Center for Applied Special Technology (CAST). (2011). *Universal design for learning guidelines version 2.0.* Wakefield, MA: Author.

Center for Universal Design. (2008). *Environments and products for all people: About UD.* North Carolina State University. Retrieved from http://www.ncsu.edu/ncsu/design/cud/about_ud/about_ud.htm

Chiasson, P. (2005). Peirce's design for thinking: An embedded philosophy of education. *Educational Philosophy and Theory, 37*(2), 207–226.

Chita-Tegmark, M., Gravel, J. W., Serpa, M. deL. B., Domings, Y., & Rose, D. H. (2012). Using the universal design for learning framework to support culturally diverse learners. *Journal of Education, 192*(1), 17–22.

Connections Academy. (2014). *Your child deserves a superior K–12 education at home.* Retrieved from http://info.connectionsacademy.com/

DeCoste, D. C. (n.d.). Universal Design for Learning in the classroom [Presentation slides]. Retrieved from https://www.montgomeryschoolsmd.org/departments/hiat/udl/UDL_intro.pdf

Individuals with Disabilities Education Improvement Act of 2004, Pub. L. No. 108–446.

Lavoie, R. D. (1989). How difficult can this be? The F.A.T. City workshop: Understanding learning disabilities [DVD]. PBS Video.

National Center for Education Statistics. (2009). *Projections of education statistics to 2018* (37th ed.). Washington, DC: Author.

Rose, D. H. (2014). *UDL guidelines—version 2.0.* Retrieved from http://www.cast.org

Rose, D. H., & Meyer, A. (2002). *Teaching every student in the digital age: Universal design for learning.* Alexandria, VA: Association for Supervision and Curriculum Development.

RECOMMENDED READINGS

* Goeke, J. L., & Ciotoli, F. (2014). Inclusive STEM: Making integrative curriculum accessible to all students. *Children's Technology and Engineering, 18,* 19–22.

* McGuire, J. M., Scott, S. S., & Shaw, S. F. (2006). Universal design and its applications in educational environments. *Remedial and Special Education, 27*(3), 166–175.

* Rappolt-Schlichtmann, G., Daley, S. G., Lim, S., Lapinski, S., Robinson, K. H., & Johnson, M. (2013). Universal design for learning and elementary school science: Exploring the efficacy, use, and perceptions of a web-based science notebook. *Journal of Educational Psychology, 105*(4), 1210–1225.

* Smith, S. J., & Basham, J. D. (2014). Designing online learning opportunities for students with disabilities. *Teaching Exceptional Children, 46*(5), 127–137.

* Spooner, F., Baker, J. N., Harris, A. A., Ahlgrim-Delzell, L., & Browder, D. M. (2007). Effects of training in universal design for learning on lesson plan development. *Remedial and Special Education, 28*(2), 108–116.

* U.S. Department of Education, Office of Special Education Programs. (n.d.). OSEP ideas that work: Tool kit on Universal Design for Learning. Retrieved from https://www.osepideasthatwork.org/udl/instrpract.asp

GO EVEN FURTHER WITH THIS TOPIC ON THE WORLD WIDE WEB

- www.cast.org/udl/
- www.udlcenter.org
- www.cec.sped.org
- www. marylandlearninglinks.org/1021
- www. udltechtoolkit.wikispaces.com

THE Apps WE LOVE

- UDLinks
- Toontastic
- Geoboard
- Scribble press
- Bitsboard

12

Incredible Inclusion

Amy Hanreddy

California State University, Northridge

Erin Studer

CHIME Institute

WHAT REALLY WORKS IN INCLUSION
IN THE ELEMENTARY CLASSROOM

Differentiation and Inclusion—You Can Do it!

Imagine a classroom where students who live in their school's neighborhood are all welcome, regardless of learning, emotional, or physical differences. Students respect, value, and even learn from one another. As a skillful teacher, you provide a wide range of engaging and well-planned lessons that meet the diverse needs of these students. Sound like a utopian vision from a science fiction novel? Not so! Meeting the needs of a broad range of learners doesn't have to be a future vision from a sci-fi novel but rather it can become attainable when we approach the art of instruction with an inclusive philosophy of teaching and learning. A teacher's strong content knowledge, a positive mind-set about the ability of all learners, an innovative vision of what quality instruction looks like, all supported by the proper collaborative and school-wide supports make inclusive classrooms for all learners a reality.

We need to keep in mind that inclusive classrooms are not a recent phenomenon. At prior points in U.S. history, it was not unusual for students of similar ages to attend classes together regardless of ability (Osgood, 2005). However, as our public education system has evolved, it has increasingly sought to sort students into categories of learners, so that "special" classes have been developed for students who are high achieving, struggling with academics or behavior, or have more significant disabilities (Osgood, 2007). This works under the myth that classes containing less diversity in ability will lead to more efficiency, and yet that myth is fatally flawed.

First, any teacher will tell you that his or her classroom is diverse. Within any class, there is a wide range of student skills and personalities. With or without policies regarding inclusion, elementary teachers need to learn to teach inclusively.

Second, focusing time and energy on whether a student belongs in a general education classroom detracts from our efforts to determine how to meet the student's needs. It is difficult to commit to the challenge of teaching a student who you believe should not be in the room. If we commit to teaching everyone who walks through the door, then we seek strategies, guidance, and support to that end.

Third, students who are learning English as a second language and students from nondominant cultural backgrounds are over identified as having special educational needs (Sullivan, 2011). While there is value in accurately identifying individuals with special needs, the strong bias toward identifying any struggling learner as a child with special needs leads to over identification of minority students. Inclusive educational approaches would deemphasize special education labeling and limit the segregation of any struggling student. In an inclusive class, the focus is on identifying educational resources to meet the needs of the child, whatever those needs may be.

And finally, under the old model, teachers with expertise in creative instructional strategies for teaching core content give up ownership of struggling students, leaving the instruction of struggling learners often in the hands of those with the least content area knowledge and preparation. We end up with classrooms where students who need the most amounts of help are often relegated to being taught by paraprofessionals or aides, many of whom have had no educational training whatsoever (Giangreco, 2010). The word "inclusion" is thrown around often, however; so what exactly are we talking about?

Inclusive Education is the movement toward ensuring that all students have their educational and social needs met in their general education classrooms, reducing dependence on separate classes based on students' perceived abilities. This practice was formalized with the passage of the Education for All Handicapped Act (EAHCA, 1975; later the Individuals with Disabilities Education Improvement Act [IDEIA], 2004), which describes a preference for the "least restrictive environment" and states that "to the maximum extent appropriate, children with disabilities . . . are educated with children who are not disabled" (IDEIA, 2004, 20 U.S.C. § 1412).

Inclusive teaching means considering the wide range of learners in every step of the teaching process and ensuring that all students have a way to access the curriculum, express what they know, and remain engaged and motivated throughout the process of learning. If I am beginning to teach a lesson on the solar system that involves reading from a textbook and Sam struggles to decode text, I could consider other ways for him to access the material (e.g., audio, pictures, read aloud), provide him with text that is written at his reading level, deliver a presentation that includes the content of the textbook, or support students in finding material online (including videos) that addresses the same content. The strategy that I choose might depend on Sam's interests and skills, my goal for the lesson, and the needs of other students in the class, with the intention being that whatever strategy I pick, Sam can implement it in the general education classroom without being pulled out for remediation.

Inclusive teaching also means considering the social needs of our students. Inclusive teachers facilitate a sense of membership and belonging in their classrooms, support their students' ability to resolve conflicts, and teach communication and social skills as a key piece of the curriculum. This culture of inclusion in the classroom provides the benefits of ethical and social development for all children and provides true access to education for all students. This may sound utopian, but isn't this the kind of classroom you want to teach? We certainly do!

Today, more students with disabilities are receiving their education in general education than at any other time since the passage of EAHCA in 1975 (Data Accountability Center, 2010), and more teachers are learning to teach inclusively than ever before. As students with a wide range of disabilities are increasingly educated alongside their typically developing peers, curriculum and instructional strategies are evolving to meet the changing needs of today's teachers and classrooms. In the classrooms of today and tomorrow, highly effective teachers will be those who can collaborate effectively, be knowledgeable about a wide range of learners and their abilities, and have a vision for instructional practices that meet the needs of all students. Since we are positive that you picked up this book in order to be one of those highly effective teachers (or because your principal bought it for you), keep reading and get some strategies and research-based suggestions on how to do all of these things.

RESEARCH SUPPORTS PRACTICES OF DIFFERENTIATION AND INCLUSION

Inclusive education is actually a collection of several research-based instructional practices that support learning, belonging, and positive behavior for diverse classrooms (Sailor & Roger, 2005; Theoharis & Causton, 2014).

Benefits to students without disabilities. We are sure you are thinking "wait, without disabilities?!" Yes. We are starting this section by mentioning students who do not have identified special needs because we want to show that inclusive education is not just for those with disabilities. It is for all kids. Several studies have explored the impact of inclusion and have found that nondisabled students have achieved improved academic outcomes as a result of being in an inclusive class (Cole, Waldron, & Majd, 2004; Ghandi, 2007). Sailor (2008) noted that inclusive practices such as Universal Design for Learning, Positive Behavior Interventions and Supports, and co-teaching have the potential to result in reduced special education referrals school-wide because struggling students receive assistance before they fall too far behind.

Benefits to students with disabilities. Evidence also suggests that students with disabilities demonstrate improved academic and social outcomes as a result of increased time spent in general education classes (Cosier, Causton-Theoharis, & Theoharis, 2013; Rea, McLaughlin, & Walther-Thomas, 2002), including improved social skills, communication skills, and increased interactions with typical peers (Boyd, Conroy, Asmus, McKenney, & Mancil, 2008). Although time spent in general education is linked to improved academic and social outcomes for students with disabilities, additional supports such as accommodations, modifications, peer supports, and co-teaching are all critical strategies associated with the success of students with disabilities in inclusive settings. Clearly, it is not enough to just plop a few students with disabilities into a general education elementary classroom and call it inclusion.

Practices to Support Inclusive Education. Universal Design for Learning considers the wide range of student strengths and needs when planning instruction by ensuring multiple means of representation, expression, and engagement (Center for Applied Special Technology, 2008; Edyburn, 2010).

Making Connections

Check out Chapters 7 and 11 on Technology and UDL

Accommodations and modifications (changes to the curriculum such as increased visuals, use of technology, and enhanced content) are critical tools to support student engagement and learning in general education classes (Dymond & Orelove, 2001; Suk-Hyang, Wehmeyer, Soukup, & Palmer, 2010). Even when a lesson has been developed using a "universally designed" approach, some students will continue to require individualized adjustments. For example, Joey has a physical disability and needs adequate space to move his wheelchair through the classroom. Samantha has a challenge in graphomotor (writing) skills and so is given the option to type her assignments. Max has an intellectual disability and so uses a version of the story being read in class that includes simplified text and less pictures. These adjustments are carefully designed based on individual needs, with an emphasis on access to the general education curriculum and environment. If you are concerned that you don't have the background knowledge to figure out what adjustments, accommodations, or modifications will be needed, you don't need to worry. That's why we emphasize collaboration between general educators and special education teachers and specialists!

Making Connections

Check out Chapter 13 on Co-Teaching

Special education is defined in IDEIA (2004) as "specially designed instruction" (Sect. 300.39). This definition does not state *where* this instruction can take place, and thus, individualized instruction can occur in a wide range of settings. When students who receive special education services spend all or part of their day within a general education classroom, one way to ensure that these students are receiving "specially designed instruction" is for a special education teacher to co-teach with the general education teacher (Murawski & Lochner, 2011). With strong evidence demonstrating improved outcomes for a wide range of students (Solis, Vaughn, Swanson, & McCulley, 2012), co-teaching is a critical piece to the puzzle of inclusive classrooms. Yes, this book has you covered in this regard as well! Check out Chapter 13 to read about how to effectively co-teach with a partner.

At times, additional adults (typically known as paraprofessionals, aides, or paraeducators) might be assigned to a classroom, a group of students, or even an individual student based upon an administrator and/or Individualized Education Program (IEP) team's determination that a higher level of support is needed than can be provided by a general education teacher in collaboration with a special education teacher. These paraprofessionals can be important components to ensuring that all students receive adequate supports and access to the curriculum and are viewed as essential in many inclusive classrooms and schools (Giangreco, 2010). Despite the benefits, however, there are also many drawbacks. Giangreco, Edelman, Luiselli, and McFarland (1997) examined the trend of assigning paraprofessionals in inclusive classrooms and noted common challenges: increased reliance on adults, interference with social relationships, and reduced access to instruction from credentialed teachers. In order to avoid these negative impacts, it is critical that paraprofessionals are well trained to support all students, that teachers provide high-quality supervision, and that paraprofessionals do not provide the majority of instruction for students with identified disabilities (Giangreco & Doyle, 2002).

BEGINNING TO THINK INCLUSIVELY: AVOIDING COMMON PITFALLS

Teachers

✖ **STOP confusing mere placement in a general education classroom with inclusive teaching practices.** True inclusion means that students benefit from a comprehensive approach to their educational program. This comprehensive approach includes (a) planned adult supports in co-teaching and, if necessary, paraprofessional support; (b) access to universally designed and appropriately differentiated curriculum; (c) use of carefully considered accommodations and modifications; and (d) supports by peers and any needed service providers. Placement in a general education class for students with special needs without these supports and considerations is not inclusion; it is just assigning a seat. For a checklist of critical classroom practices, check out the Classroom Quality Indicators tool.

✖ **STOP assuming that if a student with a disability is to be included in general education, they will need full-time paraprofessional support.** Carefully considered accommodations, modifications, differentiation, co-teaching, and peer supports often eliminate the need for paraprofessional supports. In fact, if these additional supports are provided without first trying less restrictive approaches, we may actually hamper students' development and growth as independent students.

✖ **STOP relying on paraprofessionals to provide instruction to students with disabilities.** Students deserve to receive instruction from highly qualified and well-trained teachers (that's you!). When assigned to classrooms or students, paraprofessionals should not be the primary deliverers of instruction. According to Giangreco, Suter, & Doyle (2010), this amounts to assigning "the least qualified personnel to students who present the most challenging learning and behavior characteristics" (p. 51).

✖ **STOP seating students with disabilities together or in the back of the classroom.** Assigned seating for students with disabilities should be determined like any other student in the classroom with any special consideration taken into account (e.g., field of vision consideration, access and mobility challenges). Grouping of students with disabilities in close proximity to one another for the ease of providing support during independent work time is really just a symptom of a larger instructional issue. Students of any one group (high achieving, English language learners, students with special needs) shouldn't all be working together all of the time. Keep this in mind when creating your seating chart.

✖ **STOP calling students "my kids" and "your kids" when referring to students with and without disabilities.** Caseloads and class rosters are of secondary importance compared to who is sitting in your classroom. In inclusive classrooms, as soon as a student sits down in your classroom, they are "our" students.

✖ **STOP considering individual learning needs after a lesson has been planned and developed.** Co-planned, universally designed lessons take into consideration the needs of the class prior to deciding "how" a lesson is going to play out. All lessons are driven by the general education curriculum ("what") and are guided by the needs present in the classroom ("who"). By taking student strengths and needs into account, you are better able to create a cohesive lesson plan that is accessible to all of your students, rather than attempting to develop "retrofitted" solutions to help a student be a part of a preexisting lesson.

- ✘ **STOP using a "one-size-fits-all" behavior management system in the classroom.** Fair isn't equal; fair is getting what you need (Lavoie, 2004). It is true for instruction, and it is true for behavior management. There will be occasions when individual students need something slightly different or in addition to your established system. Students might need a personalized checklist, reward system, or opportunities to take breaks. These adjustments are not unfair to the other students (remember those students don't *need* the additional supports) nor is it mollycoddling the student who requires the additional support. It is providing the child with a system they need to learn new behavioral skills.

- ✘ **STOP establishing prerequisites for membership in your classroom.** For example, some teachers say students are only "ready" to enter their class when they can sit quietly or work independently. Prerequisites to be included in a general education class are the classic traps of a segregated special education delivery model. Students cannot learn how to "sit quietly and work independently" in your classroom by going down the hallway and learning how to do it in the resource room with another teacher.

- ✘ **STOP treating special educators like an aide in the classroom.** Special education teachers are highly trained professionals with critical knowledge about the needs of a wide variety of learners. They are trained in strategies and approaches that help children who are struggling. Too often, they are used to merely "support" students or pull a small group of learners off to the side for help while the general education teacher instructs the rest of the class. This is a misuse of their expertise and an underutilization of the adult resources in a room.

- ✘ **STOP structuring your groups solely by ability levels.** There are times for ability or "readiness level" groupings in a classroom, but there is also ample time and reasons for mixed-ability level groupings. There is much to be gained and learned by students of varying levels and abilities working and interacting with one another. It also helps ensure that instruction remains universally designed or differentiated to allow access for all students.

- ✘ **STOP working like an independent contractor when it comes to planning instruction.** Too many teachers work in isolation when it comes to planning instruction for their classrooms. The task of differentiating for a broad range of learners and meeting their individual needs is too much for just one teacher to take on. We know that! We agree completely. To truly be effective, teachers must work with their colleagues to plan their instruction and their lessons. The most successful and sustainable approach in an inclusive classroom is to collaborate and co-plan.

✗ **STOP believing that only students with special needs will benefit from an inclusive approach.** Students across the continuum of learners often need support, differentiation, and access to various universally designed pathways to learn and express knowledge. Students from low socioeconomic backgrounds, students who have had limited access to preschool or Head Start programs, English language learners, students from migrant families, students who are high achieving/gifted, and students who are merely struggling because of prior gaps in their instruction can all benefit from inclusive education environments with carefully designed and differentiated curriculum and instruction.

Administrators

✗ **STOP integrating and including students after general education rosters are created.** This continues the sense that students with disabilities create additional work. If a maximum class size is 25 students, then any student with an IEP in the class, even if part time, should be included within that 25. Classroom assignments should include all students at a given grade level, including students who spend a portion of their day in special education settings.

✗ **STOP making placement decisions based on students' eligibility category.** Not only is this not in compliance with IDEIA and other state and federal guidelines, it is ultimately limiting to the growth and development of children. Each child's Least Restrictive Environment (LRE) requires individual considerations about their strengths and needs. Each IEP team must also consider if and how the supports and accommodations any one child needs can be implemented in the general education classroom. A presupposition of a child's placement based solely on the disability category listed on their IEP is *not* legal, educationally appropriate, or ethical.

GO TEACHING INCLUSIVELY: STRATEGIES FOR SUCCESS

✓ **REMEMBER a key tenet of special education:** Special education is *specially designed instruction* (IDEIA, 2004). Regardless of where students are receiving their instruction, their IEPs should identify the individual goals targeted during instruction, and these goals should form the foundation for the individualized supports that students will receive in class. By increasing awareness of these goals, teachers can ensure that students continue to make progress in relation to individually determined goals as well as the core curriculum.

✓ **USE tools to help you determine how IEP goals will be practiced** in the context of regularly occurring class activities. Tools such as an IEP/activity matrix are helpful for doing this. See pages 195 and 196 for examples!

✓ **ENCOURAGE any adults in the room to help all learners.** Although some students who receive special education services require additional adult support for a portion of the day, many teachers are not aware that these additional adults can support other students in the class as well. It is easy to fall into the trap of allowing a paraprofessional or special education teacher to take on the role of primary instructor for a student they support, but when this happens, general education teachers become less aware of the individual student's learning needs and might even feel less owner-ship of these students. To avoid this, ensure that all adults are responsible for all students, and make a point of providing direct instruction to students who receive special education services. The table on page 197 provides an example of how a teacher and a para-professional might share responsibility for students within a lesson.

✓ **DO break direct instruction (especially whole group instruction) into small chunks.** Delivering instruction in smaller chunks is good practice for *all* learners. It provides additional benefit for chil-dren with special needs, struggling learners, and even English language learners. Leveraging active learning, social interaction, and increased time to build and consider new knowledge allows a variety of learners to access the curriculum through a wider range of learning pathways than mere lecture or demonstration.

✓ **USE a Positive Behavior Support system in your classroom.** Teachers often cite issues of classroom man-agement as a reason for seeking seg-regated settings for students with special needs. However, challenging behavior is not solely attributable to students with special needs. Teachers who develop and implement Positive

Making Connections

Check out Chapters 8 and 9 on PBS and Classroom Management

Behavior Support systems find that any classroom environment becomes more manageable and effective, creating an environment in which all learners can succeed.

✓ **PURPOSEFULLY PLAN for ways to utilize peer supports in your classroom.** Peer modeling may be one of the most powerful and effective tools that a teacher in an inclusive classroom has at their disposal. The old teacher adage, "Never do anything a student can do for you; it's their learning experience, not yours," is never more true than in an inclusive classroom. Peer support, peer modeling, and peer collaboration is often more welcome and desired by students than support from a teacher or paraprofessional. This support also helps to establish the culture of belonging and togetherness that underpin an inclusive classroom.

✓ **COLLABORATE, co-teach, co-plan, and co-assess with your colleagues.** The style of work required to include a wide variety of learners in a classroom and to develop universally designed and differentiated lessons must be a collaborative working style (Murawski, 2010). You can't do it on your own! It's true—you must be willing to accept and in some cases seek out the support, collaboration, and genuine shared responsibility of your colleagues.

✓ **CREATE a system for adaptations to the curriculum or instruction.** Too many teachers and schools re-create the wheel every year. Instead, have a repository for all of your adapted materials at each grade level. That way, if your kindergarten teacher decides to be a third-grade teacher next year, she can look at all the materials that have already been adapted for third graders over the years. Certainly, students are different, and she may need to continue to make adaptations, but at least she doesn't have to start from scratch.

✓ **START to become well informed about the needs and concerns for students with a wide range of disabilities.** Everyone naturally has differing levels of knowledge and expertise about how to support learners across the range abilities (gifted learners, English language learners, students who have reading disabilities, etc.). One of the positives of co-teaching and collaboration is that no single teacher has to know everything. By putting all of our heads together, we are able to teach all students. Often, teachers who are uninformed about certain disability types may have apprehension or anxiety about teaching a student with that disability. Being well informed and well educated about a wide variety of learning needs is often an antidote to those fears. When teachers engage in this kind of quest for a deeper understanding about the needs of their students, they are more likely to feel prepared to work with their colleagues to meet those needs; they are also less likely to recommend that a student with special needs has to be educated by "an expert" in some other classroom down the hall.

SAMPLE GOAL/ACTIVITY MATRICES

Sample Goal/Activity Matrix for Cecilia

Class Activities: Goals:	Language Arts	Math	Social Studies	Science
Correctly respond to comprehension questions after reading a short selection of text.	Embed comprehension questions into independent and group reading activities.	When completing a word problem, highlight key words and identify what a problem is asking.	After decoding information from a selection of a nonfiction text, identify key facts.	Correctly follow written directions for science activities.
Use a checklist of assignment steps and self-monitoring strategies to complete class assignments at a similar pace as her peers.	Follow a "writer's workshop" checklist to monitor progress on an extended writing assignment.	Use a timer to "check in" on her own progress every 5 minutes while working independently on a worksheet.	When working on a group project, act as a "project manager" to ensure the group has completed all required steps and has followed the given timeline.	Follow steps to the completion of a science activity by checking off each step on a checklist.

Cecilia is a student whose goals emphasize reading comprehension and the completion of assignments in a timely manner.

Sample Goal/Activity Matrix for Rodrigo

Class Activities: Goals:	Language Arts	Math	Social Studies	Science
Use pictures to represent the understanding of modified reading material.	Identify pictures that represent the main idea and characters in a story read in class.	Correctly identify pictures to match a word problem.	Use an image search engine to select at least three pictures that represent a key topic discussed in class and share these with peers.	Follow a materials checklist using pictures to prepare for a science lab activity.
Count items with 1:1 correspondence up to 20.	Count the number of books needed for his table group and distribute these to students.	Use manipulatives to solve simple addition and subtraction problems to 20.	Identify materials needed for group members when creating a diorama.	Act as "materials manager" in lab activity. Gather and count needed materials for his small group.

Rodrigo is a student whose goals emphasize using pictures as a form of communication and counting items up to 20.

LESSON PLANNING FOR PARAPROFESSIONAL SUPPORT

Lesson Steps	Teacher	Paraprofessional
Students return to class from recess and wait for instruction.	Greets students and introduces science "warm-up" activity.	Makes sure students have put away jackets and lunchboxes. Gets individual students started on the activity.
Students work on warm-up journal/discussion prompt in pairs.	Support pairs and listen to discussion to assess current knowledge.	Prepare materials for next activity (from list provided by teacher).
Students listen as teacher introduces an activity on the "rock cycle."	Introduce the rock cycle and show examples of various types of rocks. Explain activity using pictures to illustrate steps and key concepts.	Pass around rocks and make sure all students get a chance to hold them. Help individual students to follow a checklist for the activity being described by the teacher.
Students complete "rock cycle" activity (using clay to illustrate volcanic, sedimentary, and metamorphic rocks).	Facilitate use of key vocabulary among groups. Support individual students in identifying key features of each rock type—move from group to group.	Facilitate use of key vocabulary among groups. Support individual students in identifying key features of each rock type—move from group to group.
Students debrief activity as a whole group, reviewing key features of each rock type.	Lead whole group discussion emphasizing key vocabulary. Use pictures to illustrate steps and key concepts.	Use picture checklist from the activity to remind individual students of vocabulary. Direct students to visuals used by teacher.

A teacher and paraprofessional share responsibility for all students in the class.

SELF-ASSESSMENT OF INCLUSIVE EDUCATIONAL PRACTICES

Complete the self-assessment for your classroom, indicating the degree to which each practice is currently being implemented. Once the assessment is completed, highlight two rows that will be prioritized in the weeks that follow. Continue choosing items and moving them closer to being "fully" implemented!

	Fully	Partially	Not Yet
Teachers differentiate for a variety of learners by using visual, tactile, and kinesthetic materials and experiences.			
Teachers use a variety of student groupings, such as pairs, small groups, and whole class.			
Teachers choose groupings on the basis of learning styles, abilities, interests, and curricular focus, and not on the basis of ability alone.			
Teachers plan accommodations for students with disabilities, based on their IEP, and incorporate those accommodations into lesson plans and everyday instruction.			
Teachers plan modifications to classroom instruction for students with disabilities who need it, using the same or similar, age-appropriate materials for assignments, homework, and tests.			
Teachers provide direct instruction on IEP goals, infused across subject areas within the general education curriculum.			
All students receive positive reinforcement and feedback (i.e., at least 75% positive; no more than 25% corrective).			
Teachers interact with students in ways that allow for positive peer relationships and personal dignity.			
Teachers work with paraprofessionals who are assigned to individual students to a) provide appropriate supports and b) fade adult support to increase student independence.			
Instructional staff select co-teaching methods on the basis of student need and curriculum content when two adults are instructors in the class.			
Instructional planning teams welcome parents as active team members.			

Source: Revised from the (2006) Quality Indicators of Inclusive Education. *Maryland Coalition for Inclusive Education.* Retrieved from www.mcie.org/usermedia/application/8/quality-indicators—building-based-practices-2011%28accessible-by-berman%29.pdf.

GOAL/ACTIVITY MATRIX

Directions

1. At the head of each column in the top row, identify four main activities to target throughout the day.

2. Summarize two IEP goals to be prioritized for an individual student. List these at the start of each row on the left.

3. For each goal, describe how it might be addressed within each of the main activities. Share this chart with all team members (special ed and general ed teachers, family, related service providers).

As routines are established for addressing these first two skills throughout the day, continue to add more goals and more activities!

Class Activities: → ↓ Goals:	*Activity 1*	*Activity 2*	*Activity 3*	*Activity 4*

REFERENCES

Boyd, B. A., Conroy, M. A., Asmus, J. M., McKenney, E. L. W., & Mancil, G. R. (2008). Descriptive analysis of classroom setting events on the social behaviors of children with autism spectrum disorder. *Education and Training in Developmental Disabilities, 43*, 186–197.

Center for Applied Special Technology. (2008). UDL Editions by CAST. Retrieved from http://udleditions.cast.org/

Cole, C., Waldron, N., & Majd, M. (2004). Academic progress of students across inclusive and traditional settings. *Mental Retardation, 42*(2), 136–144.

Cosier, M., Causton-Theoharis, J., & Theoharis, G. (2013). Does access matter? Time in general education and achievement for students with disabilities. *Remedial and Special Education, 34*(6), 323–332.

Data Accountability Center. (2010). Individuals with Disabilities Education Act (IDEA) data. Part B data and notes. Retrieved from https://www.ideadata.org/PartBData.asp

Dymond, S. K., & Orelove, F. P. (2001). What constitutes effective curricula for students with severe disabilities? *Exceptionality, 9*, 109–122.

Education for All Handicapped Children Act of 1975. U.S. Public Law 94–142. U.S. Code. Vol. 20, secs. 1401 et seq.

Edyburn, D. (2010). Would you recognize Universal Design for Learning if you saw it? Ten propositions for new directions for the second decade of UDL. *Learning Disability Quarterly, 33*, 33–41.

Ghandi, A. (2007). Context matters: Exploring relations between inclusion and reading achievement of students without disabilities. *International Journal of Disability, Development, and Education, 54*(1), 91–112.

Giangreco, M. (2010). One-to-one paraprofessionals for students with disabilities in inclusive schools: Is conventional wisdom wrong? *Intellectual and Developmental Disabilities, 48*(1), 1–13.

Giangreco, M., & Doyle, M. (2002). Students with disabilities and paraprofessional supports: Benefits, balance, and band-aids. *Focus on Exceptional Children, 34*(7), 1–12.

Giangreco, M., Edelman, S., Luiselli, T., & McFarland, S. (1997). Helping or hovering? Effects of instructional assistant proximity on students with disabilities. *Exceptional Children, 64*, 7–18.

Giangreco, M. F., Suter, J. C., & Doyle, M. (2010). Paraprofessionals in inclusive schools: A review of recent research. *Journal of Educational and Psychological Consultation, 20*(1), 41–57.

Individuals with Disabilities Education Improvement Act. (2004). 20 U.S.C. § 1400.

Lavoie, R. (2004). How difficult can this be? The F.A.T. City Workshop: Understanding learning disabilities [DVD]. United States: PBS Videos.

Murawski, W. W. (2010). *Collaborative teaching in elementary schools: Making the co-teaching marriage work!* Thousand Oaks, CA: Corwin Press.

Murawski, W., & Lochner, W. (2011). Observing co-teaching: What to ask for, look for, and listen for. *Intervention in School and Clinic, 46*(3), 174–183.

Osgood, R. (2005). *The history of inclusion in the United States.* Washington, DC: Gallaudet University Press.

Osgood, R. (2007). *The history of special education: A struggle for equality in American public schools.* Westport, CT: Praeger.

Rea, P. J., McLaughlin, V. L., & Walther-Thomas, C. (2002). Outcomes for students with learning disabilities in inclusive and pullout programs. *Exceptional Children, 68*(2), 203.

Sailor, W. (2008). Access to the general curriculum: Systems change or tinker some more? *Research and Practice for Persons with Severe Disabilities, 33/34*(4–1), 249–257.

Sailor, W., & Roger, B. (2005). Rethinking inclusion: Schoolwide applications. *Phi Delta Kappan, 86,* 503–509.

Solis, M., Vaughn, S., Swanson, E., & McCulley, L. (2012). Collaborative models of instruction: The empirical foundations of inclusion and co-teaching. *Psychology in the Schools, 49*(5), 498–510.

Suk-Hyang, L., Wehmeyer, M. L., Soukup, J. H., & Palmer, S. B. (2010). Impact of curriculum modifications on access to the general education curriculum for students with disabilities. *Exceptional Children, 76*(2), 213–233.

Sullivan, A. L. (2011). Disproportionality in special education identification and placement of English Language Learners. *Exceptional Children, 77*(3), 317–334.

Theoharis, G., & Causton, J. (2014). Leading inclusive reform for students with disabilities: A school- and systemwide approach. *Theory into Practice, 53*(2), 82–97.

RECOMMENDED READINGS

* Artiles, A., Kozleski, E., & Waitoller, F. (2011). *Inclusive education: Examining equity on five continents.* Cambridge, MA: Harvard Education Press.

* Downing, J. (2010). *Academic instruction for students with moderate and severe disabilities in academic settings.* Thousand Oaks, CA: Corwin.

* Halvorsen, A. T., & Neary, T. (2009). *Building inclusive schools: Tools and strategies for success.* Boston, MA: Pearson.

RECOMMENDED VIDEOS

Fabrocini, J., Adler, M., & San Giacomo, L. (2007). *Accessible IEPs for all: Gathering the experts around the table* [DVD]. Baltimore, MD: Paul H. Brookes.

Habib, D. (2007). *Including Samuel* [DVD]. Concord, NH: Author.

Habib, D. (2007). *Thaysa.* Available at http://vimeo.com/43931633

Habib, D. (2014). *All means all.* SWIFT Center. Available online at https://www.youtube.com/watch?v=v1MaeQqaygg&index=8&list=TLaazIdxYLjh5XhMuAdgDiSXQ1NXPfmPjY

GO EVEN FURTHER WITH THIS TOPIC ON THE WORLD WIDE WEB

- www.mcie.org/pubs.asp
- www.njcie.net/tools_schools.asp
- www.csie.org.uk/index.shtml
- www.theinclusiveclass.com/
- www.projectparticipate.org/handouts/TipsforParaeducators.pdf

THE Apps WE LOVE

- Clicker Docs
- Bitsboard
- Educreations
- Pictello
- Booksy

13

Creative Co-Teaching

Wendy W. Murawski

California State University, Northridge

WHAT REALLY WORKS IN CO-TEACHING IN THE ELEMENTARY CLASSROOM

Can't We All Just Get Along?

It's summer, and you are thinking about the next school year starting and reflecting a bit on last year. What will you want to improve upon? You think about your content, your students, your communications with parents, and then it hits you. There are so many adults who come into your elementary classroom on a daily basis—how can you do a better job with *them?* You feel like your classroom has a revolving door on it. Adults walk in and take your students out in the middle of a lesson, or sometimes stay and work with them in the room. There are even adults who walk in and seem to just stand around until you ask them to do something specific. Yes. This is the area that needs improvement. How can you work it so that there are fewer distractions, a more strategic use of adults, and a better way to differentiate instruction for the wide range of needs in your elementary classroom?

The reality is that schools are including more students with disabilities into general education classrooms. As those students move into the classrooms, so do special education teachers, paraprofessionals, speech/language specialists, physical therapists, and other specialists. Thus, we seriously need to reform the instructional methods used to support both students and teachers. The call for reform in both general and special education is to include evidence-based practices that are interactive, multimodal, collaborative, dynamic, and real world. Sure—we'd all agree that those sound good—but how are we supposed to do all that when we have 20 or 30 five-year-olds running around the room? How are we supposed to be real world and dynamic when some of our students have never been in a classroom, used English, learned their letters and numbers, or been asked to share before? Yikes. Don't despair. There is help. Your help comes in the form of a partner—for better or worse, richer or poorer, academics or behavior. We call this instructional marriage *co-teaching* (Murawski, 2010), and it may be the way to help you do everything you need to do in the elementary classroom while staying sane!

Co-teaching as a service delivery model is gaining ground both nationally and internationally. It offers a way to provide quality services to all students, including those with special needs, in general education classrooms. By increasing differentiation of instruction, all of your students can benefit. So we know that it can benefit students, but what exactly is co-teaching? To start, co-teaching occurs when two or more professionals teach a group of students together. But they can't just be in the room together. More is needed. In fact, Murawski (2010) (yes, that's me!) clarified that in order for true co-teaching to occur, "co-planning, co-instructing, and co-assessing," are necessary (p. 11). Teachers and students can potentially get the best of all worlds. Think about it: Pair a specialist who is highly qualified to differentiate instruction with an educator who is highly qualified in specific grade-level content and BAM! You get differentiating heaven. This chapter is about how to make that actually happen.

Let's get back to our opening scenario: You are thinking about all those adults and kiddos. You absentmindedly open your e-mail, only to find one from a colleague saying, "Hi! I just found out that we are going to share a bunch of students this coming year. Instead of me coming in and pulling students out randomly, I was wondering if you'd be interested in co-teaching with me? We could share the load and plan how to really meet everyone's needs. I'm not as strong on the grade-level standards as you are, but I'm great at coming up with strategies for learning, differentiating materials, making accommodations and modifications, and let's face it—parents love me! So, what do you say?" You pause, and as a smile crosses your face, you respond, "Heck yeah!"

KEY RESEARCH YOU SHOULD KNOW ABOUT CO-TEACHING

Think of the typical elementary classroom. Is it a room in which students are working collaboratively and critically analyzing problems, while two teachers joke as they facilitate fun and differentiated learning activities? Or is it a room with a frustrated teacher standing at the front whiteboard and raising her voice as kids sit on the carpet, poking each other and wiggling uncontrollably? I'm guessing it was more likely the latter. That's the most common scenario unfortunately.

Although findings demonstrated that students' standardized test scores were higher if teachers individualized and differentiated instruction (Pearl & Miller, 2007), research also shows that teachers continue to use traditional, whole group teaching methods even as classes become more diverse and inclusive of students with disabilities (Kennedy & Ihle, 2012; King-Sears & Bowman-Kruhm, 2011). We are talking large, whole group lessons even when students are 5 and 6 years old! Dude, what are we thinking? When you co-teach, though, you can divide and conquer. You are not always just standing in front of the kids at the same time. Co-teaching results in smaller student-teacher ratios, more cooperative group work, an increase in the use of evidence-based practices, and a stronger emphasis on essential questions, big ideas, and real-world application of content (e.g., Austin, 2001; Friend & Cook, 2012; Murawski & Spencer, 2011). Individuals who want to co-teach are expected to work as equals in the same classroom, using their parity, shared expertise, and resources to optimize outcomes for students (Cramer, Liston, Nevin, & Thousand, 2010; Rea, McLaughlin, & Walther-Thomas, 2002). Thus, co-teaching meets the call for instructional reform in the fields of both general *and* special education. Woo-hoo!

Co-teaching is in no way new, and many of you have probably heard of it before. However, research on actual implementation and outcomes remains confusing at best. Much has been written about the quality, or lack thereof, of existing research (McDuffie, Mastropieri, & Scruggs, 2009; Murawski & Goodwin, 2014). Unfortunately, it is rare for studies on co-teaching to meet all of the standards for sound, well-defined, and outcome-focused research (Scruggs, Mastropieri, & McDuffie, 2007; Weiss & Brigham, 2000). In general, collecting data on a specific treatment should not pose a problem; however, co-teaching is a service delivery option in which collaboration, personality, and student characteristics play an integral role (Friend, Cook, Hurley-Chamberlain, & Shamberger, 2010; Zigmond, Magiera, Simmons, & Volonino, 2013). These are variables that are extremely difficult to tease out and quantify. In essence, this is a doozy to collect data on! We are talking different personalities here.

In 2001, I completed the first meta-analysis on co-teaching with Dr. Lee Swanson. A meta-analysis is essentially where you take all the quantitative research you have on an intervention and boil it down to one number called an effect size to see if the intervention works or not. Ultimately, we reported an overall positive effect size of .40, though we called it an "apples and oranges" analysis (Murawski & Swanson, 2001). What that really means is that, while it seems like co-teaching has significant promise, at the time there were just not a lot of similar studies to compare. Then, in 2007, Scruggs and colleagues offered the first meta-synthesis of qualitative co-teaching data; their results reinforced the components cited in most literature as critical to co-teaching effectiveness. Not surprisingly, those studies that included administrative support, professional development, planning time, and teacher voice yielded more positive results than those that did not. Anyone here surprised? Just recently, Vanessa Goodwin and I summarized the research on co-teaching as contradictory, confusing, and cautiously optimistic (Murawski & Goodwin, 2014). In a nutshell, those teachers who have the critical characteristics and logistics present for co-teaching success (i.e., parity, planning, personalities, professional development, and presence) are successful. Those who don't, often struggle. (Yes, a big collective "no duh" is allowed.)

My job then is to provide you with the DOs and DON'Ts for co-teaching by identifying actions that I've frequently observed that actually act as obstacles for co-teaching success, as well as those actions that maximize the chance of co-teachers making a positive impact on preschool and elementary school students. Data continue to be collected on the implementation and impact of co-teaching, so that's good. In the meantime, this is your user-friendly reference for getting started or improving co-teaching at your school—unless, of course, you prefer buying a whole book called, *Collaborative Teaching in Elementary Schools: Making the Co-Teaching Marriage Work* by Murawski (2010). I hear it's phenomenal! No? Alright, I'll still provide you with numerous resources for additional reading on co-teaching at the end of this chapter for those who would like to go deeper in the topic.

WHAT YOU NEED TO AVOID AT ALL COSTS RELATED TO CO-TEACHING

Teachers

- ✗ **STOP confusing "collaboration" and "inclusion" with "co-teaching."** They are not the same thing. Collaboration is a style of interacting; you can collaborate to accomplish a mutual goal, but that goal doesn't have to be related to co-teaching. Inclusion is the philosophy that students with special needs can have those needs met in the general education setting; co-teaching might help accomplish that, but co-teaching is not the only option. Co-teaching requires "co-planning, co-instructing, and co-assessing" (Murawski, 2003, p. 10); collaboration is a major requirement.

Making Connections

Check out Chapter 12 on Inclusion

✖ **STOP thinking that all co-teaching takes is putting two people in the same classroom.** Even two fantastic teachers may not co-teach well if they do not know what it requires or if both have been taught only how to "lead" a class and not how to collaborate. If this is a collaborative marriage, it'd be nice if your two teachers actually got along, wouldn't it?

✖ **STOP calling the general education teacher the "teacher" and the special education teacher "the co-teacher."** He or she is not a copilot. Stop calling general education students "regular education"; the others are not irregular. Just say "co-teachers" and "general and special education students" or even just "students."

✖ **STOP expecting co-taught classrooms to look the same as solo taught classes.** By definition, two teachers should be interacting with each other and with students differently to get different outcomes. If I enter your room and just walk around helping kids at their desks, how is that any different than what an aide or parent volunteer would do?

✖ **STOP looking at co-teaching as *the* method for inclusion.** Inclusive schools use a variety of in-class service delivery options for students. Not all students with disabilities need to be in a co-taught class, nor do all teachers need to co-teach. Some kids are great with just monitoring, assistance from a paraprofessional, or minor accommodations.

✖ **STOP blaming administrators, parents, or other teachers if they are not on board with co-teaching.** They may just not know what to do. Teach them. Get them on board.

✖ **STOP trying to wait to see if you'll be required to co-teach.** This train has left the station. It's happening. You'd be better off to try it now while there are resources and professional development offered, rather than when it's fait accompli.

✖ **STOP having the general education teacher lead and the special educator become the aide.** This is a major complaint in co-teaching. It's really common when the general educator is with the kids all day and the special educator is only in there during language arts or math. However, we each need "face time" with the kids, and we each have something to contribute.

✖ **STOP complaining that you don't have time to co-plan.** If you are not co-planning, you are not truly co-teaching. It's as simple as that. So either quit calling it co-teaching (say "in-class support" instead) or go to your administrator and brainstorm ways to get co-planning time. Let them know that you need help in finding time to collaborate and plan together.

✘ **STOP having some kids on one roster or gradebook and others on another.** They are all "your" (collective) kids. This may mean going and talking to your administrator again about how to accomplish this.

✘ **STOP making the room feel like it belongs to one of you.** Yes, the fourth-grade teacher is in there all day, and the Special Education teacher only comes in for 1 hour, but it is so simple to put both names on the door and inside the room. When the Special Educator walks in, it will help with parity; for the rest of the day, the kids simply won't care.

Administrators

✘ **STOP breaking up great teams.** Just because they are good together doesn't mean they will be equally effective with other partners (Murawski & Dieker, 2013). Leave them alone to keep doing their magic!

✘ **STOP using special education co-teachers to substitute classes where no sub is available.** These individuals are in the general education classes for a legal and academic reason. They need to stay there or you're asking for trouble.

✘ **STOP putting teachers together without their knowledge, input, or any professional development.** Partnerships matter. Give teachers a voice in their partnerships, and then give them some training on what to do and what to expect, preferably before they are standing in front of a class of students together.

✘ **STOP putting teachers into co-teaching teams with no opportunity or time for planning and expecting different outcomes.** What you will get is called merely "in-class support" in which the special educator shows up and asks, "What are we doing today?" If you want something different, they need time to plan for that.

(GO) STRATEGIES FOR MAKING YOU SUCCESSFUL WITH CO-TEACHING

(or "If I could only get you to do these things, all would be well with the world")

Teachers, DO This

✓ **KNOW the essential question for co-teaching!** Murawski and Spencer (2011) provide it as: "How is what co-teachers are doing together substantively different and better for students than what one teacher would do alone?" (p. 96). We emphasized that instruction with two teachers should look differently than it does with one. I know I've said that frequently, but I'm hoping it's sinking in. Has it? Does your co-teaching look different? Self-evaluate. If not, what do you need to do? Figure it out and get to it!

✓ **INTRODUCE the class as being taught by two teachers,** not as being taught by a special educator and general educator. Make sure parents know that a co-taught class can be a boon to all students, including those who are gifted, because teachers are more able to individualize and differentiate. Define co-teaching during Back to School night or on letters home to parents.

✓ **READ** *10 Tips for Efficient Use of Co-Planning Time* (Murawski, 2012) to learn how to use time more effectively. Embrace the "What/How/Who" approach to co-planning.

✓ **USE the SHARE worksheet** (provided on page 212) to communicate your preferences, pet peeves, and ultimate desires for the classroom. Doing this proactively before students enter the room will help you be on the same page and reduces the chances of them "playing mom against dad." Reduce, not eliminate.

✓ **SHOW parity.** Have both names on the door, both names on report cards, and space for both of you to keep your things. Make sure both of you have access to the hardcopy or electronic gradebook and both teachers' names are on materials sent home to parents. Practice using "we" language, instead of "I" language to demonstrate that you are a team.

✓ **COMMUNICATE, communicate, communicate!** Talk to each other about HOW to talk to each other. How will you share problems, concerns, observations, and constructive criticisms before they become real obstacles? Remember, students will pick up on any negative vibes!

✓ **TRY new things.** Co-teachers are notorious for sticking with "One teach/One support." That's understandable when you don't have time to co-plan, but step away from large group instruction and embrace small groups. Mix it up, and try all of the different instructional approaches (Cook & Friend, 1995; see page 211). Then come up with some of your own!

✓ **INCREASE your toolbox.** In addition to professional development (PD) on co-teaching, the general educator should go to PD on differentiation, UDL, and other typically special education focus areas. The special educator should go to PD on the general education content area, especially as it relates to Common Core.

✓ **DETERMINE your roles and responsibilities.** All teachers have preferred areas. Talk to each other. If one of you loves technology, that person can be in charge of updating the class website, creating PowerPoints,

Making Connections

Check out Chapters 1–6 on content areas and Chapter 11 on UDL and finding worthwhile YouTube videos. The other might take on making all photocopies, creating the daily warm-up activities, and calling parents. When you've established basic roles, it will save you time in co-planning.

✔ **USE technology in planning.** There is never enough time to plan. It will rock if you are given a common time for planning, but many elementary teachers never get that. So turn to GoogleDocs, Skype, Facetime, Dropbox, or similar tools that will enable you to co-plan even when getting in the same room at the same time is a barrier.

✔ **LET GO of the reins.** We are teachers. We like control. It is very hard to let go and try something new—especially if you are the classroom teacher and you've been teaching something the same way for a while! But students learn differently and to meet their individualized, differentiated needs, you may need to try something new. Listen to your co-teacher's ideas with an open mind. Try it. You may like it.

Administrators, DO This

✔ **When scheduling, PUT students with disabilities into the master schedule first.** This is critical. You can hold spots by calling up to 30% of the class "Ghosts" and filling in those spots with students with special needs later if needed. Do not have more than 30% of the class have special needs or you run the risk of the class feeling more like a special education class than an inclusive one (Murawski & Dieker, 2013).

✔ **GIVE planning time!** Make ways for co-teachers to have regular time together to plan (after school, lunch meetings, time in the week when students are at an assembly or at PE or an elective, once a month subs). Need more ideas? Check out *Leading the Co-Teaching Dance: Leadership Strategies to Enhance Team Outcomes* by Murawski and Dieker (2013).

✔ **BE STRATEGIC in scheduling.** Start by reducing the number of partners and subjects with which you are expecting your teachers to engage. Remember that scheduling for successful co-teaching does not always require more faculty. It does typically require a lot of thought and often the willingness to try something new. Finally, be sure to work with special educators to make sure they know how to manage their entire workload while co-teaching. Help them with scheduling so that they can plan, assess, attend IEPs, make accommodations, talk to paraprofessionals, and otherwise manage their caseloads, in addition to co-teaching.

Plugged In

www.2TeachLLC.com

✔ **HOOK 'EM UP!** Give teachers who are co-teaching priority for new technology, access to the computer lab, perks in scheduling or planning, co-teaching materials and books, and first dibs on upcoming professional development. Co-teaching takes time and energy, and these teachers are often working with the most difficult population of students. Respect this by helping them in any way you can.

AT-A-GLANCE: CO-TEACHING APPROACHES TO INSTRUCTION

Co-Teaching Approach (Cook & Friend, 1995)	Class Setup	Quick Definition
One Teach, One Support (OT/OS)	Whole Class	One teacher is in front of the class leading instruction. The other is providing substantive support (e.g., collection or dissemination of papers, setting up labs, classroom management). Both are actively engaged.
Team Teaching	Whole Class	Both teachers are in front of the class, working together to provide instruction. This may take the form of debates, modeling information or note taking, compare/contrast, or role-playing.
Parallel Teaching	Regrouping	Both teachers take half of the class in order to reduce student-teacher ratio. Instruction can occur in the same or a different setting. Groups may be doing the same content in the same way, same content in a different way, or different content (Murawski, 2010).
Station Teaching	Regrouping	Students are divided into three or more small, heterogeneous groups to go to stations or centers. Students rotate through multiple centers, though teachers may rotate also. Teachers can facilitate individual stations or circulate among all stations.
Alternative Teaching	Regrouping	One teacher works with a large group of students, while the other works with a smaller group providing reteaching, preteaching, or enrichment as needed. The large group is not receiving new instruction during this time so that the small group can rejoin when finished.

Source: Murawski & Spencer (2011, p. 97).

S.H.A.R.E. WITH YOUR COLLEAGUES: SHARING HOPES, ATTITUDES, RESPONSIBILITIES, AND EXPECTATIONS

Directions: Take a few minutes to individually complete this worksheet. Be honest in your responses. After completing it individually, share the responses with your co-planning partners by taking turns reading the responses. Do not use this time to comment on your partners' responses— merely read. After reading through the responses, take a moment or two to jot down any thoughts you have regarding what your partners have said. Then, come back together and begin to share reactions to the responses. Your goal is to (a) agree, (b) compromise, or (c) agree to disagree.

1) Right now, the main *hope* I have regarding this co-planning situation with my colleagues is the following:

_____

_____

2) My *attitude*/philosophy regarding sharing my time, plans, and materials with my colleagues is the following:

_____

_____

3) I would like to have the following *responsibilities* in a co-planning situation:

_____

_____

4) I would like my colleagues to have the following *responsibilities:*

_____

_____

5) I have the following *expectations* for our co-planning relationship
   (a) regarding punctuality:

   _____

   (b) regarding managing materials:

   _____

   (c) regarding homework (work prior to meeting):

   _____

   (d) regarding planning time:

   _____

   (e) regarding reflection on process and lessons:

   _____

    (f) regarding adaptations for individual students:

   _____

   (g) regarding grading/assessments:

   _____

   (h) regarding communication skills (listening, sharing, electronic, and in person):

   _____

   (i) regarding organization:

   _____

   (j) regarding giving/receiving feedback to each other:

   _____

   (k) other important expectations I have:

   _____

Source: Murawski (2010, p. 71).

DO'S AND DON'TS OF CO-TEACHING

Co-Teaching Is . . .	Co-Teaching Is Not . . .
Two or more coequal (preferably credentialed) faculty working together.	A teacher and an assistant, teacher's aide, or paraprofessional.
Conducted in the same classroom at the same time.	When a few students are pulled out of the classroom on a regular basis to work with the special educator. It is also not job-sharing, where teachers teach different days.
Conducted with heterogeneous groups.	Pulling a group of students with disabilities to the back of the general education class.
When both teachers plan for instruction together. The general education teacher (GET) is the content specialist while the special education teacher (SET) is the expert on individualizing and delivery to various learning modalities.	When the general education teacher (GET) plans all lessons and the special education teacher (SET) walks into the room and says, "What are we doing today, and what would you like me to do?"
When both teachers provide *substantive* instruction together—having planned together, the SET can grade homework, teach content, facilitate activities, etc.	When the special education teacher walks around the room all period as the general education teacher teaches the content. Also, not when the SET sits in the class and takes notes.
When both teachers assess and evaluate student progress. IEP goals are kept in mind, as are the curricular goals and standards for that grade level.	When the GET grades "his" kids and the SET grades "her" kids—or when the GET grades all students and the SET surreptitiously changes the grades and calls it "modifying after the fact."
When teachers maximize the benefits of having two teachers in the room by having both teachers actively engaged with students. Examples of different co-teaching models include team-teaching, station-teaching, parallel-teaching, alternative-teaching, and one teach-one support (see Friend & Cook, 2000).	When teachers take turns being "in charge" of the class so that the other teacher can get caught up in grading, photocopying, making phone calls, creating IEPs, etc.—or when students remain in the large group setting in lecture format as teachers rotate who gets to "talk at them."
When teachers reflect on the progress and process, offering one another feedback on teaching styles, content, activities, and other items pertinent to improving the teaching situation.	When teachers get frustrated with one another and tell the rest of the faculty in the teachers' lounge or when one teacher simply tells the other teacher what to do and how to do it.

Source: Murawski (2002, p. 19).

REFERENCES

Austin, V. L. (2001). Teachers' beliefs about co-teaching. *Remedial and Special Education, 22*(4), 245–255.

Cook, L., & Friend, M. P. (1995). Co-teaching: Guidelines for creating effective practices. *Focus on Exceptional Children, 28*(3), 1–16.

Cramer, E., Liston, A., Nevin, A., & Thousand, J. (2010). Co-teaching in urban secondary school districts to meet the needs of all teachers and learners: Implications for teacher education reform. *International Journal of Whole Schooling, 6*(2), 59–76.

Friend, M., & Cook, L. (2000). *Interactions: Collaboration skills for school professionals* (3rd ed.). White Plains, NY: Longman.

Friend, M., & Cook, L. (2012). *Interactions: Collaboration skills for school professionals* (7th ed.). Boston, MA: Pearson.

Friend, M., Cook, L., Hurley-Chamberlain, D., & Shamberger, C. (2010). Co-teaching: An illustration of the complexity of collaboration in special education. *Journal of Educational and Psychological Consultation, 20*, 9–27.

Kennedy, M. J., & Ihle, F. M. (2012). The Old Man and the Sea: Navigating the gulf between special educators and the content area classroom. *Learning Disabilities Research and Practice, 27*, 44–54.

King-Sears, M. E., & Bowman-Kruhm, M. (2011). Specialized reading instruction for adolescents with learning disabilities: What special education co-teachers say. *Learning Disabilities Research and Practice, 26*, 172–184.

McDuffie, K., Mastropieri, M. A., & Scruggs, T. E. (2009). Promoting success in content area classes: Is value added through co-teaching? *Exceptional Children, 75*, 493–510.

Murawski, W. W. (2002). Demystifying co-teaching. *CARS+ Newsletter, 22*(3), 19.

Murawski, W. W. (2003). *Co-teaching in the inclusive classroom.* Bellevue, WA: Bureau of Education and Research.

Murawski, W. W. (2010). *Collaborative teaching in elementary schools: Making the co-teaching marriage work!* Thousand Oaks, CA: Corwin.

Murawski, W. W. (2012). 10 tips for using co-planning time more efficiently. *Teaching Exceptional Children, 44*(4), 8–15.

Murawski, W., & Dieker, L. (2013). *Leading the co-teaching dance: Leadership strategies to enhance team outcomes.* Arlington, VA: Council for Exceptional Children.

Murawski, W. W., & Goodwin, V. A. (2014). Effective inclusive schools and the co-teaching conundrum. In J. McLeskey, N. Waldron, F. Spooner, & B. Algozzine (Eds.), *Handbook of research and practice for inclusive schools* (pp. 292–305). New York, NY: Routledge.

Murawski, W. W., & Spencer, S. (2011). *Collaborate, communicate, and differentiate! How to increase student learning in today's diverse classrooms.* Thousand Oaks, CA: Corwin.

Murawski, W. W., & Swanson, H. L. (2001). A meta-analysis of co-teaching research: Where are the data? *Remedial and Special Education, 22*(5), 258–267.

Pearl, C. E., & Miller, K. J. (2007). Co-taught middle school mathematics classrooms: Accommodations and enhancements for students with specific learning disabilities. *Focus on Learning Problems in Mathematics, 29*(2), 1–20.

Rea, P. J., McLaughlin, V. L., & Walther-Thomas, C. (2002). Outcomes for students with learning disabilities in inclusive and pull-out programs. *Exceptional Children, 72*, 203–222.

Scruggs, T. E., Mastropieri, M. A., & McDuffie, K. A. (2007). Co-teaching in inclusive classrooms: A metasynthesis of qualitative research. *Exceptional Children, 73*(4), 392–416.

Weiss, M. P., & Brigham, F. J. (2000). Co-teaching and the model of shared responsibility: What does the research support? In T. E. Scruggs & M. A. Mastropieri (Eds.), *Advances in learning and behavioral disabilities* (pp. 217–245). Greenwich, CT: JAI.

Zigmond, N., Magiera, K., Simmons, R., & Volonino, V. (2013). Strategies for improving student outcomes in co-taught general education classrooms. In B. G. Cook & M. Tankersley (Eds.), *Research-based strategies for improving outcomes in academics* (pp. 116–124). Upper Saddle River, NJ: Pearson.

RECOMMENDED READINGS

* Conderman, G., & Hedin, L. (2012). Purposeful assessment practices for co-teachers. *Teaching Exceptional Children, 44*(4), 18–27.
* Murawski, W., & Dieker, L. A. (2008). 50 ways to keep your co-teacher. *Teaching Exceptional Children, 40*(4), 40–48.
* Murawski, W. W., & Hughes, C. E. (2009). Response to intervention, collaboration, and co-teaching: A necessary combination for successful systemic change. *Preventing School Failure, 53*(4), 67–77.
* Nevin, A. I., Cramer, E., Voigt, J., & Salazar, L. (2008). Instructional modifications, adaptations, and accommodations of coteachers who loop: A descriptive case study. *Teacher Education and Special Education, 31*(4), 283–297.

GO EVEN FURTHER WITH THIS
TOPIC ON THE WORLD WIDE WEB

* www.cec.sped.org
* www.2teachllc.com
* www.coteach.com
* www.specialconnections.ku.edu
* www.arcoteaching.com

THE Apps WE LOVE

* Explain Everything
* Edmodo
* Screen Chomp
* Pinterest
* Remind101
* Socrative

14

Amazing Assessment

Brooke Blanks

Radford University

WHAT REALLY WORKS IN ASSESSMENT IN THE ELEMENTARY CLASSROOM

I Know What I Taught, But What Did They Learn?

It is time to talk about something we love to hate: Assessment. What is it, and how should we use it? Some days it feels like everyone, everywhere, is talking about educational assessment ALL THE TIME. The frustrating thing is that while everyone agrees that we need to know what kids learn when we teach them stuff, we actually don't get practical suggestions about what assessments are and how they should be used. What is most troublesome, however, is that while everyone is fussing about the importance of assessment, very little information is out there to describe how to use assessment to support the most important responsibilities we have as educators: teaching kids important stuff that (a) they don't know and (b) helps them become interesting, productive, happy people. It also does not help that the "experts" write about educational assessment in language that no one really understands. Never fear! In this chapter, we are going to explore assessments you can and should use in your classroom.

FORMATIVE ASSESSMENT
VERSUS SUMMATIVE ASSESSMENT

Formative and summative assessments are very much connected to one another. Both are important to understanding students' learning in response to our instruction. But, while most of the emphasis in policy discussions and mandates is on summative assessments (e.g., high-stakes testing), formative assessment is what really has the greatest impact on student learning (Hamilton et al., 2009). This actually makes a lot of sense when you think about it because formative assessment is assessment used *for* student learning while summative assessment is assessment *of* student learning (Fisher & Frey, 2010). A quick review of the following essential characteristics of each drives the point home:

Formative Assessment	Summative Assessment
Checks students' understanding in order to plan instruction	Offers teachers and students with information about mastery of content knowledge
Results inform next steps in instruction to ensure students' success, which means they have significant practical value but usually have low emotional impact or value	Results often inform grading which means they have significant evaluative importance and thus, often have high emotional impact and value
Must be part of an instructional framework that is responsive to students' ongoing growth and current needs	Evaluates students' learning at the end of an instructional unit and compares the results to some standard or benchmark
Examples of formative assessment: • Revision-based assignments, projects, and performances • Diagnostic interviews and asking questions	*Examples of summative assessment:* • Capstone assignments, final projects, senior recitals • Final exams

Source: Adapted from Kharbach (2014).

Our goal as teachers is to use formative assessment to learn about our students so that we know what and how to design and provide instruction that meets their needs. If we do that well, the summative assessments will show us, the kids, the parents, the school, and the state that, indeed, the students did learn this material.

WHAT DOES THE RESEARCH TELL US?

Assessment can be one of our most challenging professional responsibilities. As teachers, we worry about the impact that testing may have on our students' academic, emotional, and developmental well-being. Nowadays, we also worry about the impact the testing results will have on our careers and paychecks. Despite our concerns, however, knowing how to effectively design, administer, and use assessments to improve our instruction is an essential element of our teaching practice.

Let's face it; testing is a political hot-button issue. Unfortunately, much of the discussion overlooks the fact that testing and assessment mean different things to different stakeholders. Politicians talk about using this test or that test to evaluate the quality of teachers and schools. Community members and parents understand assessment to mean high-stakes tests that determine if students go on to the next grade level. Students with disabilities and their families are familiar with testing that has been the path to receiving special education services. Two significant school improvement initiatives in the last decade, Positive Behavior Intervention and Supports (PBIS) and Response to Intervention (RTI) are

Making Connections

Check out Chapter 8 on Positive Behavior Support

grounded in the idea that we must use assessments to provide measures of students' behavior and/or learning in order to make decisions about what students need and how we will work to meet those needs. Finally, among students, assessment scores are often viewed as the means by which classmates compete against one another rather than mileposts on their path to knowledge and critical thinking. Clearly all of these stakeholders have legitimate perspectives on the form and function of assessment in our classrooms and schools. While it is important that we understand that no single assessment or type of assessment will address all of these purposes well, it is important (and I personally think it is also very cool) that much of the research on assessment indicates that what is really important is what we do with those results! Thus, for our purposes as teachers, we will focus on what research tells us are effective assessment practices that we can use to drive our instruction in our classrooms—yep, we're going to look at what really works in assessment. Over and over again, research tells us that effective teachers know how to use the results provided by the consistent use of classroom-based formative assessments (Hamilton et al., 2009; Hoover & Abrams, 2013). So let's figure out how to do just that.

Focus on classroom assessments that are appropriate, easy to use, and fun for young children. Before we can plan instruction, we must explore and document what students already know. Understanding their knowledge is essential for planning instruction that will lead to their full understanding of concepts (Black & Wiliam, 1998). Using assessment information to ask questions and understand students' progress is the only reasonable way to mold your instruction to fit your students. That is, you should use assessment data to measure students' progress and to inform instructional practice (Stiggins, Arter, Chappuis, & Chappuis, 2004).

Effective classroom assessments. Effective classroom assessments require skill and practice. However, remember that formative assessment is something most of us do every single day, without even realizing it sometimes. The following guidelines are a great way to explain all that we already know and do related to formative assessment.

Focus on teaching and the curriculum. All assessments should be tied to the curriculum, which is based on your state's academic standards (Randel & Clark, 2013). Most of us are already pretty familiar with which standards are assessed on our end-of-course tests. If you aren't, start looking into it now. Next, look at those standards and decide what skills and knowledge students need to meet those standards (Popham, 2006). This step is really important if your formative assessments are going to provide information you can use to plan instruction.

Know your objectives. High-quality objectives are directly and obviously linked to your instruction and they provide your students with a roadmap of exactly what they need to do to demonstrate their mastery of those objectives (Marzano, 2009). By the way, this is a great activity for a team of teachers to work on throughout the year. Everyone can share ideas and work to develop a "bank" of assessment tasks that work for a variety of students with a range of strengths and needs. No need to re-create the wheel in every classroom!

Involve students. Making the invisible process of testing and assessment visible to students is a huge change in the way we think about and use assessment. Games and kinesthetic assessments such as "Four Corners" are an excellent way to engage kids in the process of formative assessment. Students should be taught to use rubrics and checklists that clearly describe how their work will be evaluated (Randel & Clark, 2013). Models of excellent work, work that needs revision, and work that is below standard are fabulous tools when we spend time unpacking them with our students. Transparency helps students realize that assessments are useful because they help us understand how to be successful (Stiggins et al., 2004).

Question frequently. Questioning is an excellent formative assessment (Burns, 2005). You can use verbal or written questions to probe students' knowledge and tease out students' reasoning. Asking students meaningful questions helps us better understand their thinking. In turn, these insights guide our future planning for instruction (Center for Comprehensive School Reform and Improvement, 2014). Don't forget to differentiate your questioning based on the different learners you have.

Provide meaningful feedback. We provide students with a lot of feedback every day. The trick is to make sure we are providing feedback that helps students understand what they are doing now and what they can do in the future to increase and/or enhance their learning and performance. High-quality instructional feedback is timely, useful, and appropriate. Feedback is most helpful to students' learning when it emphasizes the features of the task (Brookhart, 2008) and shows students how their performance of the assessment task compares to the standard. This approach to feedback helps students see the gaps that exist between their goals and their current levels of performance and understanding. It also provides a guide to help students through the process of meeting those goals (Brookhart, 2008). The most effective feedback is that which occurs either during the learning experience or immediately after. Timing is everything! Our goal as teachers is to find that sweet spot in which we are giving students enough time to really work through the task they are trying to accomplish, but not so much time that we are allowing them to either practice doing things incorrectly or waiting until it's too late for them to correct course.

Understand and use your data. The information you get from regularly using formative assessments provides a ton of information about your teaching: what worked, what did not, and what you should do next and with which students. Do not make this more difficult than it has to be! Fancy looking data that are hard to gather and impossible to read are useless. Use what you know how to use. . . . And if you don't know what to use, checklists and graphs are a great place to start! Create a checklist that captures the essential information you want all students to know, and write a series of conversational questions to use during conferences with your students. When you talk with your kids, use the checklist to keep track of their answers to the questions. Look for patterns or trends in your data over time. Ask yourself questions, such as, "Are all of the kids missing the same question?" If so, your response can be, "Great, now I know what I need to reteach!" The point is to use formative assessments so that students' responses, particularly errors, provide you with information about specific student needs that you can use to guide your instruction (Center for Comprehensive School Reform and Improvement, 2014; Popham, 2006).

Change your instruction based on your assessments. Knowing what to do with your data is one of the most challenging aspects of assessment. When your students' results indicate the need for reteaching, we need to provide instruction that is different from our initial instruction, as well as additional opportunities for students to demonstrate their learning (Guskey, 2007). After all, a definition of insanity (attributed to a range of thinkers from Benjamin Franklin to Albert Einstein) is doing the same things over and over while expecting different results! If lecture was used for the initial lesson, think about using manipulatives or an interactive center for your follow-up instruction. Use groups effectively! Tomlinson and Imbeau's (2010, pp. 90–91) recommendations include using multiple ability tasks, assigning individual roles, using accessible content, and assigning competence. Classwide peer tutoring is also an excellent instructional approach for a range of students in a differentiated classroom (Maheady & Gard, 2010). The aim is to reach all students by using a variety of teaching strategies. Your assessments help you figure out how to do this.

ASSESSMENT PRACTICES THAT TEST OUR PATIENCE!

Teachers

- ✘ **STOP confusing *formative* and *summative* assessments.** Summative assessments are snapshots of what students know at a particular point in time. They are spread out and occur after instruction. Summative assessments are too far removed from instruction to be helpful in adjusting your teaching and making intervention decisions. Formative assessments are for instructional planning. They provide information about how students are responding to instruction while there is still time to adjust your teaching. Formative assessment helps teachers determine the next steps in their instructional process and for whom.
- ✘ **STOP confusing *assessment* with *grading*.** The purpose of grading to get a measure of performance. Grades do not necessarily measure learning because they often include criteria such as attendance, participation, and effort, which are related to, but not indicative of, what students actually know. The purpose of assessment is to improve student learning by looking at multiple formal and informal indicators of what students know and what they can do as a result of your instruction and then using this information to improve instruction.
- ✘ **STOP using assessments that only test students' ability to memorize random snippets of information . . . that's what the Internet is for.** Classroom-based assessments should measure students' abilities to *use* and *apply* what they have learned from you. So what if they need to look up some of the facts or use some tools—those are skills we all use in the REAL WORLD! Oh c'mon, admit it. How many times have you Googled something today alone?
- ✘ **STOP using assessments to play "gotcha" with kids, particularly kids who (let's be honest here) get on your nerves in the classroom.** Testing to reward "good" kids for paying attention, turning in homework on time, and so on, is pretty useless, especially

if the purpose of your assessment is to inform your instruction. If you already know that certain kids won't know the information you are assessing because they didn't engage with your instruction, punishing them with a bad grade is really just a form of bullying and a waste of everyone's time. Don't worry; I'll give you alternative strategies in the "DO" section.

✖ **STOP assuming that you have to do the same thing to assess all students.** We easily accept the idea that students are going to access and learn information in different ways. The same is true for assessment. Differentiate your assessments to make sure that you are getting as comprehensive a picture as possible of what each student knows and what each student still needs from your instruction. Individual conferences with students are an excellent way to assess and provide

Plugged In

www.youtube.com/ watch?v=Pad1eAcsHho

feedback to your students. Check out the video in the Plugged In box in which the teacher spends just 3 minutes talking with the student about exactly what the student did well and where the student needs more practice in very specific, concrete terms. Even very young children can participate and benefit from this type of direct conversation about their own work. Don't be afraid to adapt anything you find at the end of this chapter to meet the needs of your kids!

Administrators

✖ **STOP confusing preparation and motivation when it comes to high-stakes assessment.** There is little evidence to suggest that motivation strategies like pep rallies, pizza parties, and "Test Day" breakfasts on high-stakes assessment days result in improved achievement. Instead, focus your efforts and attention on supporting teachers' use of formative assessments for effective instruction throughout the year. That doesn't mean you can't keep motivating; just be sure you aren't doing that in lieu of providing true value to your teachers.

✖ **STOP thinking about student assessments as an effective way to evaluate your teachers.** We have a substantial body of evidence to suggest that student achievement scores and "Value Added Models" are not valid and reliable measures of teacher effectiveness (Darling-Hammond, Amrein-Beardsley, Haertel, & Rothstein, 2012). Ask any teacher anywhere. Their work is so much more than their students' test results. And we'll be a very different society if we encourage teachers to look at their students as more than their test scores.

ASSESSMENT PRACTICES THAT STAND THE TEST OF TIME

GO

Teachers, DO This

✓ **THINK about assessment as a process that is directly and clearly useful with students rather than a tool that is used to fill in blocks in your gradebook.** Assessment is a process that helps students and teachers understand students' progress toward learning goals when it is ongoing and diagnostic. Remember, the goal is to make instruction more responsive to learners' needs (Tomlinson & Imbeau, 2010).

✓ **OBSERVE your students.** Observation is an essential element of classroom-based assessment. Observation at a distance involves periodically taking 5 minutes or so to watch students (individually or in groups). Close-in observation involves observing an individual student for about 5 minutes (adapted from Venn, 2004). In fact, Friend and Cook (2012) suggest that teachers who are co-teaching occasionally use a model wherein one teacher leads instruction while the other observes and collects data on students.

✓ **USE a steady cycle of different assessments to identify students who need help in specific domains and/or with specific content.** We can always assess and monitor student learning in our classrooms. We do it pretty naturally; it's how we make decisions and judgments about our kids. Get deliberate, and record these observations, thoughts, students' responses to your questions, and so on, and get creative about opportunities to provide more support and instruction when students need additional help to master the content.

✓ **USE different types of informal assessment to monitor students' progress.** Exit Cards, Response Cards, Diaries, Learning Logs, and Student Progress Monitoring Charts are all excellent and easy to use informal assessments. Check out the resources at the end of this chapter on pages 227–230.

✓ **TEACH students to be directly involved in the assessment of their learning.** Incorporate activities into your instruction that ask students to think and talk about (a) what they have learned and (b) how they have learned it. This can include answering a set of questions, visually representing their learning processes with pictures or other forms of visual media, talking with a partner, or keeping a journal. Check out the first site on Exemplars in the Plugged In box for some great advice and tools for teaching self-assessment to very young children. The second site in the Plugged In box is one of my all-time favorite teacher blog posts. It's Larry Ferlazzo's *"We Should Celebrate Mistakes"* in which he talks about a unit he did with his students on the mistakes they make in class.

✓ **DECIDE when to use checklists, rubrics, portfolios, annotated notes, or percentage accuracy.** These are all valuable tools for your assessment toolbox, but it can be overwhelming to think about when to use each one. The third link in the Plugged In box will take you to a great document that explains in detail how and when to use each tool.

Plugged In

www.exemplars.com/ resources/rubrics/ student-rubrics

larryferlazzo.edublogs. org/2011/12/06/we-should- celebrate-mistakes/

www.calhoun.k12.al.us/makes%20 sense/Adobe%20Reader/DO%20 NOT%20OPEN%20program%20 files/Assessment/Assessing%20 skills.pdf

teresaemmert.weebly.com/ elementary-formative-assessment- lessons.html

✓ **USE formative assessments to give students second (or more) chances to be successful!** Formative assessments should not be a one-time, high-stakes proposition for students. Students should have a second chance to demonstrate their new level of competence and understanding that results from differentiated reteaching. This not only benefits the students but it also helps teachers determine the effectiveness of the follow-up instruction (Guskey, 2003). Essentially, that second chance shows you how well you retaught that student.

✓ **GET CREATIVE about managing the time for and implementation of assessment and follow-up activities.** Use more student-directed learning activities to reduce the amount of time spent on review for formative assessments. Instead, shift that time to follow-up instruction and enrichment (Guskey, 2007). Check out the fourth link in the Plugged In box for great examples of lessons that you can use to assess your kids' knowledge of math concepts and their math skills in your elementary school classroom. *Pay attention to the big ideas in these lessons and adapt for other content areas!*

Administrators, DO This

✓ **LOOK for classrooms where students can demonstrate what they know in a variety of ways.** We tend to dismiss instructional practices we are not familiar with. Talk with your teachers about their assessment practices. Tests are not always the answer.

✓ **PROVIDE ongoing professional development for teachers on multiple ways to assess student learning and how to move from data to instruction.** Get creative about making space in the weekly or monthly schedule for teachers to collaborate over their data, and get creative about solving instructional problems.

✓ **RECOGNIZE AND CELEBRATE teachers' creative use of formative assessments.** Ask questions, spend time in classrooms, dig deeply into key assignments, and talk with students about their learning outcomes. Ask teachers who have evidence that their use of formative assessment is improving learning outcomes in their classrooms to share their ideas, experiences, and resources with their colleagues.

✓ **FOCUS your staff supervision and evaluation processes on teaching and learning.** Look for evidence in your classrooms of the following high-impact instructional activities that are based on the results of formative assessments: reteaching, individual and group tutoring, peer tutoring, cooperative teams, alternative textbooks/ media resources, academic games, learning kits, learning centers and laboratories, and instructional computer activities (Guskey, 2007). Ask teachers how they determined who was going to do what, at what level, and why. Their responses should include words like "data, answers, responses, or assessments."

AWESOME IDEAS FOR QUICK AND EASY FORMATIVE ASSESSMENTS IN YOUR CLASSROOM

Methods for Observing and Recording

- *Anecdotal Record:* A descriptive narrative of a student's behavior or learning; details are useful for teacher's planning, conferencing, and so on.
- *Running Record:* A sequential record recorded while the behavior or learning is occurring; documents what a child might do in a particular situation.
- *Checklist:* A list on which the teacher checks the behaviors, traits, or learning targets observed during a lesson or activity.
- *Rating Scale:* A list of behaviors made into a scale that features frequency of behavior or level of mastery.

Whole Group Informal Assessments

- *Thumbs Up/Thumbs Down:* Students give a thumbs up or a thumbs down to show their level of understanding with respect to a previous, current, or upcoming task.
- *Think-Pair-Share:* Students are given time to think about a question or prompt, then to share information with a partner, and finally to share their thoughts with the whole group for discussion.
- *Response Cards:* Teacher-made or student-made cards used to show responses to teacher prompts.

Some examples of *premade response cards* are

- Multiple-Choice: students can show A, B, C, or D by clipping a clothespin on the letter of their choice.
- Categories: good for comparisons such as mammal or reptile, fantasy or realism, dependent or independent, and so on.

Individual Informal Assessments

- *Study Cards:* Study cards are created by students to synthesize information learned in a lesson. After creating them, students can use them to quiz a classmate or review for an assessment. As a teacher, you can collect and review the Study Cards to assess a student's understanding of a concept. www.theteachertoolkit.com/index.php/tool/study-cards

- *Fun and Easy Formative Assessment:* Provide students with challenging activities for increasing their skills in various areas such as math, spelling, or science. The presentation at this link provides fun, free, and easy activities that you can use in class with older students to promote engagement to assess students' learning at the end of instruction. www.nwea.org/blog/2013/22-easy-formative-assessment-techniques-for-measuring-student-learning/
- *Buddy Journals:* This tool, which is a written correspondence between two classmates, gives students a purpose for their writing. Buddy Journals promote student interaction and collaboration, and they can also help improve students' grammar, punctuation, and spelling. www.theteachertoolkit.com/index.php/tool/buddy-journal
- *3–2–1:* Ask students to jot down 3 facts they learned, 2 examples of their learning, and 1 question or confusion they still have. www.readingquest.org/strat/321.html
- *Four Corners:* Pose a question and offer four possible answers. Students show their answers by traveling to the corresponding corner. Discuss why each group chose that corner and how they could convince others that they are correct. www.youtube.com/watch?v=gkk7hoh7RXY
- *Classroom Whip-Around:* The whip-around strategy is a quick gauge of how your students understand your instruction. It can be used as a formative assessment because it monitors achievement. It can also be used as a check of understanding because it provides a snapshot of what your students are absorbing in the lesson. ontheroadtoaccomplishedteaching.blogspot.com/2012/11/whip-around-teaching-toolkit-strategy.html
- *Tableau:* The name of this strategy comes from the term *tableau vivant* which means "living picture." In this activity, students create a still picture, without talking, to capture and communicate the meaning of a concept. Students must truly understand the meaning of a concept or idea in order to communicate it using physical poses, gestures, and facial expressions rather than words. This collaborative strategy is appealing to kinesthetic learners and allows all students to be creative while strengthening their comprehension of a concept. www.theteachertoolkit.com/index.php/tool/tableau

SAMPLE OBSERVATION FORMS

Student Name: _____ Subject Area: _____

Date	Observations

Name	Reads fluently	Self-corrects missed words	Rereads when story is unclear	Describes main character	Retells story with accuracy
1.					
2.					
3.					
4.					
5.					

SAMPLE RESPONSE CARDS

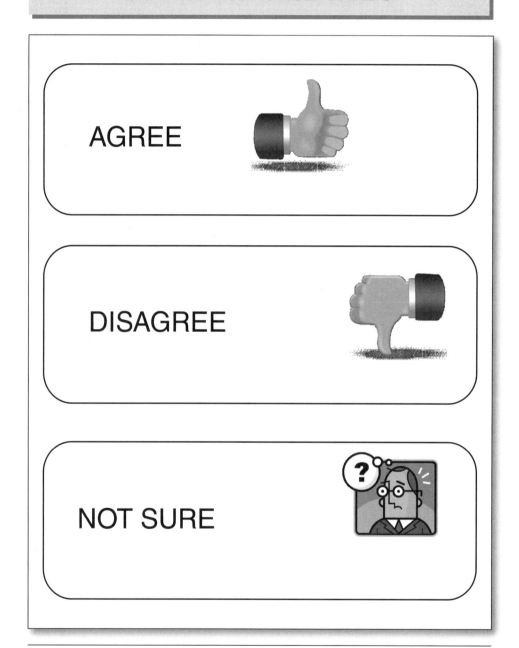

AGREE

DISAGREE

NOT SURE

Source: Auton, Beck, & West (2010).

REFERENCES

Auton, K., Beck, S., & West, T. (2010). Informal assessment strategies. Handout prepared for Summer 2010 (RES 5560–375) Appalachian State University— Dr. George Olson, Instructor.

Black, P., & Wiliam, D. (1998). Inside the black box. *Phi Delta Kappan, 80*(2), 139–148.

Brookhart, S. (2008). *How to give effective feedback to your students.* Alexandria, VA: Association for Supervision and Curriculum Development.

Burns, M. (2005). Looking at how students reason. *Educational Leadership, 63*(3), 26–31.

Center for Comprehensive School Reform and Improvement. (2014). *Using classroom assessment to improve teaching.* Retrieved from http://www.education .com/reference/article/Ref_Using_Classroom/

Darling-Hammond, L., Amrein-Beardsley, A., Haertel, E., & Rothstein, J. (2012). Evaluating teacher evaluation. *Phi Delta Kappan, 93*(6), 8–15.

Fisher, D., & Frey, N. (2010). *Enhancing RTI: How to ensure success with effective classroom instruction and intervention.* Alexandria, VA: Association for Supervision and Curriculum Development.

Friend, M., & Cook, L. (2012). *Interactions: Collaboration skills for school professionals* (7th ed.). San Francisco, CA: Pearson.

Guskey, T. R. (2003). How classroom assessments improve learning. *Educational Leadership, 60*(5), 6–11.

Guskey, T. R. (2007). The rest of the story. *Educational Leadership, 65*(4), 28–35.

Hamilton, L., Halverson, R., Jackson, S., Mandinach, E., Supovitz, J., & Wayman, J. (2009). *Using student achievement data to support instructional decision making* (NCEE Publication No. 2009–4067). Washington, DC: National Center for Education Evaluation and Regional Assistance, Institute of Education Sciences, U.S. Department of Education.

Hoover, N. R., & Abrams, L. M. (2013). Teachers' instructional use of summative student assessment data. *Applied Measurement in Education, 26*(3), 219–231.

Kharbach, M. (2014). A visual chart on summative vs. formative assessment. Retrieved from http://www.educatorstechnology.com/2014/02/a-visual-chart-on-summative-vs.html

Maheady, L., & Gard, J. (2010). Classwide peer tutoring: Practice, theory, research, and personal narrative. *Intervention in School and Clinic, 46*(2), 71–78.

Marzano, R. J. (2009). *Designing and teaching learning goals and objectives.* Bloomington, IN: Solution Tree.

Popham, W. J. (2006). All about accountability/phony formative assessments: Buyer beware! *Educational Leadership, 64,* 86–87.

Randel, B., & Clark, T. (2013). Measuring classroom assessment practices. In J. H. McMillan (Ed.), *SAGE handbook of research on classroom assessment* (pp. 145–164). Thousand Oaks, CA: SAGE.

Stiggins, R. J., Arter, J. A., Chappuis, J., & Chappuis, S. (2004). *Classroom assessment FOR student learning: Doing it right—using it well.* Portland, OR: ETS Assessment Training Institute.

Tomlinson, C. A., & Imbeau, M. B. (2010). *Leading and managing a differentiated classroom.* Alexandria, VA: Association for Supervision and Curriculum Development.

Venn, J. (2004). *Quick, easy, and accurate classroom assessment for all students: A resource guidebook for teachers.* Retrieved from http://www.johnvenn.com

RECOMMENDED READINGS

* Bennett, R. E., & Gitomer, D. H. (2009). Transforming K12 assessment: Integrating accountability testing, formative assessment and professional support. In C. Wyatt-Smith & J. Cumming (Eds.), *Educational assessment in the 21st century* (pp. 43–61). New York, NY: Springer.

* Enger, S. K., & Yager, R. B. E. (2009). *Assessing student understanding in science: A standards-based K-12 handbook.* Thousand Oaks, CA: Corwin.

* Popham, W. J., & Popham, J. W. (2005). *Classroom assessment: What teachers need to know.* Boston, MA: Allyn & Bacon.

GO EVEN FURTHER WITH THIS TOPIC ON THE WORLD WIDE WEB

- www.wvde.state.wv.us/teach21/ExamplesofFormativeAssessment.html
- www.nctm.org/uploadedFiles/Research_News_and_Advocacy/ Research/Clips_and_Briefs/Research_brief_04_-_Five_Key%20 Strategies.pdf
- www.nwea.org/blog/2013/mapping-formative-assessment-strategies-to-the-common-core-state-standards-part-one/
- www.edutopia.org/blog/formative-assessments-importance-of-rebecca-alber

THE Apps WE LOVE

- For all Rubrics
- Voicethread
- Formative Feedback for Learning
- Geddit
- Kahoot!

SECTION III

What Really Works With Special Populations

15

Great Gifted Education

Claire E. Hughes

College of Coastal Georgia

WHAT REALLY WORKS IN GIFTED EDUCATION IN THE ELEMENTARY CLASSROOM

Fluff Versus Stuff: Problems With Definitions and Practice

Have you heard the saying, "All children are gifted. They just open their packages at different times and in different ways"? Yeah, well, that may be simplifying the notion of giftedness just a tad. In fact, although teachers and parents might identify giftedness in children by the differences that they demonstrate in a classroom, the definition of *giftedness* is a challenging one. Children with gifts and talents are not required to be identified or served through federal law, so each state has a slightly different version of definition and service. Some theorists state that giftedness is an internal quality, one that is highly inheritable and measureable (Terman, 1925), while others say that it is a result of development of a combination of factors (Renzulli, 1978). Others have noted that the idea of giftedness is very dependent on one's culture (Peterson, 1999). When we talk about a "gifted student," we tend to mean children who are precocious or learn very quickly, notice things faster and with greater intensity, have the ability to concentrate for long periods of time, have areas of significant interest, have strong memory and imaging skills, and who can work with abstract information and ideas—all above their age peers (Poh, 2008). In addition, they tend to be more flexible in their thinking and more intuitive in their learning than other students.

So, if there is no standard way to identify a child with gifts and talents, why should we serve them? The reason is an ethical one: All children deserve an education that meets them where they are and moves them forward. In fact, in the case of gifted students, not doing so as a public school system leaves the development of talent up to parents, which means that only children from advantaged backgrounds would be provided advanced and enriched opportunities. That's certainly not okay. One of the greatest ways to provide equality of educational growth is to offer gifted education. There is an old adage out there attributed to Rick Lavoie (2004), "Fair does not mean the same; fair means giving each child what he or she needs." You've heard this in the chapter on inclusion, UDL, and co-teaching; now you're hearing it again here.

Making Connections

Check out Chapters 11, 12, and 13 on UDL, Inclusion, and Co-Teaching

This is particularly true, in my humble opinion, for gifted children because they are often the most frequently left out of education. A gifted child is more likely to be "left behind" than any other subgroup of children— meaning that they are the least likely to make a year's worth of gains in a year. They come into school ahead, but then their relative position slips. Children who begin school knowing 75–85% of the content for that grade are the least likely to make significant academic gains over that year. Perhaps most concerning is that gifted students from poverty are the most likely to slip in their achievement levels over time (Spielhagen & Cooper, 2005). This loss of talent and ability is significant—both for the individual and for our nation. Developing the talents and abilities of *all* students is the work of education, which includes those children who learn faster than their age peers. No pressure, right?

There is no "one-size-fits-all" program or practice that is guaranteed to work. Often, a teacher just wants to keep a gifted child busy and out of trouble, so she or he may end up using materials that are marketed "for gifted kids," are attractive, and yet have no real substance. According to a project sponsored by the U.S. Department of Education and described in the book *Best Practices in Gifted Education* (Robinson, Shore, & Enerson, 2007), there are 29 strategies that have been proven effective in identifying and serving gifted students. These research-grounded strategies offer specific guidance to teachers, administrators, policy makers, and parents. While many educational practices and packaged programs employ these strategies, there are even more that are based in pseudoscience, reputation, or just busywork with no substance.

According to Robinson et al. (2007, p. 2) these 29 strategies can be broken down based on where they are used: home, classroom, and school. While addressing each of these 29 strategies—even just the ones in the classroom category—would be too much for this chapter to attempt, I do recommend you check out their book. It's an excellent resource for you and for parents. In the meantime, don't fret. This chapter will take many of these research-based strategies and make them "real" for you. I'm sure that you want to meet ALL of your students' needs; let's not let any group of students lag behind in their educational growth.

STOP THE FLUFF! HERE ARE YOUR GIFTED "DON'TS"

Teachers

- ✖ **STOP thinking that gifted kids can do it all.** "Well, if you're so gifted, you should be able to ____" is a common statement that gifted kids hear all the time. "Giftedness" is a way of describing significantly strong performance in one area or a way of describing how fast their processing or memory might be. There are gifted children with learning disabilities, which means that it is fairly likely that there will be a gifted child in class who might be a very strong reader, but lousy at math . . . or a kid who knows everything about fusion and fission, but can't remember the multiplication tables. Gifted children are strong learners—in their area of strength. C'mon, aren't *you* good at some things and lousy at others?

- ✖ **STOP thinking that you can do it all.** It takes lots of ideas to come up with new ways to advance and enrich material. It may mean collaborating with another teacher to help find the time, the material, and the ideas about what to do (Hughes & Murawski, 2001). Don't think you have to be a gifted ed teacher, or gifted yourself, to teach students who are gifted.

- ✖ **STOP having them be the "peer tutor" because they finish early.** Some gifted kids are great teachers and genuinely love to help others. But not all of them. Some of them are terrible tutors because they can't explain how they learned it . . . *they just "knew it."* They often end up doing the work for other kids, which doesn't help other children actually learn the content. Worst case scenario? They actually embarrass the other kids by saying, "Seriously? You don't know this? It's so easy!"

- ✖ **STOP having them do work that they already know how to do.** Every child deserves to learn something new every day. Gifted kids start each grade knowing approximately 75–85% of that year's content. That means that there is only about 15–25% of content that is new to them. Be sure to pretest them. If they can already do the work, let them go ahead.

✘ **STOP thinking that they're not "emotionally mature" enough to work with older children.** Often, a gifted kid is trying so hard to fit in with peers who are less developed than they are, they overdo it, and their behavior looks silly. Or they're incredibly sensitive, due to their giftedness rather than their chronological age. That won't go away with time. Research finds again and again that students who are advanced (e.g., moving ahead in content or even skipping a grade) do much better—both academically and emotionally—than their gifted peers who are not advanced. Older kids tend to understand them better, and any sensitivities are put down to youth, not to being "weird." Not so when they are with their age-level peers.

✘ **STOP identifying giftedness with one measure or a set of measures that use "teacher-pleasing" behaviors.** Oftentimes, gifted kids are not the "good" kids, but are the ones who ask questions, don't study but know the answers, exhibit leadership, and challenge authority. Untrained teachers are not very good at identifying giftedness separate from "good" classroom behavior that is typical of the majority culture. If any of you are familiar with the cartoon of Calvin and Hobbes, Calvin (the precocious trouble-maker child) is undoubtedly gifted—but also a serious handful. Any of you have kids like that?

✘ **STOP thinking that only kids who get As must be gifted.** Often, gifted children are unmotivated to learn grade-level material and will "check out" of school, do the minimum, or throw something together at the last minute. Gifted children who are not of the same cultural or language background of the teacher are particularly at risk for disengaging from content they do not see as relevant. Look at their content knowledge, abilities, and potential, not their grades.

Administrators

✘ **STOP spreading your gifted kids across classes.** It might help a teacher's test score average, but it doesn't help the student. Gifted children must have an opportunity to work together at some point during the day. That means that grouping has to be flexible. Heterogeneous groups are great for some things, but gifted learners need to have like-minded peers around to challenge them.

✘ **STOP holding kids back with policies that discourage advancement or programs that only focus on kids who are struggling.** All children deserve to have their needs met, and gifted children deserve the right to an education as well. Open your minds—and your policies.

✗ **STOP treating parents who ask for "more" as "pushy" parents.** They are asking for educational interventions that are appropriate for where their child is. This is what *all* parents ask. They are not asking for "more"; they are asking for "learning opportunities."

✗ **STOP saying "We don't have any gifted kids here."** If you are an administrator in a low-performing or low-socioeconomic school, or none of your children meet the state or district criteria, that doesn't mean you don't have gifted children. Giftedness is defined in context, and there will be children who are performing in the top 10% of your school. Treat them as "at-promise" children and celebrate their strengths.

GO DO THE GOOD STUFF!

Teachers, DO This

✓ **DIFFERENTIATE *up* as well as down.** To differentiate means to change the instruction according to the characteristics of the child. Gifted children need differentiation as well. The "age-level/grade-level" expectations are frequently not appropriate. Remember, all kids have the right to an education that is focused where they are learning.

✓ **ASK higher order thinking questions.** The most important thing you can do to help a gifted child grow is to ask higher order thinking questions. These are questions without limits that force a child to use understanding and information to answer, but can't be "looked up" and don't have a "right" answer. Try to avoid closed yes/no and multiple-choice questions.

✓ **COMPACT the curriculum.** Time is extremely important. You want to be able to use your time most effectively, and the best way to do this is spend a little time with your advanced learners. Get them started on projects that they can do independently. The critical element is the time you spend with them upfront. Gifted children need teachers; they cannot be expected to go in a corner and teach themselves.

✓ **USE flexible grouping.** Gifted children aren't gifted at everything. You may have a child who is gifted in math, but not in reading. You might have a child who is gifted in astronomy, but not in geology. You might have a child who is gifted in social leadership, but not in math. Grouping should follow the students, not their label. Similarly, you can't just "sprinkle" gifted kids throughout your class in the hope that they can teach other students. Often, they're terrible tutors because they already knew the information and can't remember learning it. Gifted children should spend part of their day with other gifted kids with differentiated curriculum. Beyond academic benefits, using gifted grouping provides social benefits. Often, a gifted kid will become arrogant when they're the only one with the answers. Being around other gifted children may be a shock, but they can then make friends with other children who have esoteric interests, too!

✔ **USE instructional technology.** Computers and other technology allow opportunities for gifted children to use their thinking abilities with infinite resources and information. Technology allows them to gather, present, and share information in ways that extend beyond the classroom walls. A challenge that I give teachers who teach traditional classes is this: Do something with kids that cannot be duplicated online. That typically means face-to-face presentation, real-time discussions, sensory experiences, and hands-on material work.

Making Connections

Check out Chapter 7 on Engagement and Technology

✔ **ENCOURAGE creativity.** We should encourage creativity in our talented children. Our future society depends on these children learning how to use their knowledge in new and novel ways. Creativity is much more than the traditional "arts" but is a way of thinking innovatively and inventively in all areas (Feldman & Benjamin, 1998).

✔ **PROVIDE opportunities for advancement.** Colangelo, Assouline, and Gross's (2004) groundbreaking review of studies found that gifted children who were advanced—whether through acceleration or subject-level advancement—far exceeded their peers both in academic achievement over a lifetime and in their social benefits to students. Schools are known for being rigid in their policies, and teachers are often uncomfortable with allowing children to move ahead. This research validates that children may indeed need, and deserve, acceleration.

✔ **PROVIDE emotional support for being "different."** While we all know that struggling children need emotional support in order to achieve, gifted students, too, need emotional support to develop their talents and abilities. They are different, and these differences should be understood and celebrated. Conversely, research has found that when gifted kids are told how "smart" they are, they do not choose challenging work and perform less well than when they were given feedback on their use of learning strategies. So we need to stop saying they are smart and instead give them opportunities to show us.

Administrators, DO This

✓ **TRAIN teachers to understand characteristics and needs of gifted learners.** They are not all straight-A students, and not all straight-A students are gifted. Encourage teachers to create opportunities for advanced work. Some children who had previously not demonstrated motivation or interest might show their abilities when they are not bored.

✓ **ENCOURAGE the staff and teachers to focus on student strengths.** Children are more likely to show you what they can do, instead of only focusing on areas of deficit. Encourage a climate of achievement and success from everyone.

✓ **EMPLOY the use of identification protocols that use more than teacher recommendations, IQ requirements, and achievement.** Using performance assessments over time can reveal much more about a child's potential for more complex work than a single score or a teacher's perception. Ask teachers to give children a project or a large problem to solve, and then document how the children go about solving the project. Create identification strategies to seek to find and serve children in the upper 10–25% of the school, regardless of actual label requirements by the state or district.

Making Connections

Check out Chapter 14 on Assessment

✓ **OFFER advanced classes or enrichment opportunities.** Does your school have an Odyssey of the Mind program, a chess club, or a Latin class? Do you have a partnership with the local library? If not, look to see what other opportunities you can give advanced learners. Start a program, such as the Schoolwide Enrichment Program (Renzulli & Reis, 1985) or a cluster grouping approach to implement in your school.

✓ **ENCOURAGE parents and families to think about possibilities for their talented children.** Often, parents and families are afraid that they will "lose" their child to a broader world. Encourage them to look at careers that challenge and interest the child. Provide families with specific activities that they can do to help their child develop their abilities. Show them programs and opportunities available within the local and greater community. Provide childcare and transportation information to access these resources.

DOS AND DON'TS FOR WORKING WITH GIFTED CHILDREN

Do NOT	DO
Give the same assignment to be done in the same amount of time for all students.	You can provide a series of tiered activities—all of which focus on the same objective. One strategy has been to use the • EVERYONE must do_____ • MOST should do _____ • SOME could do _____ Another option has been to provide a tic-tac-toe board for all children with directions to gifted children that they MUST use the center square and make a tic-tac-toe or an X, while other children might only have to do corners or three in a row. See the Tic-Tac-Toe Board on page 245 for an example of how squares can be differentiated. The question in the middle requires one of the higher levels of reasoning.
Expect "good enough."	Challenge gifted kids with new content and innovative ways for them to show their understanding. They need to understand that there is always something new to learn and an infinite variety of ways to communicate the concepts. They also need to understand how content connects to other content and to see the complexity of what they're learning. Ask "How could this be better?"
Teach content in isolation.	Focus on adapting the content connected by concepts. Make connections between math and history, such as the History of Zero (Kaplan, 2000), or teach the history of the letters as you teach phonics (Robb, 2007). Or teach the concept of "Change" as it relates to math, language arts, science, and social studies (VanTassel-Baska, 1998).
Ask: "What/where/who."	Ask "What could happen if /Why/How did ____ happen?"
Tell the answer.	Wait for the answer.
Just accept an answer to a higher order question.	Not all answers to higher order questions are of the same quality. Ask "Why is that the best answer? How can you prove your answer?"
Always be the one asking questions.	Encourage your gifted children to ASK questions about the content. "What do you think professional ____ asked when they were studying this?" Teach them how to ask good questions, not just provide answers.

(Continued)

(Continued)

Do NOT	DO
"Wing it," or wait for a teachable moment for question-asking.	Use Bloom's Taxonomy or the Elements of Thought wheel to plan questions ahead of time. See page 246 for Elements of Thought and page 247 for ideas from Bloom's Taxonomy.
Teach what is already mastered.	Pretest. Children who get above an 85% on the pretest can focus only on the skills they don't know and can be freed up for a specified period of time. See page 248 for a Compacting Contract.
Use your gifted children as peer tutors.	Gifted children need to be able to grow as well. They should be able to either move ahead when content is already mastered or free themselves up for research and independent work.
Expect a gifted child to sit quietly when they're done with the expected work.	The use of an independent project can provide a set of "what to do when you're done" activities. EVERY child should be learning during a class period. "Free time" should not be provided only for those children who have done the expected task. They should have some activities to continue to work on: • Create a PowerPoint or Prezi • Vocabulary work • Learning packets • Listening Stations/Interest Centers • Computer links • Journals or Learning Logs • Content-related silent reading • Artistic or creative applications to content • Investigations—Independent Research
Put all of your gifted kids together in a group for the whole year.	Group according to the unit and according to their pretest scores. Not all gifted kids are gifted at everything. Using the label to justify the grouping doesn't allow other children with those strengths to engage at high levels and doesn't allow the gifted child to receive supplementary instruction in areas of more challenge.
Spread your gifted kids around the groups for "cooperative" grouping or to be the role models.	Group according to the unit and according to their test scores. A bored gifted child is an arrogant gifted child, and often, they make terrible role models because they can't explain to their peers how they got the answers. If they already know that content, they should have the opportunity to work with others who are also advanced and can work on more challenging problems together.

Do NOT	DO
Use the computer to babysit gifted students.	Work with gifted children to show them new skills and expectations. Gifted children need a teacher—they cannot teach themselves.
Treat the computer as a "toy" or as a distraction.	The computer is an incredible source of information and presentation. If you are asking children to do something that they can find on the computer, you need to change your assignment so that they do something with the information that they find: Analyze it, present it, make meaning of it.
Assume the computer is only a tool.	Computer programs can help children create new knowledge and demonstrate. Page 249 also shows how different apps from an iPad can align with Bloom's Taxonomy.
Mistake creativity for silliness or as a challenge of authority.	Understand that "why" and "what if" questions from gifted children are part of their characteristics. While they should learn courtesy, they are often looking for novel solutions to old ways. If they have a good idea, listen to them and respect them.
Provide one way and only way to do something.	Provide open-ended ways to solve problems. Focus on the goal, not the way to get there. If a gifted kid asks, "Can I do this assignment this way?" decide if the child will still meet the objective of the lesson.
Provide the problems to be solved.	Encourage children to FIND problems and figure out how to solve them. Problem-finding is one of the most critical skills in creativity (Starko, 1999).
Accept a short or incomplete answer or make a derogatory comment about their answer.	Ask for elaboration, another way of thinking about a situation, or more ideas. Increasing fluidity, flexibility, elaboration, and originality of ideas and thinking can help gifted children stretch creatively (Torrance, 1966). However, share the purpose of the questions; when children know that their creativity is being developed, they are more likely to participate. See page 250 for visuals of creativity.
He's already advanced cognitively. Don't insist that he be advanced physically and emotionally as well before you give him work that is where his mind is.	Give advanced opportunities as a child shows you that he or she can do the work. Often, a gifted child is more accepted by older children because they do not expect that child to be like them. Same-aged children may label the child as "weird" or apply pressure to achieve at their level—which means that the gifted child is underachieving.

(Continued)

(Continued)

Do NOT	DO
Punish or mock a child for being "arrogant" or a "know-it-all."	Allow the child different ways to show you what they know. They can't dominate or interrupt the learning of other children, but they, too, have the right to learn something new every day. Ask them to do things like write down their ideas to share with you later, create a PowerPoint to share information, or put information on a class blog or web page.
Expect the gifted child to know everything.	First, give them instruction in what they don't know. Gifted children have strengths, but they also experience struggles and confusion while they are learning.
	Second, teach them that making mistakes is HOW we learn. If you can already do it, you aren't learning.
	Understand that some gifted children are "twice-exceptional" and may have learning and social disabilities as well as gifts and talents (Hughes, 2011). Provide accommodations and modifications in their areas of challenge, and challenge their abilities at the same time.
Tell them how smart they are, and expect things to be easy for them; if it's too easy, it's too low.	Focus on their learning; emphasize the process they use to learn something. If they learn quickly, they are using effective strategies. Encourage them to try challenging things and to learn from mistakes. Gifted children sometimes feel they won't be gifted anymore if they don't "get it" and have to work hard at something.
Expect them to be like everyone else; tell them to "stop thinking so much."	It can be very lonely being the only one to make jokes that only the teacher gets or to be interested in random things. You can do the following: • Encourage connections with other people interested in a topic through the Internet. Some gifted children find university professor mentors or find groups of people interested in their topic. • Encourage the gifted children to hang out together. They should learn how to be friends with others, but they also need to find friends like themselves. They're not being exclusionary, they're finding peers. Understand that they may comprehend things that they have no control over. These are the kids who can get very upset about world hunger, war, poverty, and issues in the news. Give them outlets and opportunities to help.
Expect them to always be perfect at everything.	Gifted kids are kids, first and foremost. That means they will be silly and goofy and terrible at some things and, on occasion, make wrong choices. It doesn't make them less gifted; it means that they're kids.

TIC-TAC-TOE BOARD

Describe what _____ might have looked like.	How could you tell _____ from _____?	How might you see _____ in real life?
Restate _____ in your own words.	What is another perspective on _____?	What is the purpose of _____?
List the reasons why. _____	What evidence do you see for_____?	If _____ happened, what might have been the end?

THE ELEMENTS OF THOUGHT

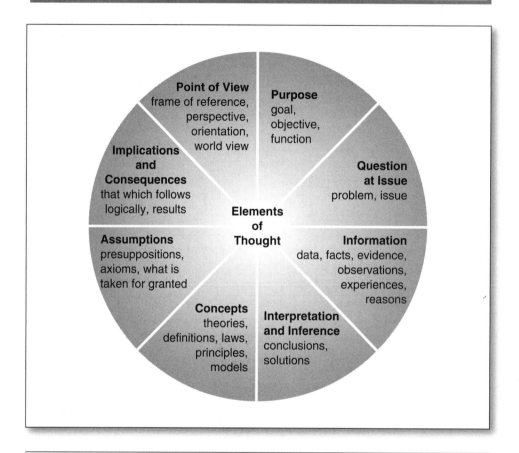

BLOOM'S TAXONOMY

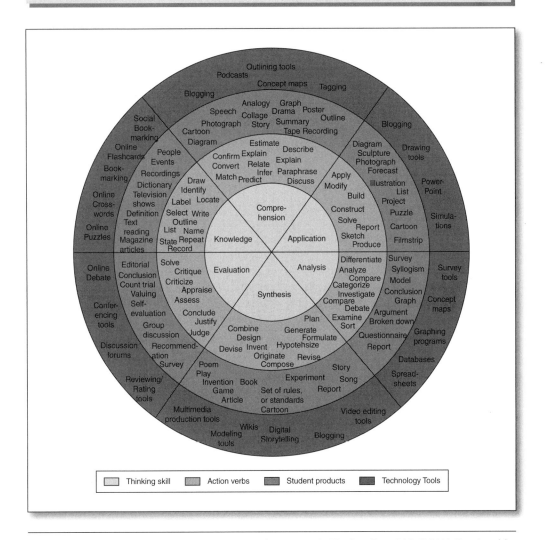

Source: Graphic created by Emily Hixon, Janet Buckenmeyer, & Heather Zamojski, © 2011. Reprinted by permission of the authors.

COMPACTING CONTRACT

Name:

Content Area:

Score on Pretest (Must be above a 90%)_____

I would like to research the following question:

I will need the following resources:

The time I will need is:

I will present my findings in this way:

To get an A, I will need to do:

If I do not use my time wisely, I understand that I will be asked to either revise my project or join the rest of the class and receive a(n) _____ for my efforts.

BLOOM'S TAXONOMY AND IPAD APPS

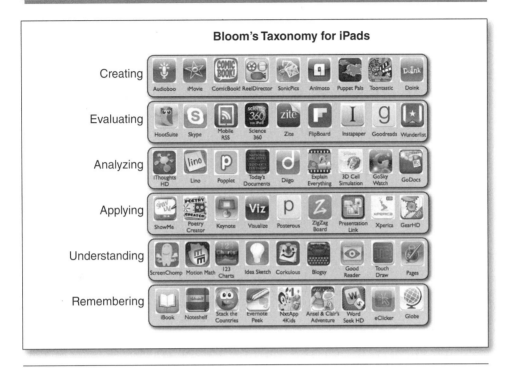

Source: Bloom's Taxonomy for iPads. Sylvia Rosenthal Tolisano. globallyconnectedlearning.com. Adapted from Dave Mileham. Used with permission.

ELEMENTS OF CREATIVITY

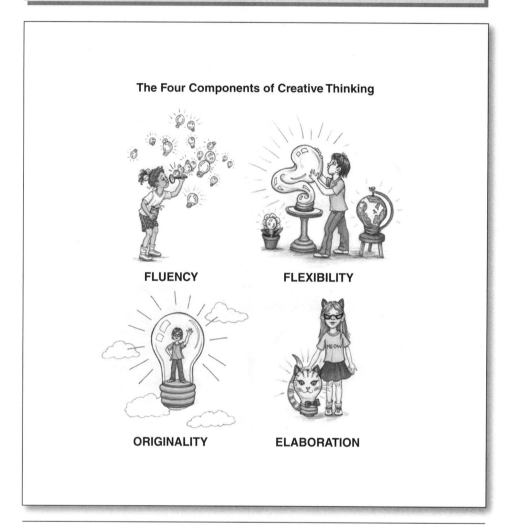

The Four Components of Creative Thinking

FLUENCY

FLEXIBILITY

ORIGINALITY

ELABORATION

Source: ©Jr Imagination. From "Creative Genius:How to Grow the Seeds of Creativity Within Every Child" by Marjorie Sarnat. www.jrimagination.com Used by Permission.

REFERENCES

Colangelo, N., Assouline, S., & Gross, M. (2004). *A nation deceived: How schools hold back America's brightest students.* Templeton National Report on Acceleration. Iowa City, IA: University of Iowa Press.

Feldman, D. H., & Benjamin, A. C. (1998). Letters from the field. *Roeper Review, 21,* 78–88.

Hughes, C. E. (2011). Twice-exceptional learners: Twice the strengths, twice the challenges. In J. Escalante (Ed.), *A kaleidoscope of special populations in gifted education: Considerations, connections, and meeting the needs of our most able diverse gifted students* (pp. 153–174). Austin, TX: Prufrock Press.

Hughes, C. E., & Murawski, W. W. (2001). Lessons from another field: Applying co-teaching strategies to gifted education. *Gifted Child Quarterly, 45*(3), 195–204.

Kaplan, R. (2000). *The nothing that is: A natural history of zero.* London, England: Oxford University Press.

Lavoie, R. (2004). How difficult can this be? The F.A.T. City Workshop: Understanding learning disabilities [Video]. United States: PBS Videos.

Peterson, J. S. (1999). Gifted—Through whose cultural lens? An application of the postpositivistic mode of inquiry. *Journal for the Education of the Gifted, 22,* 354–383.

Poh, P. S. (2008). Cognitive characteristics of the gifted. In J. A. Plucker & C. M. Callahan (Eds.), *Critical issues and practices in gifted education: What the research says* (pp. 57–83). Waco, TX: Prufrock Press.

Renzulli, J. S. (1978). What makes giftedness: Reexamining of a definition. *Phi Delta Kappan, 60,* 180–184, 261.

Renzulli, J. S., & Reis, S. M. (1985). *The schoolwide enrichment model: A comprehensive plan for educational excellence.* Mansfield Center, CT: Creative Learning Press.

Robb, D. (2007). *Ox, house, stick: The history of our alphabet.* London, England: Charlesbridge.

Robinson, A., Shore, B. M., & Enerson, D. L. (Eds.). (2007). *Best practices in gifted education: An evidence-based guide.* Waco, TX: Prufrock Press.

Spielhagen, F., & Cooper, B. (2005). The unkindest cut: Seven stupid arguments against programs for the gifted. *Education Week, 24*(31), 47–48.

Starko, A. (1999). Problem-finding: A key to creative productivity. In A. S. Fishkin, B. Cramond, & P. Olszewski-Kubilius (Eds.), *Investigating creativity in youth: Research and method* (pp. 75–96). Cresskill, NJ: Hampton Press.

Terman, L. M. (1925). *Mental and physical traits of a thousand gifted children: Genetic studies of genius: Vol. 1.* Stanford, CA: Stanford University Press.

Torrance, E. P. (1966). *Torrance tests of creative thinking: Norms technical manual.* Princeton, NJ: Personnel.

VanTassel-Baska, J. (1998). *Excellence in educating gifted and talented learners* (3rd ed). Denver, CO: Love.

RECOMMENDED READINGS

* Castellano, J. A. (2003). *Special populations in gifted education: Working with diversified learners*. Boston, MA: Allyn & Bacon.
* Csikszentmihalyi, M. (1996). *Creativity*. New York, NY: Harper.
* Gallagher, J. J. (1985). *Teaching the gifted child* (3rd ed.). Boston, MA: Allyn & Bacon.
* Gross, M. U. M. (1993). *Exceptionally gifted children*. London, England: Routledge.
* Sternberg, R. J. (1985). *Beyond IQ: A triarchic theory of intelligence*. New York, NY: Cambridge University Press.
* Tannenbaum, A. J. (1972). A backward and forward glance at the gifted. *National Elementary Principal, 51*, 14–23.

GO EVEN FURTHER WITH THIS TOPIC ON THE WORLD WIDE WEB

- www.nagc.org
- www.cectag.com/
- www.sengifted.org/
- www.hoagiesgifted.org
- www.prufrock.com

THE Apps WE LOVE

- Wolfram Alpha
- Mathemagics
- Night Sky
- TED
- Stick Picks
- Words with Friends
- Khan Academy

16

Engaging English Language Learners

Shartriya Collier

California State University, Northridge

WHAT REALLY WORKS IN ELL INSTRUCTION IN THE ELEMENTARY CLASSROOM

Who Are English Language Learners?

Bonjour! Buenos Días! Guten Morgen! 早安! In the 2011–2012 school year, 9.1% of students in the United States (an estimated 4.4 million students) were identified as English language learners (ELLs). Seven of the eight states with the highest percentages of ELL students in their public schools were in the West (National Center for Education Statistics, 2014). In eight states—Alaska, California, Colorado, Hawaii, Nevada, New Mexico, Oregon, and Texas—10% or more of public school students were English language learners. For example, currently in California, the 1,346,333 English learners represent 21.6% of the total enrollment. Moreover, an estimated 2,685,899 students speak a language other than English in the home. Thus, 43.1% of the public school systems' total enrollment consists of students who have parents who may or may not speak English as a first language. Clearly, this is a group of students we need to be able to teach, and I'm just the one to help you with that.

English learners are a diverse population. While the majority of English learners in states such as California are Spanish speakers, additional common language backgrounds include Vietnamese, Korean, Russian, Farsi, Arabic, Urdu, as well as other languages and dialects (California Department of Education, 2014). This diverse array of linguistic and cultural backgrounds, varied family dynamics, and personal experiences can make it overwhelming for a teacher to determine how to effectively support the needs of this population. Not many of us are able to learn 21 different languages in order to hold parent-teacher conferences!

Moreover, with the looming pressure of implementing the Common Core Standards and lingering regulations associated with the No Child Left Behind legislation, many teachers have difficulty determining how to develop content knowledge in subjects such as reading, math, science, and social studies in addition to developing the English skills that second language learners need to excel in school. . Furthermore, the new standards require an increased emphasis on textual analysis, critical thinking, and developing effective arguments in addition to using and applying academic vocabulary (California Department of Education, 2013). Thus, education is constantly evolving, and elementary teachers need to stay current and increase their teacher toolkits of strategies.

At one point in time, the most common approach to teaching English as a second language to students was referred to as the Pull-Out Model. Specifically, a designated teacher would remove the child from the classroom for an hour or so and reinforce key vocabulary and grammatical concepts in English. While the Pull-Out Model is still common in many secondary schools, it is not as common at the elementary school level. Due to the increasing numbers of English language learners, students are often no longer pulled out of the classroom for separate language instruction. That's good in that it reduces the inconsistencies of instruction and the feeling of exclusion of these students, but as a result, classroom teachers are now tasked with integrating key academic skills with key language teaching methods for all of their learners.

Making Connections

Check out Chapters 6 and 10 on Integrating the Arts and Cooperative Learning

Currently, the most common model used to address the needs of English learners in typical grade-level classrooms is referred to as content-based instruction or sheltered instruction. There are many different types of sheltered instruction: Content-Based Instruction (CBI), Sheltered Instruction Observation Protocol (SIOP), and Specially Designed Academic Instruction in English (SDAIE). Regardless of the approach used, the key premise remains the same for all—teachers must integrate language *and* content in a meaningful way.

Yet such a task is not an easy one because several factors impact the process. First, most teachers are required to use a mandated curriculum such as Treasures, Houghton Mifflin, and SRA Reading. Although these curricula are useful, many do not include modifications for ELLs. Additionally, most of the lessons and activities are designed as whole-class direct instruction. A whole-class approach may not provide the time needed for sheltered instructional strategies such as cooperative learning, project-based learning, total physical response, and drama. Yet these are all strategies that have been shown to support the learning needs of ELLs. Second, students must be provided opportunities to develop academic language in context. In others words, much instruction in mandated curricula focuses on teaching vocabulary in an isolated manner. Third, many mandated curricula emphasize comprehension skills but minimally address writing, listening, and speaking (Calderon, Slavin, & Sanchez, 2011).

This chapter explores key research and theories of best practices for addressing the needs of English learners in typical classrooms. Common misconceptions regarding ELLs in schools are highlighted. Finally, strategies teachers may use to create an authentic context for students to utilize, apply, and master the English language while also learning English content are discussed. Let's go! (Allons-y! Lass uns gehen! Vamonos! 我们走吧! And so on.)

EFFECTIVE SECOND LANGUAGE LEARNING IN SCHOOL: THEORIES AND RESEARCH

Many researchers of second language acquisition draw upon theories of first language acquisition to explain the language learning process. The most central concept you need to know in order to understand the academic needs of ELLs is scaffolding. *Scaffolding* is the root of sheltered instruction. Particularly, scaffolding must be used within what Vygotsky refers to as the *zone of proximal development* (Barr, Eslami, & Joshi, 2012). This is critically important when developing academic reading comprehension skills and multiple literacies in addition to content knowledge. In other words, students can grow as second language speakers only with the modeling, support, and guidance of the teacher and their more experienced peers. For example, Walqui (2006) argues that effective scaffolding for ELLs must occur on three levels:

Scaffold 1: Planned curriculum progression over time (e.g., a series of tasks over time, a project of classroom ritual)

Scaffold 2: The procedures used in a particular activity (an extension of Scaffold 1)

Scaffold 3: The collaborative process of interaction (the process of achieving Scaffold 2). (Walqui, 2006, p. 164)

Similarly, Sibold (2011) argues that in order to scaffold vocabulary instruction, teachers must provide simplified definitions, allow students to draw pictures of the words, and use the words frequently. Moreover, Dong (2013) found that activating prior knowledge, concept mapping, and utilizing students' first language were key tools needed for ELLs to learn science vocabulary in English. Don't you think these techniques sound like ones that would benefit most of your learners, not just those identified as ELL? Me too.

World-renowned second language acquisition theorist, Stephen Krashen (1982) also addressed the idea of scaffolding. Krashen and Terrell developed what is known as "The Natural Approach" to second language teaching. The premise behind this approach is essentially that *comprehension precedes production.* Teachers are responsible for providing *comprehensible input* to their students (Echevarria, Vogt, & Short, 2008). Depending on the language level, teachers must vary their questioning techniques as to require little output at the early stages of language development. Krashen argues that forcing a child to speak too soon may raise their "affective filter" or anxiety level. Comprehensible input must occur at the student's instructional level or slightly beyond. Comprehensible input is essentially this: How slow or fast does a teacher speak? What type of support materials are being used? What visual support and realia are included? What thinking maps can be used to support cognitive development? How can the teacher simplify but not "water down" academic content? The best way to conceptualize comprehensible input is to imagine arriving in a foreign country in which you do not know the language. What would it take to communicate? What supports would you need from your peers to survive? A teacher must have a pedagogical knapsack of scaffolds or input strategies he or she can use. Yet just as important is how a teacher effectively implements a variety of strategies to teach content. Students must be provided with multiple opportunities to practice, use, and apply language and content. Merrill Swain (1993, 2000) refers to this as *comprehensible output.* Comprehensible output emphasizes the need for learners to develop metalinguistic awareness. Therefore, they must become aware of their own language learning skills and challenges. They then begin to "hypothesis test" language by applying what they know from their first language to their second language. In the process of making errors, they begin to notice their own strengths and weaknesses. Opportunities for oral discourse and feedback from peers and teachers are central to this process. Shin (2010) found that the use of songs and poems to teach English significantly increased the oral language production, or comprehensible output, of her students.

Swain's focus on learner linguistic self-awareness and experimentation with language was groundbreaking. It challenged teachers and instructors to begin rethinking traditional questioning and pedagogical techniques. Teachers realized that instead of speaking for 90–100% of the day, they needed to provide more opportunities for students' linguistic output. They then had to ask, "How can we create meaningful interactions in the classroom? What opportunities can I create to encourage students to self-evaluate their own language learning? How can students not only evaluate themselves but also assess and evaluate their peers?" We now know that both comprehensible input and comprehensible output are important.

Thus, many sheltered instructors employ a variety of structured grouping strategies so that English learners may have opportunities to practice using language together. Chamot's (1996) Cognitive Academic Language Learning Approach (CALLA) to language teaching expanded this concept by emphasizing the integration of cognitive, social/affective, and metalinguistic awareness in the development of academic language. Eventually, we began to see an increased emphasis on the use of thinking maps to assist in reading comprehension, cognitive-based study skills, and writing (Williams & Pilonieta, 2012). Regardless of how it is packaged, second language theorists and researchers have acknowledged the cognitive, sociocultural, and affective factors that influence second language acquisition, particularly in the school context.

Jim Cummins's (1991) Model of Academic Language is one of the most widely employed theoretical paradigms in the world. It examines the cognitive demands English learners face when acquiring academic content. It also considers the context for learning that teachers must create in order for students to understand and apply the content. Cummins's model consists of four quadrants (Quadrant A: high context, low cognitive demand; Quadrant B: high context, high cognitive demand; Quadrant C: low context, low cognitive demand; and Quadrant D: low context, high cognitive demand).

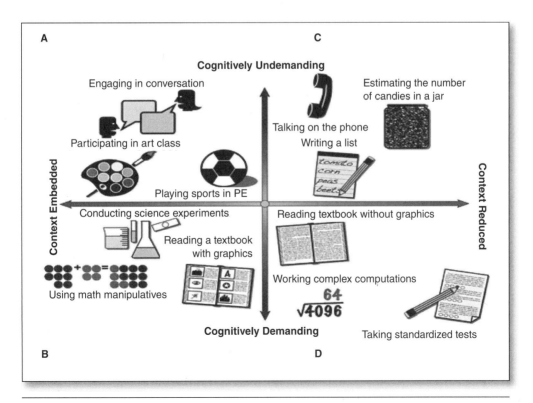

Source: Cummins, J. (n.d.). Quadrants Framework. Used with permission. Retrieved from http://iris.peabody.vanderbilt.edu/module/ell.

In many modern classrooms, instruction often falls in Quadrant D: low context, high cognitive demand. This includes lecture-based instruction, little visual support, tests and quizzes, minimal vocabulary instruction, and whole-class instruction only. However, according to Cummins (1991), effective instruction for ELLs must occur in Quadrant B: high context, high cognitive demand. Therefore, instruction must be hands-on and teachers should use a variety of realia and pictures. Teachers must also implement project-based and inquiry-based learning. As a result, students are learning and applying language in a contextualized manner.

In sum, effective teachers of English learners must consistently seek activities to scaffold the content and support the language development of students. Teachers must use comprehensible input strategies, such as using slower speech and effective questioning techniques, to relay the content to their students. Opportunities for comprehensible output, such as group interaction, are key so students may become more aware of their own language learning strategies. Finally, teachers must make sure content is high context, high cognitive demand. Yet in order to do this, teachers need to be aware of their own personal biases. The following section explores common myths and assumptions about ELLs and their families.

"WE ARE MORE THAN BLANK SLATES": MISCONCEPTIONS AND ASSUMPTIONS REGARDING ELLs

Teachers

- ✘ **STOP assuming that English learners are a homogenous group (specifically, Spanish speakers).** As previously mentioned, English learners represent a variety of cultural and linguistic backgrounds. Did you know that over 20 countries speak Spanish? Each one has its own unique culture. We need to show students that we respect their differences.

- ✘ **STOP believing that the parents of English language learners do not care about their children's education.** Many parents are recent arrivals to the country. As a result, they are in the process of securing housing and acclimating to a new culture. Therefore, they are not aware of the parent/teacher rules and norms of interaction. Part of your task is to inform them of what your expectations are for their child (Collier & Auerbach, 2011). Unfortunately, a new current trend is that many parents are not identifying their children as ELLs for fear of getting them "stuck in the system." This means that, even though some students are not identified as

English language learners, they may still need language learning support.

✖ **STOP saying you are using Specially Designed Academic Instruction in English (SDAIE) just because you have integrated a few pictures and realia.** Sheltered Instruction focuses on the long-term processes of language acquisition. Teachers must consider the social/affective, cognitive, and metalinguistic strategies used over time. Overwhelmed by this? Don't be. Talk to a SDAIE teacher or ELL coach; ask them to collaborate or co-teach.

✖ **STOP viewing English learners as "blank slates" because they do not speak English.** Many students have received extensive schooling in their first language. Thus, it is your job to determine what skills they have when they arrive. You must use a variety of authentic, formal, and informal assessment tools in the first and second language (if possible) to determine their status. Also, research shows that what students have in their first language, transfers over to their second language (Burchinal, Field, Lopez, Howes, & Pianta, 2012).

✖ **STOP expecting interpreters or other students to teach your students.** You are the teacher. Be sure to interact directly with all of your students. Do not defer their instruction to individuals who speak their language.

✖ **STOP sitting the English learners in the back of the room.** As previously discussed, interaction with fluent English speakers is essential to language development. Think about where your English learners will best be able to participate, be surrounded by helpful peers, and ask questions when needed.

Administrators

✖ **STOP isolating your English learners into one classroom or tracking them with students at the same language proficiency level.** ELLs need exposure to a variety of language speakers at a variety of language levels in order to produce comprehensible output. I know that some districts find it more manageable to cluster students, but this simply flies in the face of what research tells us is best practice.

✖ **STOP isolating your English language development (ELD) program.** In some states, schools have a separate ELD time in addition to a 90-minute mandated literacy block. While it is helpful for teachers to have allocated ELD time, teachers should be encouraged to use sheltered strategies throughout the day in *all* subject areas. The ELD program should be aligned with the literacy program.

✗ **STOP assuming that parents of ELLs do not care.** Your school must provide a variety of services to inform, instruct, and empower parents regarding what it takes for their child to excel in school. What are you doing to work with those parents?

✗ **STOP providing a one-time professional development inservice for ELL strategies (aka the "dog and pony show").** If you are in a school with a high number of ELLs, you must provide opportunities for teachers to receive consistent professional development, work as teams, and build a school community to support the needs of this population.

BECOMING A MULTILINGUAL AND MULTICULTURAL ADVOCATE: STRATEGIES FOR SUCCESSFULLY INSTRUCTING ELLs

Teachers, DO This

✓ **CELEBRATE the diversity in your classrooms.** Use your students as "cultural ambassadors." They are all experts in their own language and cultural traditions. Have a weekly cultural ambassador who can teach the class a few words in their first language and share key cultural traditions. You can invite parents to take part in this process, thereby extending your classroom to the community. You could also have a multilingual bulletin board in which you encourage students to learn a new word in another language.

✓ **KEEP parents informed of your classroom expectations by sending a monthly or weekly newsletter.** This can be a one-page sheet in which you include a strategy or "Tip of the Week" that parents may use to help their child. Make sure all correspondence is translated into at least one other language. Google translate and Babblefish.com are decent translation tools, but you should get a native language speaker to review them if possible. If not possible, don't give up on this idea. Something is better than nothing, even if there are errors. Make sure parents understand you are there to support them and not judge them.

Making Connections

Check out Chapter 20 on Collaborating With Families

✓ **KNOW that Sheltered Instruction may be packaged in a variety of ways.** Regardless of which approach you use, remember second language learning strategies must occur before, during, and after a lesson. To remember, use Shartriya Collier's PEACE Model:

PEACE MODEL

Preteach	Vocabulary;
Expand upon	Students' background knowledge by modeling key concepts using authentic literature, videos, and other visual support;
Apply	Students have opportunities to work in pairs, in groups, and individually to practice the concepts;
Connect	Students are encouraged to make connections from what they are learning to the real world; and
Evaluate	Use a variety of assessments such as rubrics, checklists, self-evaluation, and other authentic tools to determine where students need more support and what changes you need to make to your instruction.

- ✓ **USE the SIOP checklist for planning.** I've provided you a checklist on page 263.
- ✓ **USE structured cooperative groups to encourage positive interaction.** Just placing students in groups does not make it structured. Some structures of cooperative grouping are think-pair-share, four corners, numbered heads together, and inside-circle outside-circle. Also, always assign group roles and change groups frequently.

Making Connections

Check out Chapter 6 on Arts Integration

- ✓ **KNOW that vocabulary instruction is essential.** A nice model is Kinsella's Vocabulary template (2005). I've provided you a resource in the back of this chapter on page 266.
- ✓ **USE the writing process and writing workshops to model effective writing for students.** Do not penalize students for errors because that is part of the process. Nonetheless, frequently provide mini-lessons in which you highlight specific writing strategies.
- ✓ **INTEGRATE the arts.** Dance, drama, music, and art are a wonderful way for English learners to master the language while having fun. The rest of your students will likely appreciate this as well!
- ✓ **USE a variety of authentic literature in English as well as other languages.** If possible, include bilingual books as part of the class library. Ask your students if they have books in their first language they would like to share in the class library.

Administrators, DO This

- ✓ **USE thematic instruction to bridge the various curricular programs used in your school.** For example, if you have an overarching theme of family and community for one month, teachers can highlight family themes in the reading program, the ELD program, and even the math and science programs. This helps to bridge the gaps and reinforce key skills across the content areas.
- ✓ **BEGIN to view your school site as an extension of the community.** Hold parent literacy nights and parent-child luncheons. Invite local businesses for a community education town hall. Begin to move from the individualist framework to the collectivist paradigm, thereby making parents, teachers, and administrators accountable for the success of the children. Don't know much about individualism versus collectivism? Educate yourself by checking out Rothstein-Fisch and Trumbull's (2008) book, *Managing Diverse Classrooms: How to Build on Students' Cultural Strengths.*
- ✓ **PROVIDE a teachers' "show-and-tell" at the beginning of your staff meetings in which teachers may share new and interesting resources they have discovered about effective instruction.** Make sure they specifically mention how this instruction is appropriate for students who are ELL or are gifted or have disabilities, in addition to the typical learners.
- ✓ **FOCUS on good instruction, not just the numbers.** Applaud and share widely when teachers have a success in their class. Use the train-the-trainers model in which your most effective teachers train their colleagues in the skills they are using successfully.

SIOP LESSON PLANNING SHEET

Name:_____   Date:_____

Assignment:_____

LESSON PREPARATION

1. *Write* **content objectives** clearly for students.

2. *Write* **language objectives** clearly for students.

3. Choose **content concepts appropriate** for age and educational background level of students.

4. Identify **supplementary materials** to use (graphs, models, visuals).

5. **Adapt content** (e.g., text, assignment) to all levels of student proficiency.

6. Plan **meaningful activities** that integrate lesson concepts (e.g., surveys, letter writing, simulations, constructing models) with language practice opportunities for reading, writing, listening, and/or speaking.

BUILDING BACKGROUND

7. **Explicitly link concepts** to students' backgrounds and experiences.

8. **Explicitly link past learning** and new concepts.

9. **Emphasize key vocabulary** (e.g., introduce, write, repeat, and highlight) for students.

COMPREHENSIBLE INPUT

10. Use **speech** appropriate for students' proficiency level (e.g., slower rate, enunciation, and simple sentence structure for beginners).

11. **Explain academic tasks** clearly.

12. Use a **variety of techniques** to make content concepts clear (e.g., modeling, visuals, hands-on activities, demonstrations, gestures, body language).

STRATEGIES

13. Provide ample opportunities for students to use **strategies**, (e.g., problem-solving, predicting, organizing, summarizing, categorizing, evaluating, self-monitoring).

14. Use **scaffolding techniques** consistently (providing the right amount of support to move students from one level of understanding to a higher level) throughout lesson.

15. Use a variety of **question types including those that promote higher order thinking** skills throughout the lesson (literal, analytical, and interpretive questions).

INTERACTION

16. Provide frequent **opportunities for interactions** and discussion between teacher/student and among students, and encourage elaborated responses.

17. Use **group configurations** that support language and content objectives of the lesson.

18. Provide sufficient **wait time for student responses** consistently.

19. Give ample opportunities for **students to clarify key concepts in L1** as needed with aide, peer, or L1 text.

PRACTICE/APPLICATION

20. Provide **hands-on materials** and/or manipulatives for students to practice using new content knowledge.

21. Provide activities for students to **apply content and language knowledge** in the classroom.

22. Provide activities that **integrate all language skills** (i.e., reading, writing, listening, and speaking).

LESSON DELIVERY

23. **Support content objectives** clearly.

24. **Support language objectives** clearly.

25. **Engage students** approximately 90–100% of the period (most students taking part and on task throughout the lesson).

26. **Pace** the lesson appropriately to the students' ability level.

REVIEW/ASSESSMENT

27. Give a comprehensive **review of key vocabulary**.

28. Give a comprehensive **review of key content concepts**.

29. Provide **feedback** to students regularly on their output (e.g., language, content, work).

30. Conduct **assessments** of student comprehension and learning throughout lesson on all lesson objectives (e.g., spot checking, group response.)

COMMENTS

Source: Adapted from Echevarria, Vogt, & Short (2008).

KINSELLA'S VOCABULARY TEMPLATE

Workshop: _____ **Reading Selection:** _____

Word	Meaning	Example(s)	Image

☙VERBAL PRACTICE

✎WRITING PRACTICE

Source: Adapted from Kinsella (2005).

REFERENCES

Barr, S., Eslami, Z. R., & Joshi, R. M. (2012). Core strategies to support English language learners. *Educational Forum, 76*(1), 105–117.

Burchinal, M., Field, S., Lopez, M. L., Howes, C., & Pianta, R. (2012). Instruction in Spanish in pre-kindergarten classrooms and child outcomes for English language learners. *Early Childhood Research Quarterly, 27*, 188–197.

Calderon, M., Slavin, R., & Sanchez, M. (2011). Effective instruction for English learners. *The Future of Children, 21*(1), 103–127.

California Department of Education. (2013). California Common Core State Standards. Retrieved from http://www.cde.ca.gov/re/cc/

California Department of Education. (2014). Facts about English learners in California. Retrieved from http://www.cde.ca.gov/ds/sd/cb/cefelfacts.asp

Chamot, A. U. (1996). The Cognitive Academic Language Learning Approach (CALLA): Theoretical framework and instructional applications. In J. E. Alatis (Ed.), *Georgetown University Round Table on Languages and Linguistics, 1996* (pp. 108–115). Washington, DC: Georgetown University Press.

Collier, S., & Auerbach, S. (2011). "It's difficult because of the language:" Language use and bilingual family program development in the post-proposition 227 era. *Multicultural Education, 11*(2), 9–14.

Cummins, J. (1991). Language development and academic learning. In L. M. Malavé & G. Duquette (Eds.), *Language, culture and cognition* (pp. 161–175). Clevedon, England: Multilingual Matters.

Dong, Y. R. (2013). Powerful learning tools for ELLs: Using native language, familiar examples, and concept mapping to teach English language learners. *Science Teacher, 80*(4), 51–57.

Echevarria, J., Vogt, M., & Short, D. (2008). *Making content comprehensible for English Learners: The SIOP model* (3rd ed.). Needham Heights, MA: Allyn & Bacon.

Kinsella, K. (2005). Teaching academic vocabulary. Aiming high: Apsirando a lo major resource. Retrieved from http://www.scoe.org/docs/ah/AH_kinsella2.pdf

Krashen, S. (1982). *Principles and practice in second language acquisition.* New York, NY: Pergamon.

National Center for Education Statistics. (2014). English learners: Fast facts. Retrieved from http://nces.ed.gov/fastfacts/display.asp?id=96

Rothstein-Fisch, C., & Trumbull, E. (2008). *Managing diverse classrooms: How to build on students' cultural strengths.* Alexandria, VA: Association for Supervision and Curriculum Development.

Shin, S. J. (2010). Teaching English language learners: Recommendations for early childhood educators. *Dimensions of Early Childhood, 38*(2), 13–21.

Sibold, C. (2011). Building English language learners' academic vocabulary: Strategies and tips. *Multicultural Education, 18*(2), 24–29.

Swain, M. (1993). The output hypothesis: Just speaking and writing aren't enough. *Canadian Modern Language Review, 50*(1), 158–164.

Swain, M. (2000). The output hypothesis and beyond: Mediating acquisition through collaborative dialogue. In J. P. Lantolf (Ed.), *Sociocultural theory and second language learning* (pp. 97–114). Oxford, England: Oxford University Press.

Walqui, A. (2006). Scaffolding instruction for English language learners: A conceptual framework. *International Journal of Bilingual Education and Bilingualism, 9*(2), 159–180.

Williams, C., & Pilonieta, P. (2012). Using interactive writing instruction with kindergarten and first-grade English language learners. *Early Childhood Education Journal, 40*, 145–150.

RECOMMENDED READINGS

* Auerbach, S., & Collier, S. (2011). Bringing high stakes from the classroom to the parent center: Lessons from an intervention program for immigrant families. *Teachers College Record, 114*(3), 1–40.

* Kelley, A., & Kohnert, K. (2012). Is there a cognate advent for typically developing Spanish-speaking English-language learners? *American Speech-Language-Hearing Association, 43*, 191–204.

* Peterson, M., Brandes, D., Kunkel, A., Wilson, J., Rahn, N. L., Egan, A., & McComas, J. (2014). Teaching letter sounds to kindergarten English language learners using incremental rehearsal. *Journal of School Psychology, 52*, 97–107.

* Roy-Campbell, Z. M. (2013). Who educates teacher educators about English language learners? *Reading Horizons, 52*(2), 255–280.

GO EVEN FURTHER WITH THIS TOPIC ON THE WORLD WIDE WEB

- www.tesol.org
- www.cal.org
- www.ncela.us/
- www.webenglishteacher.com/esl.html
- www.davesESLcafe.com
- www.nabe.org
- www.everythingesl.net
- www.colorincolorado.org
- www.colorincolorado.org/educators/content/cooperative/
- www.edu-sources.org/engagement-strategies/
- www.esl.about.com
- www.onestopenglish.com
- www.breakingnewsenglish.com
- www.moramodules.com

THE Apps WE LOVE

- Phonetics Focus
- FluentU
- Conversation English by the English App
- Puppet Pals
- Adventures for Kids by WireCloud

17

Addressing Autism Spectrum Disorder

Emily Iland

California State University, Northridge

WHAT REALLY WORKS WITH ASD
IN THE ELEMENTARY CLASSROOM

Meeting the Needs of Students With Autism Spectrum Disorders

You can't live in America without hearing about the increase in the rate of autism, unless maybe you live in a box or in the woods. Nope. Even if you live there, it's likely you know that autism cases are skyrocketing. More children are being diagnosed with Autism Spectrum Disorder (ASD) than ever before. The Centers for Disease Control (2014) reports that 1 in 68 children is now diagnosed with ASD. Because ASD is five times more common in boys than girls, 1 in 42 eight-year-old boys now meets the criteria for ASD. This astounding figure has a far-reaching impact for society in general, for the education system, and for teachers.

Most teachers now know that children with disabilities should be educated with their nondisabled peers to the greatest extent possible, and this means that more children with ASD will take their places in general

269

education classrooms than ever before. Think about that. If 1 in 42 boys has ASD, that means a child with ASD will be part of almost every classroom. While this reality becomes more obvious year after year, it does not mean that teachers, specialists, administrators, or even classmates are prepared to understand, accept, and meet the needs of students on the spectrum. Once educators are aware of the growing need, it takes a personal commitment to help these students be successful, realize their potential, be appreciated, and truly be included at school.

Good teaching for students with ASD is no longer a mystery. What really works is becoming more and more clear. This will be discussed in detail later in the chapter, but before getting to that, it is essential to realize that students on the spectrum have multiple needs that are very closely tied to the diagnostic features of ASD. Identifying the features of autism that an individual student exhibits and then finding effective ways to address each of those areas is the key to success! With a clear understanding of the student's strengths and needs, methods, strategies, and solutions can be selected to help him or her develop skills, access his or her education, and be part of the school community (Doyle & Iland, 2004).

One of the most important things a teacher can do to help a student with ASD be successful in a general education classroom is to shift focus beyond academics (gasp!). Autism is a developmental disability, so prioritizing the developmental needs of a student with ASD is necessary to support the child's growth, progress, and meaningful inclusion. This chapter offers insight into the features of ASD and practical ways to meet the educational needs of students with ASD, while at the same time enhancing the educational experience of every student in the classroom. A lofty goal indeed, but a worthwhile one.

UNDERSTANDING ASD

Although teachers are not supposed to diagnose disabilities, understanding the official criteria for ASD can provide useful insight into the differences that distinguish a child on the autism spectrum from a typically developing child. Two areas of difference, social communication/interaction and behavior/sensory issues, are at the core of ASD. In 2013, new research-based criteria for Autism Spectrum Disorder were developed to create a reliable, consistent method to identify the features of the disability (American Psychiatric Association, 2013). One of the most controversial changes is that formerly separate diagnoses like Autistic Disorder, Asperger Syndrome, and Pervasive Developmental Disorder were replaced by a single dimensional category: Autism Spectrum Disorder (Iland, 2013b). As you read on to learn about the features of ASD, you may recognize features of the disorder in students you already know and will be better prepared to understand students you will teach in the future.

Whether or not a student has a formal diagnosis, impairments in these three areas of *social communication and social interaction* can be noted (or have been noted) in all individuals on the spectrum, with varying levels of severity:

1.   A deficit in *social-emotional reciprocity* means that the individual does not understand and engage in back-and-forth social exchanges and/ or does not seem to match and reflect the emotions of others. Examples of this feature include not knowing how to have a back-and-forth conversation, problems initiating social interactions, or a lack of response to the initiations of others. People on the spectrum may seem content to be alone, but this "aloneness" is actually a symptom of the lack of reciprocity: the reduced sharing of interests, emotions, or affect with others.

2.   A lack of eye contact is one of the most noticeable deficits in *nonverbal communicative behaviors used for social interaction* in ASD. Imagine the problems that can arise from difficulties or even an inability to use and read facial expressions, body language, and gestures. Someone on the spectrum may have poorly integrated verbal and nonverbal communication (matching body language and facial expression with their words) or even a total lack of nonverbal communication.

3.   Deficits in *developing, maintaining, and understanding relationships* is a central feature of ASD with a significant impact. For example, the student may have difficulties making friends and may even appear disinterested in peers. The student may not know how to play (imaginative play or other games). The student may also have difficulty adjusting behavior to suit various social contexts (for example, not being deferential to authority figures).

The second area of developmental deficit in ASD is called *restricted, repetitive patterns of behavior, interests, or activities.* Of the possible four areas of impact, a person with ASD will exhibit at least two of these features (now or in the past) with varying levels of severity:

1.   Examples of *repetitive (or stereotyped) motor movements, use of objects, or speech* range from lining up toys, flipping objects, echoing what others say, repeating phrases or dialogue from movies, or using unusual "idiosyncratic" phrases. This criterion also includes repetitive movement of the body or hands, such as flapping, rocking, and pacing.

2.   People with ASD may exhibit an *insistence on sameness, inflexible adherence to routines, or ritualized patterns of verbal or nonverbal behavior.* They may need to take the same route or eat the same food every day, repeat greetings or other rituals, have difficulties with transition, and experience extreme distress at small changes in their routine or the environment. Rigid thinking patterns, also called black-and-white thinking, is another example of how this criterion may be manifested.

3. The *highly restricted, fixated interests seen in ASD* might look like "obsessions" to others, but are actually a behavior feature of ASD (not mental illness). These interests are *abnormal in intensity* (fixated on something that others like, such as video games) or *abnormal in focus* (fixated on something that few others like, such as vacuum cleaner parts). These interests are described as "excessively circumscribed or perseverative," meaning that the person has a narrow focus of interest and wants repeated, continuous engagement with it (whether it is Legos® or water towers). This feature may also include a strong attachment to, or preoccupation with, unusual objects (for example, always carrying a particular item such as a toy car or plastic spoon).

4. *Hyperreactivity or hyporeactivity to sensory input or unusual interest in sensory aspects of environment* is included for the first time in the diagnostic manual. Hypersensitivity is noted when the student has an adverse response to specific sounds, smells, tastes, or textures (or other input) and may result in avoidance. Hyposensitivity is seen when the student does not register sensation, such as under responding to heat, cold, or pain. "Sensory seeking" is seen in students who want more sensory input. Examples include excessive smelling or touching of objects and visual fascination with lights or movement.

Just as the diagnostic criteria have evolved, findings made through scientific advances are contributing to an even more complete understanding of ASD. For example, advances in neurology have led to the view of autism as a disorder of information processing (Minshew & Williams, 2008). Processing difficulties can include auditory information, language, text, social information, and even motor planning. The more complex the information is, the more difficult it is to process. This finding helps explain why people with ASD may master basic skills (such as factual memory) but struggle with more complex learning (such as higher order thinking skills). Focus on detail over the big picture, problems with time concepts and time management, disorganization, and difficulty processing multimodal input are being linked to neurological features of ASD (National Education Association, 2006). So what are you supposed to do with all this information, you ask? Read on.

MAKING THE MATCH BETWEEN NEEDS AND INTERVENTION

The Individuals with Disabilities Education Information Act (IDEIA, 2004) is the law that governs special education. The Individuals with Disabilities Education Improvement Act (IDEIA) guides the development of the Individualized Education Program (IEP) to meet the educational needs of students with disabilities. One of the most relevant issues in considering how to effectively educate students with ASD is the fact that education is *not* just academic. According to the federal regulations that tell states how to follow IDEIA law, education is *academic, developmental, and functional* (U.S. Department of Education, 2005). Note that functional needs include skills that help the student throughout the day, including hygiene, eating, and so forth. Ignorance of this fact may be one of the greatest obstacles faced by students with ASD and their families. When schools focus only on the academic needs of a student and neglect their developmental or functional needs, they are not only disadvantaging students with ASD, they are breaking the law!

That said, there are many competing views about *how* to effectively meet the multiple needs of students on the spectrum. It is widely agreed that no single treatment is effective for everyone (National Research Council, 2001). There is a great deal of variation among kids with autism, so what works for one may not work for another. As autism expert Lorna Wing often said, "If you've met one person with autism, you've met one person with autism."

After having a panel of experts analyze 775 research studies, the National Autism Center published the National Standards Report (NSR; Wilczynski et al., 2009). The NSR may be a welcome tool to help educators, parents, and service providers make treatment decisions for children and adolescents on the spectrum. The NSR identified 11 interventions with sufficient empirical research behind them to be considered "Established" for addressing communication, interpersonal, play, higher cognitive functions, learning readiness, motor skills, personal responsibility and self-regulation skills, and to expand placement options. Check out page 280 for short definitions on each of these interventions, but refer to the report itself for more information.

Plugged In

www.nationalautism center.org/national-standards-project/

Another category of evidence identified in the NSR is "Emerging" treatments, which may be effective but have not yet been demonstrated sufficiently. It may be reasonable to choose these interventions for a particular student, but additional studies are needed to consider whether these treatments are truly effective.

Finally, the third category of intervention identified in the NSR is "Unestablished" practices. The NSR cautions against assuming that these treatments are effective. In fact, the report states that there is no way to rule out the possibility that these treatments are actually ineffective. The five unestablished interventions are: Auditory Integration Training, Facilitated Communication, Gluten- and Casein-Free Diet, the Sensory Integrative Package, and Academic Interventions. I've included definitions on page 282, but guess what? You're right! I'd still like to recommend you to the report itself.

Reports like the NSR are a source of guidance, not a prescription or mandate. When choosing interventions, the information about research should be integrated with individual considerations, professional judgment, values and preferences of families, and student data. The ability to implement a particular intervention faithfully should also be considered (Wilczynski et al., 2009). Even if you as the teacher prefer one treatment over another, you'll need to keep in mind that the family will need to consider what works best for them and the student.

It will also be important to refer to updates to research reports as they are published. The next update from the National Autism Center is

Plugged In

autismpdc.fpg.unc
.edu/sites/autismpdc
.fpg.unc.edu/files/2014-EBP-
Report.pdf

expected to include a review and analysis of treatments for ASD based on research conducted between 2007 and 2012 and will include the evaluation of treatments for adults (age 22+). Also be on the lookout for similar reviews of the literature prepared by other organizations to help guide parents and educators, like the 2014 report from The National Professional Development Center on Autism Spectrum Disorders found at the URL in the Plugged In box.

 WHAT TO DO (*AND NOT DO*)

Now that you know what ASD is all about, and now that you know what the research literature suggests, here are some quick DOs and DON'Ts to help you every day.

✘ **STOP doubting your ability to teach and relate to students on the spectrum.** Too many teachers defer their students to the special education teacher thinking, "I don't know anything about autism." Kids on the spectrum are still kids, and they are still your students. It's your job to teach them and connect with them. You may get a happy surprise when you get to know students with ASD, who often have many endearing qualities and talents.

✘ **STOP thinking you already know everything you need to know about ASD.** Every kid is different; every family has information you can use to help teach that child. Take the opportunity to learn by talking to them, collaborating with specialists, attending conferences, reading articles, or checking out books, films, or plays that address the human side of ASD, such as *The Curious Incident of the Dog in the Night-Time* by Mark Haddon (2004).

✘ **STOP focusing only on academics.** As IDEIA regulations state, education must address the academic, developmental, and functional needs of the student. Students with ASD may be "uneven," with both unexpected strengths and surprising areas of need. A student who is an expert on planets may not understand how we humans get along here on earth, so be sure to take these kinds of needs into account!

✖ **STOP thinking of inclusion as geography (a place or a placement).** It is sad to see students with ASD in general education settings who are truly alone. Inclusion does not happen automatically or by chance by just physically putting children with and without disabilities in the same space. Real inclusion happens when the student is taught to play, communicate, and interact with others. Classmates also need to be clued in about autism in general and even be directly told about some traits of a particular child so that those differences are understood and don't lead to bullying or rejection.

✖ **STOP thinking that a student with ASD who is alone *wants* to be alone.** Solitude is more often a result of poor play and social skills than a choice. After enough failure and rejection, and having few alternatives, students on the spectrum often resort to pacing the playground, seeking out the company of adults, or retreating alone into their special interest. Social isolation can only be reversed through conscious efforts of the teacher and the class.

Making Connections

Check out Chapter 19 on Social Skills

✖ **STOP assuming that a student who is not following instructions is refusing or defiant.** Sometimes there is a major mismatch between demands in the classroom and the social, communication, sensory, and behavior issues of ASD. When the student is frustrated or overwhelmed, he or she may just give up. A shutdown that looks like refusal can really mean the student can't cope at the moment. It is not a challenge to authority; it is more like a turtle going into its shell.

✖ **STOP ignoring what the student is trying to communicate to you through behavior.** Students who have communication challenges may resort to communicating with their actions, not words. A child who covers her ears and rocks can be signaling that she is feeling overwhelmed; a child who pushes away other kids in line for the slide may be signaling that he wants his turn. Don't wait for the child to "use his words" or insist that he do so, especially when stressed. Learning to read and respond to the student's nonverbal communication can nip all kinds of problems in the bud.

✖ **STOP ignoring/shutting out/judging the parents.** You know that when a child has a problem at school, one of the first things teachers do is blame the parents. When a child has a lot of difficulties, the parents may be on the receiving end of negativity and judgment. In fact, most parents of children with ASD have their hands full and are doing the best they can. They may also actually be experts in one particular area: their child. Their experiences often help them understand their child's needs. They may be able to tell you what worked and what didn't work in the past so you don't have to figure it out on your own.

✗ **STOP minimizing the developmental needs of bright students with ASD who don't seem to have academic needs.** Elementary school is an excellent time to build skills in socialization, communication, behavior, and self-regulation that will help the child be a more successful student and classmate. Closing the developmental gap and the divide with the peer group is as important as any academic goal. This will stay with them the rest of their lives!

GO Teachers, DO This

✓ **WORK WITH A TEAM to prioritize the developmental and functional needs of the student** (play, social communication, social interaction, even toilet training and eating). This can be a formal team (like an IEP team) or even just a group of concerned teachers and family members. At a time when there is tremendous pressure to focus only on academics and test scores, you can feel like you're swimming upstream to address nonacademic needs. In addition to the fact that educational law supports this approach, this shift in thinking can have a significant impact on the student's well-being, progress, and lifetime outcomes.

✓ **BE PROACTIVE to create true social inclusion.** The teacher's attitude about "who belongs" sets the tone for the entire class. Classmates may be concerned about differences they can see but do not understand, which can get in the way of friendships and relationships. If you can only do one thing differently than you are doing now, consider implementing a Peer Training Program that teaches nondisabled peers how to play with, relate to, and include students with ASD in every school environment. Such programs are usually free or low cost, easy to implement, and have benefits for all students involved, not just the student with ASD. For example, the Ohio Center for Autism and Low Incidence Disabilities (OCALI) website has a free module with information, videos, and resources to help you implement a Peer-Mediated Instruction Intervention (PMII), in which the adults step back and trained peers take the lead to improve the target student's social, communication, and play

Plugged In

OCALI
www.autisminternet
modules.org

skills. Visit www.autisminternetmodules.org for more information on PMII and just about any other topic on ASD.

✓ **MONITOR the child in all environments, and protect him or her from bullying and ostracization.** A recent study found that 63% of children with ASD from ages 6 to 15 had been bullied at some point in their lives, and 39% had been bullied in the previous month (Anderson, 2012). A student with limited social understanding, limited communication skills, and a small circle of friends can be the perfect target, especially in unstructured settings like the playground or the locker room. The need for supervision will range from constant adult supervision to trained peer support and mentoring. Consider occasionally eating lunch near your students or observe students on campus to watch what goes on! Seeing the student outside the classroom is vital to understanding the student's social inclusion or recreation skills. It is also important to ensure that a student with ASD does not bully others.

✓ **MAKE the learning environment tolerable.** A highly structured, sensory-friendly setting is essential for students with ASD and can benefit every student in the classroom (Mesibov & Shea, 2008). What does it mean to be tolerable? Read on for some helpful tips.

✓ **CREATE structure** so the student knows what will happen and when. Visual supports like schedules, task lists, checklists, and color coding help the student know how much work to do, when he or she is finished, where things belong, and what happens next.

✓ **CREATE sensory comfort.** An occupational therapist can help design a sensory diet of desirable input to help the student stay engaged and avoid becoming overwhelmed.

✓ **USE scales, charts, or other tools to express types and intensity of emotions.** Help the student choose and use relaxation strategies and coping strategies to reduce stress and maintain self-control. Be sure to make these strategies age appropriate.

✓ **USE positive behavioral supports**, like the Premack principle: Alternate between preferred and nonpreferred activities. Give the student two good choices to give a sense of control, like "Do you want to do your math first or your science?" Use favorite interests for rewards, breaks, and relaxation. Let the student shine by helping others in areas of strength, from math to passing out supplies.

✓ **ADDRESS comprehension in ASD.** Multiple features of ASD contribute to problems understanding what is read, even for individuals on the spectrum who decode very well and read with expression. Do not underestimate the impact of this issue. Check out the evidence-based and promising ways to help in *Drawing a Blank: Improving Comprehension for Readers on the Autism Spectrum* (Iland, 2011).

✓ **PRIORITIZE safety from a young age.** Picture what your student would do at the age of 18 in an encounter with the police. At any age, be sure to include goals for following instructions like "stop" and "go," answering "yes" and "no" reliably, and taking "no" for an answer. Check out the *Be Safe* movie (Iland, 2013a) for video modeling tools to teach teens and adults with disabilities how to interact safely with the police.

Plugged In

www.BeSafeTheMovie.com

✓ **LISTEN to the parents and others who know the child well.** For example, ask the mom to lend you the one book she really wants you to read, ask the dad what goals he has for his child, and ask if the child has friends outside of school. These three simple questions will let the parents know that you truly care about their concerns and their child.

✓ **LISTEN to others who have experience with the child or expertise in ASD.** Ask last year's teacher the #1 thing that worked and the #1 thing to avoid. Ask educational specialists what advice they have for you. Consider important information shared by behaviorists, therapists, or team members outside of school who know what works for the child to help create consistency across environments. Collaboration is key when it comes to working with all kids, especially those with special needs (Murawski & Spencer, 2011).

✓ **LISTEN to the child.** He or she may not be able to explain their thoughts and feelings with words, so be aware of the communicative intent of things the student does. Watch for signs that the student is becoming overwhelmed, and step in to prevent a meltdown. Notice the materials and activities that the child prefers, and use these things as rewards or teaching tools. Build on the child's strengths and abilities to help with more difficult tasks.

✓ **UNDERSTAND that sometimes the student simply can't comply with instructions or keep it together.** This is not refusal or defiance; it can be called *variability of performance*. If you see it as *can't* versus *won't*, you won't take it personally! Instead, figure out what might have brought on a difficulty and how to make things go more smoothly next time. For more insights like this one, check out "Helpful Handouts" at www.barbaradoyle.com/.

✓ **ASK for help.** Sometimes teachers are reluctant to ask, perhaps fearing that they might be judged as less capable. Just like parents, however, you are likely to know very little about autism until you have a child/student who has it, and you need to learn quickly! In addition, every child with ASD is different than the one before.

Take advantage of professional development opportunities so you feel more comfortable. Ask program specialists and special educators what they can do to help and support you and your student.

✓ **LOOK for resources.** There is an increasing amount of information about ASD on the web. Some of it is incredibly helpful, while others appear to be whack-a-doodle. Make sure it is from credible sources! In addition to OCALI, there are readings, vignettes, and modules in a variety of other sources, like the Iris Center www.iris.peabody .vanderbilt.edu.

Plugged In

www.iris.peabody
.vanderbilt.edu

AT-A-GLANCE

A Quick Guide to Established, Emerging, and Unestablished Autism Treatments (adapted from Wilczynski et al., 2009)

Established Treatments: Treatments with sufficient empirical evidence to demonstrate effectiveness	
Term	*Quick Definition*
Antecedent Package	Modifying a situation that typically precedes a problematic behavior to avoid its occurrence
Behavioral Package	Applying basic principles of behavior change to reduce problem behavior and teach appropriate replacement behavior
Comprehensive Behavioral Intervention for Young Children (CBIYC)	Treating children under the age of 8 using a comprehensive combination of behavioral techniques; also known as Applied Behavioral Analysis (ABA) programs or early intensive behavioral intervention
Joint Attention Intervention	Teaching the individual to respond to the nonverbal social initiations of others or initiate interactions with shared attention
Modeling	Having an adult or child model a behavior for the individual with ASD to copy
Naturalistic Teaching Strategies	Using child-directed interactions in a natural environment to teach skills; examples include modeling play and providing a stimulating environment
Peer Training	Teaching children without disabilities how to play and interact with children with ASD; includes programs such as Integrated Play Groups™ and peer-mediated social interaction (PMII)
Pivotal Response Treatment (PRT)	Building skills and producing behavior improvements by targeting key (pivotal) areas such as motivation to engage in social interaction; focus includes parental involvement in natural environments
Schedules	Presenting task lists or steps to complete a specific activity
Self-Management	Teaching individuals with ASD to regulate their own behavior by tracking when they are on-track or off-track for meeting a particular goal using such things as tokens and checkmarks; includes a reward (reinforcement system)
Story-Based Intervention	Using written descriptions of expectations for a particular situation; examples include Social Stories that explain the "who," "what," "where," when," and "why" of a situation

Emerging Treatments: Treatments that may be effective, but without sufficient empirical evidence to demonstrate this	
Term	*Quick Definition*
Augmentative and Alternative Communication Device (AAC)	Using low-tech devices like pictures or high-tech devices like computers to facilitate communication
Cognitive Behavioral Intervention Package	Changing thought patterns that are unrealistic or negative to positively impact emotions and/or life functioning
Developmental Relationship-Based Treatment	Techniques based on developmental theory that emphasize the building of social relationships; also referred to as Denver Model, Developmental, Individual Differences, Relationship-Based (DIR) Floortime, Relationship Development Intervention (RDI), or Responsive Teaching
Exercise	Increasing physical activity to increase positive behavior or reduce inappropriate behavior
Exposure Package	Requiring the individual to face anxiety-provoking situations while preventing the person from responding with inappropriate strategies used in the past
Imitation-Based Interaction	Teaching by having a child imitate the words and/or actions of an adult
Initiation Training	Directly teaching the individual to initiate interactions with peers
Language Training (Production or Production and Understanding)	Using techniques such as oral communication training or echo relevant word training to increase speech or to increase both speech and comprehension of language
Massage/Touch Therapy	Providing deep tissue stimulation
Multi-Component Package	Combining more than one treatment from different fields of interest
Music Therapy	Using music, rhythm, or songs to teach skills and meet goals
Peer-Mediated Instructional Arrangement	Also called peer tutoring, involving same-age peers in teaching academic skills
Picture Exchange Communication System	Using behavioral principles and words/images to teach functional communication; also called PECs

(Continued)

(Continued)

Term	Quick Definition
Reductive Package	Reducing problem behaviors using materials such as water mist and ammonia without trying to teach a new "positive" behavior
Scripting	Developing scripts for a specific skill or situation that are practiced in advance
Sign Instruction	Directly teaching sign language as a form of communication
Social Communication Intervention	Targeting specific areas of social communication such as reading social context or choosing topics of conversation; also referred to as social pragmatic interventions
Social Skills Package	Targeting basic social responses to build social interaction skills. Examples of targeted skills range from eye contact to maintaining conversation
Structured Teaching	Modifying the environment, materials, and presentation of material to make thinking, learning, and comprehension easier for individuals with ASD; also referred to as TEACCH method (Treatment and Education of Autistic and related Communication-Handicapped Children)
Technology-Based Treatment	Using computers or technology to present instructional material
Theory of Mind Training	Developing perspective-taking and "mind reading," the ability to imagine the thoughts and mental states of others

Unestablished Treatments: Treatments with little or no evidence in the scientific literature that allows for firm conclusions about the effectiveness of these interventions

Term	Quick Definition
Auditory Integration Training	Presenting modulated sounds through headphones to improve sensitivity to sound and sound distortion, retraining the person's auditory system
Facilitated Communication	Using a computer or keyboard while a facilitator supports the hand or arm
Gluten- and Casein-Free Diet	Eliminating foods containing gluten (wheat and related grain) and casein (milk protein) from the diet
Sensory Integrative Package	Addressing environmental over-stimulation or under-stimulation by challenging the individual to use all of his or her senses
Academic Interventions	Using traditional teaching methods to improve academic performance

Source: Adapted from Wilczynski et al. (2009).

INTERVENTION SELECTION CHECKLIST

Answer these questions to help select an intervention that is most appropriate to teach social skills to a particular student with ASD.	
Question	*Answer*
Which specific skills will be targeted?	
Is the intervention well matched to teach those skills?	
Is the intervention well matched to the student's developmental level (language and cognitive functioning)?	
Is the intervention appropriate to the learner's status as a beginner or intermediate?	
Is the strategy supported by research?	
If the strategy is *not* supported by research, what is the rationale or logic for using it?	
Other considerations	

Source: Adapted from Bellini (2008).

REFERENCES

American Psychiatric Association. (2013). *Diagnostic and statistical manual of mental disorders* (5th ed.). Arlington, VA: Author.

Anderson, C. (2012). IAN research report: Bullying and children with ASD. Retrieved from http://www.iancommunity.org/cs/ian_research_reports/ian_research_report_bullying

Bellini, S. (2008). *Building social relationships: A systematic approach to teaching social interaction skills to children and adolescents with autism spectrum disorders.* Shawnee Mission, KS: Autism Asperger.

Centers for Disease Control. (2014). Autism spectrum disorder: Data and statistics. Retrieved from http://www.cdc.gov/ncbddd/autism/data.html

Doyle, B. T., & Iland, E. (2004). *Autism spectrum disorders from A to Z.* Arlington, TX: Future Horizons.

Haddon, M. (2004). *The curious incident of the dog in the night-time.* New York, NY: Vintage Books.

Iland, E. (2011). *Drawing a blank: Improving comprehension for readers on the autism spectrum.* Shawnee Mission, KS: Autism Asperger.

Iland, E. (2013a). *Be safe teaching edition.* Saugus, CA: Camino Cinema.

Iland, E. (2013b). *No more Asperger's?* What educational therapists need to know about the DSM-V. *Educational Therapist Journal, 34*(1), 12–17.

Individuals with Disabilities Education Improvement Act of 2004. 20 U.S.C. §1401 *et seq.* (2004).

Mesibov, G., & Shea, V. (2008). Structured teaching and environmental supports. In K. D. Buron & P. Wolfberg (Eds.), *Learners on the autism spectrum: Preparing highly qualified educators* (pp. 114–137). Shawnee Mission, KS: Autism Asperger.

Minshew, W., & Williams, D. L. (2008). Brain-behavior connections in autism. In K. D. Buron & P. Wolfberg (Eds.), *Learners on the autism spectrum: Preparing highly qualified educators* (pp. 44–65). Shawnee Mission, KS: Autism Asperger.

Murawski, W. W., & Spencer, S. (2011). *Collaborate, communicate, and differentiate: How to increase student learning in today's diverse schools.* Thousand Oaks, CA: Corwin.

National Education Association. (2006). The puzzle of autism. Retrieved from http://www.nea.org/assets/docs/HE/autismpuzzle.pdf

National Research Council. (2001). *Educating children with autism.* Washington, DC: National Academy Press.

U.S. Department of Education. (2005). Part 300/D/300.324. Retrieved from http://idea.ed.gov/explore/home

Wilczynski, S., Green, G., Ricciardi, J., Boyd, B., Hume, A., Ladd, M., . . . Rue, H. (2009). *National Standards Report:* The national standards project—Addressing the need for evidence-based practice guidelines for autism spectrum disorders. Retrieved from http://www.nationalautismcenter.org/pdf/NAC%20Standards%20Report.pdf

RECOMMENDED READINGS

* Prizant, B. M., Wetherby, A. M., Rubin, E., Laurent, A. C., & Rydell, P. J. (2006). *The SCERTS® model: A comprehensive educational approach for children with autism spectrum disorders.* Baltimore, MD: Paul Brookes.

* Sargent, L. R., Perner, D., Fesgen, M., & Cook, T. (2012). *Social skills for students with autism spectrum disorders and other developmental disabilities.* Arlington, VA: Council for Exceptional Children.

* Winner, M. G. (2006). *Thinking about you thinking about me.* San Jose, CA: Author.

GO EVEN FURTHER WITH THIS TOPIC ON THE WORLD WIDE WEB

- www.autisminternetmodules.org
- www.autism-society.org
- www.autismnow.org
- www.cdc.gov/ncbddd/autism/index.html
- www.BeSafeTheMovie.com

THE Apps WE LOVE

- Aacorn
- Choiceworks Calendar
- Heckerty
- Rufus Robot
- Autismapps.wikispaces.com

18

Developing Deaf Education

Flavia Fleischer, Will Garrow, and Rachel Friedman Narr

California State University, Northridge

WHAT REALLY WORKS IN DEAF EDUCATION IN THE ELEMENTARY CLASSROOM

Who Are the Deaf Students?

Xavier, a third-grade student, has just moved to your school from another state. Normally that wouldn't concern you at all; you are used to, and welcome, new students all the time. This time, however, you're nervous. You've just found out that Xavier is Deaf—and you don't know sign language at all! Actually, you don't even know if he signs. What if he reads lips? Or has a cochlear implant? You certainly assume he will have an interpreter with him all day. Wait. Can you? You know you want Xavier to have the best experience in your class possible, but you're at a loss. What will you do? The first thing you will do is breathe. Next, you'll read this chapter.

Deaf students, who also include hard-of-hearing* children, constitute approximately 78,000 of the U.S. public school population in the 50 states who receive services under Individuals with Disabilities Education Act (IDEA) Part B (Government Accountability Report, 2011). There are even more if you include the number of Deaf children in the District of Columbia, schools of the Bureau of Indian Education, and the U.S. territories (Government Accountability Report, 2011). Don't fret. To teach students who are Deaf, you don't need to be an expert. Leave that to specialists. You are Xavier's teacher; you just need to know how to teach *him* best.

Key Term

* The term *Deaf* is an umbrella term that includes both Deaf and hard-of-hearing people from diverse backgrounds. The authors believe that the other terms used to describe or refer to Deaf people are artificial and not how the community identifies themselves. So, avoid any issues, and just use the term Deaf.

Despite varying amounts and types of hearing losses, most Deaf children are naturally attuned to information that they can access spatially in their environment using various ways of perception. Though most Deaf students access information through visual perception (their eyes), Deaf-Blind children access information spatially using tactile perception (their hands). Auditory access (getting information through their ears) for Deaf children is unnatural, limited, and exhausting, even for children who use hearing aids or cochlear implants. Let's stop there for a second. This bears repeating. *Getting information aurally is unnatural and difficult, sometimes extremely so, <u>even</u> for kids who have hearing aids or cochlear implants!* Most Deaf children with hearing aids and/or cochlear implants do not acquire an auditory language naturally. So what does that mean to you, as Xavier's teacher? Well, many studies have shown that Deaf children are better able to learn auditory languages, if they are accessible, when they have signed language(s) (Humphries et al., 2014; Johnson, 2006; Lane, 1999). So one of the things you can do is find out pretty quickly if Xavier uses American Sign Language (ASL), and then you can support a continuation of the use of ASL in addition to English.

Deaf children need access to a community that will enable them to naturally acquire knowledge and tools to capitalize upon their skills. If you don't sign and there are no other children in the third grade who do, where will Xavier find this community? His parents? Actually, in contrast to most families, Deaf children are primarily born into families who do not immediately have the socially based experience, knowledge, and tools to raise Deaf children who are spatially oriented. In other words, they are born into hearing families where the Deaf child is probably the first Deaf person that family has ever met. Did you know that approximately 96% of Deaf children have hearing parents (Mitchell & Karchmer, 2004)? Because our society is primarily a hearing one, and therefore has a socially constructed bias toward hearing, Deaf children are often put through various early intervention and rehabilitative programs in hopes that they can change their natural spatial inclination to become more auditorially inclined (Lane, 1999; Lane, Hoffmeister, & Bahan, 1996), but they frequently struggle in auditory-based programs, leaving them language delayed, psychologically traumatized, and unprepared for socialization and lifelong education (Komesaroff, 2007; Lane, 1999; Leigh, 2009; Schick, Marschark, & Spencer, 2006). Eek! You don't want that. So again, you struggle with what you can do for Xavier to help him be successful in your traditional third-grade classroom.

You look at Xavier's cumulative file and find out that, like most other Deaf students, Xavier's family is indeed hearing. You make a note to yourself to meet right away with the parents to find out what types of opportunities Xavier has to be with other people who are Deaf. You also realize that, just as you tried to learn more about Latino/a culture when Juan joined your class 6 years ago and Armenian culture when Ashot joined your class last year, you are going to have to pretty quickly learn more about Deaf culture and how it will impact you and Xavier. Why don't we give you a quick introduction now?

First of all, very few Deaf children are born into an environment where they can gain access to and acquire the socially based experience, knowledge, and tools to support their spatial orientation, enabling them to become successful adults. Families and schools can attain these perspectives, but it requires a commitment to understanding the world from a Deaf-centric perspective. Yep—Deaf-centric. If you are not Deaf, you are likely understanding the world from the position of a hearing-centric perspective. That's an important thing to realize right from the get-go. To provide Xavier with the valuable tools he may need, it would help if you are familiar with what is called Deaf Community Cultural Wealth (DCCW). DCCW is adapted from Yosso's (2005) work on Community Cultural Wealth, which addresses the rich knowledge, skills, and tools that minority communities pass down through generations. The Deaf community has naturally developed DCCW through centuries of navigating and networking through global spaces that are not designed by, for, and of Deaf people. DCCW allows Deaf people to navigate and flourish in hearing-centric spaces and to be productive, contributing citizens in our society. Because most Deaf kids are born and raised in hearing-centric societies, most don't have access to DCCW. As a result, they are less able to acquire and develop the essential tools that will allow them to navigate through various spaces—including a mainstream school environment—successfully. To complicate matters further, we have seen the practice of placing Deaf children in general education classrooms with hearing children become more commonplace since the inception of Public Law 94–142 in the early 1970s, also known as the Education for all Handicapped Children Act, later revised as the Individuals with Disabilities Education Act (IDEA). This practice was first known as mainstreaming and later called inclusion. Although it is by far the most common educational practice for Deaf children, it rarely provides them with optimal education access. We know, we know. You are thinking, "What?! But that's why Xavier is in my general education third-grade class! Does this mean he shouldn't be there? Or that I can't teach him?" Patience, our friend. Read on for more information.

As of 2002, approximately 75% of Deaf children were mainstreamed and received special education services for support in general education classrooms for at least a part of their day (Karchmer & Mitchell, 2003). The goal of a Deaf child's education tragically becomes mitigating hearing loss, rather than utilizing and optimizing their strengths as spatial beings (Johnson, 2006). We say "tragically" because this means schools are operating from a deficit perspective, rather than a strengths approach. Because we are, for the most part, a hearing-centric society, we think of being Deaf as a disability, rather than helping kids capitalize on their spatial strengths.

Furthermore, Deaf children in mainstream environments do not have access to peers and adults who are able to model, teach, and discuss with them how to navigate through society. This doesn't mean that Xavier won't have friends or adults who care; it does however mean it may be unlikely that Xavier will have other peers or adults who are Deaf to show him the way, to connect with him on a spatial level, or to understand his challenges. And man, there will be challenges! Between mainstream education and the children's home environment, there are several barriers for Deaf children that prevent them from accessing, acquiring, and developing DCCW, the way they might if they were in a Deaf school or Deaf environment.

The goal of this chapter is to help familiarize you with the common challenges in educating Deaf children so that YOU can facilitate a Deaf child's acquisition and access to DCCW, in this case, Xavier. So, what's your first step—before Xavier even enters your classroom? Understanding what DCCW is and then using this as a foundation for working with Xavier, or any other Deaf children you may teach in the future, will help mitigate some of their challenges. The goal, as with any of your other students, is to support their learning and socialization processes and needs.

Let's start. DCCW is comprised of six capitals: linguistic, social, familial, navigational, aspirational, and resistant (adapted from Yosso, 2005). Whoa, wait. Let's back up. What is capital? In a nutshell, capitals are socially accumulated assets and resources that can help you move forward in society. In this situation though, we are talking about those capitals that promote DCCW. Each capital constitutes an integral part of building a whole, well-rounded Deaf child with the skills and tools to flourish and succeed.

DEAF COMMUNITY CULTURAL WEALTH: THE SIX CAPITALS

Each example of capital is important for Deaf students to move forward academically, behaviorally, emotionally, and socially. Our job as teachers is to learn more about them and consider how we can maximize them in our classrooms. Here, we briefly introduce each one, but check out Six Capitals for Building Deaf Cultural Capital Wealth (DCCW) on page 298, where we offer concrete strategies for what you can do.

Linguistic Capital. Developing complex cognitive skills, socialization for positive self-development, and self-awareness are arguably the most critical aspects of development in childhood. These skills cannot be attained without linguistic capital. Even with hearing aids and cochlear implants, Deaf children do not have full and natural access to spoken languages. Naturally developed signed language is crucial to help ensure their linguistic and cognitive development. This means that you will want to encourage Xavier, his classroom peers, and his family members to use sign language in addition to any spoken language that is used around or with him. This may be the time to sign up for that ASL course you've always thought of taking!

Social Capital. Having access to and gaining social capital allows children to meet their social developmental milestones all the way into adulthood. Most Deaf children do not have full, natural access to language, causing linguistic delays, which frequently result in cognitive delays, thus making it very difficult for Deaf children to make sense of their social experiences and environment. Clearly then, you need to make sure that Xavier has an opportunity to communicate frequently with his grade-level peers. What interests him? If all the boys in your class are into Legos, talk to Xavier's mom about hosting a Lego party and inviting some of his classmates.

Familial Capital. Familial capital involves the concept of kinship composed of a network of people who are caring, invested in, and supportive of the community and of the individuals within the community. Kinship can be fostered within and between families, friends, and through sports, school, and other social community settings (Yosso, 2005). Kinship comes from a networked support system that provides the ability and opportunity to discuss one's feelings, thoughts, and ideas in depth, and to receive supporting feedback in return. Kinship provides encouragement to try new ideas or experiences, as well as to overcome challenges. In this case then, you need to make sure that Xavier knows that you care about him, that you are open to discuss his feelings, and that he is part of a bigger network of very successful Deaf individuals.

Aspirational Capital. Aspirational capital allows one to have dreams, hopes, and goals "in face of perceived and real barriers" (Yosso, 2005, p. 77). This ability allows a child to persevere and resist negativity, to go beyond their immediate circumstances complete with social barriers to attain higher education and better opportunities. Despite good intentions, but poor educational environments for Deaf children, current society has inherently low expectations for Deaf children. This sends a message that their futures are limited. Of course, this is unfounded and has been proven to be incorrect again and over again by Deaf people who have held on to their aspirational capital. Yes, being in a Deaf school might provide Xavier with a peer group who can communicate with him more easily, but the reality is that he is with you in the typical mainstream classroom. So, let's make the most of it! Never assume being Deaf means Xavier cannot do what other children do. It's just a difference—like the fact that Sarah has two moms, Gunther just moved here from Germany, and Roberto is an albino. So what? What is more important is that Xavier knows, like all of your third graders, that he can be whatever he wants to be—if he does his homework tonight, that is!

Navigational Capital. Navigational capital is the ability to maneuver through social institutions (Yosso, 2005). Social institutions are designed for people who have been perceived as representing the norm. Imagine you are Deaf. How would you navigate your school? How many bells ring to tell you to come in from recess? How many teachers raise their voice to tell you to get in line for lunch? How many videos are shown for fun without any captioning? Hmmmm. A lot, right? So, what can you do to change this?

Resistant Capital. Resistant capital provides the emotional and psychological ability to resist and challenge negative slights toward a person and their communities. It allows a person the opportunity to maintain their dignity and to create spaces that transform negative views of themselves into an understanding of their own great potential. Deaf children often don't acquire resistant capital because they don't have opportunities to socialize with peers and adults who have such skills and/or knowledge. Bullying is rampant in both elementary and secondary schools. Anyone who is different in any way has a strong chance of being a target. So, knowing that, prep your class. Prep Xavier. Prep his family members. Be proactive and *teach* him how to respond. That's something you can certainly do—you're a teacher after all!

🛑 WHAT YOU SHOULD AVOID AT ALL COSTS

- ✘ **STOP thinking that the Deaf world is just the Hearing world without sound.** Go back and reread the part where we remind you that you need to try to be Deaf-centric for a bit in order to realize that your entire frame of reference is one of a hearing person. Then, when you've got the right frame of mind, come back and read the rest of our tips.
- ✘ **STOP having tunnel vision** on the development of spoken language, focusing on repetitive drills of listening and speaking skills, rather than on comprehension and analysis of content. Instead, we should view spoken language development as a supplementary skill that may or may not provide overall benefits to a Deaf child. Signed language is the only fully accessible language

that Deaf children, regardless of their hearing abilities, will be able to access, acquire, learn naturally, and use to express themselves naturally. (That means without intense amounts of remediation, exhaustion, and potential frustration.) Having a high aptitude in signed languages starting at an early age has been proven to be a bona fide linguistic and cognitive foundation and platform for the acquisition of many other integral educational and life skills, such as literacy skills. Yes, being able to sign actually helps Deaf kids read too!

✗ **DON'T think that just because a Deaf student has a cochlear implant or hearing aid, he can easily hear what you are saying.** Cochlear implants and hearing aids are not miracle cures. More often than not, they can't understand what you are saying because the ability to hear is not the same as the ability to understand speech. Even if a child can repeat what you've said, that doesn't mean they *understand* what you've said. The very assumption that the ability to hear equates to the ability to understand sounds often leads to late detection of actual language delays and overlooks many other learning issues. We are reminded of a student we recently worked with who has a cochlear implant and told us (through sign), "I have no idea what my teacher says most of the time!"

✗ **STOP assuming that signed language is the cause of problems in developing English literacy skills.** The level of Deaf children's actual linguistic and cognitive skills is the root of the problem. Many Deaf children are linguistically and cognitively delayed because of late access, exposure, and use of a fully accessible language (spoken languages are rarely accessible to them), and the delays complicate the encoding and the decoding required to make meaning from print. Deaf people with early and robust access to signed language develop high levels of literacy.

✗ **STOP thinking that signed language can be acquired and learned by Deaf children at any age.** Late acquisition of signed language by Deaf children is often marked by grammatical errors across all linguistic aspects. Deaf children rarely catch up with the native signers in overall linguistic competency as well as in literacy skills. Linguistic delay causes Deaf children to struggle with acquiring spoken languages too. Ultimately what we are saying is, just like it is important for hearing children to learn language right way, the same holds true for Deaf children—just with signed language!

✗ **STOP assuming that Deaf children struggle with socialization because they are Deaf.** Deaf children are frequently in an environment that doesn't allow for the socialization processes to occur naturally. Again, the inaccessibility of the language used in the environment and the misunderstandings our society has about Deaf children lead to struggles with socialization. Help them make friends!

✖ **DON'T assume that if Deaf children are playing with other children, they are able to fully access the processes and norms to acquire and learn the integral social skills and strategies.** Just because Deaf children may participate in playtime with hearing children does not mean they are able to make sense of the norms, conventions, and processes. Check to find out what is actually happening and how you might better facilitate the experience.

✖ **DON'T assume that Deaf children have opportunities to socialize outside of school.** Many Deaf children grow up feeling isolated from their peers and, sadly, from their families. Deaf children may be able to participate in playtime together with hearing children, but as they get older, they are frequently set aside from other children because of a lack of communication and presence of social stigma that is generally associated with Deaf children. They may have acquaintances, but they rarely develop close, deep bonds with their peers.

✖ **STOP leaving the responsibility of learning how to communicate and socialize with Deaf children to the peers.** Many teachers and administrators assume that if Deaf children and hearing children are left to socialize, they will learn how to communicate with each other. When a situation complicates the Deaf children's ability to participate fully in groups, such as not having interpreters present, this often leads the teacher to allow Deaf children to work individually. This is detrimental to Deaf children, as well as to the other children, as opportunities for them to learn how to work in groups are lost.

✖ **DON'T assume Deaf children have access to familial support system to talk about issues that concern them.** Many Deaf children struggle to communicate openly and freely with their families due to lack of language access. A vast majority of the parents of Deaf children do not make the time to learn signed language, limiting the communication opportunities for Deaf children. It may be helpful to Deaf children if you are able to provide their families, for example, with ways to learn signed language, information on Deaf community events, contacts for counselors and psychologists who sign, or helpful videos that are captioned.

✖ **DON'T limit the potential of Deaf children.** There are so many misconceptions about Deaf children and their abilities or potential. For instance, many adults cannot conceive Deaf children as pilots for big airline companies or as trial lawyers. These societally imposed limitations and barriers only serve to restrict the potential of Deaf children, and our society loses the valuable contributions that they could have made.

- ✖ **DON'T assume that Deaf children have an understanding of how to navigate through spaces.** Since nearly all of our spaces in our society are designed for and cater to hearing people, Deaf children must acquire a different set of tools and skills that allows them to navigate with success and without sacrificing their dignity. Try to figure out what changes can be made to your school, curricula, processes, and rules that will enable *all* of your children, including those who are Deaf, to be successful.

- ✖ **STOP leaving teaching, feedback, and assessment responsibilities to the interpreters, teacher aides, itinerant teachers, and tutors.** Because many teachers and administrators do not have opportunities to receive an in-depth training and education to prepare them to work with Deaf students in their classrooms, it is naturally easier to leave it to others who may be viewed as having more experience and access. However, remember that teacher aides and interpreters do not have the extensive training to do what teachers and administrators do. Furthermore, in leaving teaching, feedback, and assessment responsibilities to others, a message is sent to Deaf children that you are not invested in them.

- ✖ **STOP talking to the interpreter.** They are there purely as a way for you to communicate to the student. They are not there to edit your communication, share the child's feelings without their permission, or tattle on the child. Nor are they there to design curriculum, grade papers, or tutor the student. That's your job!

- ✖ **STOP using materials designed solely for hearing children.** Many teachers don't think in advance about how many times they rely on their voice, or the bell, or even audio in a movie. Put on headphones and see what you are missing.

- ✖ **STOP raising your voice when speaking to a student who is Deaf.** It doesn't help.

- ✖ **DON'T allow Deaf children to succumb to or accept negative views of their abilities.** Many people find it difficult to support Deaf children due to their lack of experience, knowledge, and realistic expectations, making it a challenge to turn negative views into positive ones. With all of the negativity that Deaf children face every day from others, it is very easy for them to internalize and believe in the messages.

SO WHAT EXACTLY AM I SUPPOSED TO DO WITH XAVIER AND OTHER DEAF CHILDREN?

- ✓ **RETHINK how you introduce and teach English literacy skills to Deaf children.** Our current approaches often employ hearing-centric approaches that generally work well and consistently only for hearing children but are not applicable or beneficial for Deaf children. Instead, seek strategies that capitalize on their strengths, like using American Sign Language early and consistently in childhood. Ask your school to offer ASL classes for families. They will certainly be helpful to families of Deaf children, but they may also be beneficial for those families who want to become better friends with individuals who are Deaf.

✓ **OFFER signed language instruction to all students.** Signed language has consistently been proven as the most accessible language and the only modality that ensures full and natural linguistic and cognitive development for Deaf children. It's guaranteed and risk free! Deaf children with a strong foundation in signed language are better able to acquire literacy skills in their second, third (and even more!) languages. Why not offer it to all children so more students are learning this important language and learning to communicate with one another?

✓ **IMPROVE socialization processes by including signs in social situations.** To make social situations and events more fully accessible to Deaf children, signed language is necessary. To ensure a linguistically accessible social environment that is more inclusive of all children, teach them ways to communicate without requiring hearing. Football, basketball, and baseball players all have signs they use (e.g., "T" for time out), so capitalize on that and teach students ways to communicate so all can play and participate.

✓ **DO directly address and discuss social norms and processes with all children.** Explicit discussions of the social norms and processes in a given environment will help ensure that all children, including Deaf children, gain an understanding of the processes employed by society. How can you get Deaf children's attention without yelling at them? What are some ways we can know that it is time to clean up without a bell sounding? What do you do if someone has been mean or bullied you?

✓ **PROVIDE parents with ideas and support for various socialization opportunities that are fully accessible for Deaf children to use after school.** Many parents do not know where they can find socialization opportunities for their Deaf children after school. Develop a list of opportunities to share with them and encourage them to be proactive in seeking out various Deaf community events as well as connecting with other parents raising Deaf children. Often, Deaf community events will provide exposure to a wide range of peers, both Deaf and hearing, that allows for positive and accessible interactions. You may even want to attend some of these events yourself!

✓ **COMMUNICATE!** Learning how to interact and communicate with diverse people is an important skill for any child to acquire and have. Create opportunities to expose and teach everyone different

Making Connections

Check out Chapter 12 on Inclusion

methods of communication. As an example, instead of only using spoken language for group discussions, encourage the use of gestures, writing, drawing, and other communication skills to ensure that Deaf children have direct opportunities to participate.

✓ **INCLUDE signed language lessons in your curriculum.** Lessons in signed language will allow you to create an environment where Deaf children feel valued and included and at the same time provide wonderful linguistic and cognitive benefits to all children. Not only that—think about how much more smoothly your class will run if all of your students use the hand sign to quietly ask to go to the bathroom, instead of yelling out "May I go potty?"

✓ **CREATE opportunities for Deaf children to receive positive emotional and psychological support.** When needed, serve as a resource for the child's familial network to help them develop tools and skills for providing Deaf children with the appropriate, positive, and nurturing support system. It is not always transparent where a family can go to get support, so be the person who provides clear and consistent support. Call on Deaf adults to help you navigate the community and supports.

✓ **EMPOWER Deaf children to understand their great human potential, intellect, and the important role they play in our society.** Incorporate lessons and discussions about the great contributions that Deaf people have made to our society and how they accomplished such contributions. Outline the ways that Deaf children are to be valued as they do bring a unique perspective to our society as do all children. Honor Deaf Americans during Deaf Awareness Month and regularly incorporate Deaf-centric themes in your curriculum. For example, introduce, teach, and discuss real-life role models that Deaf children can relate to in order to support their aspirations, and outline the various ways they can chase their dreams.

✓ **MODEL and foster behaviors that emphasize the value of civic responsibility to our society.** When Deaf children are valued as important contributors to our society because of their unique relationship with the world (instead of as a problem that needs to be treated and fixed), we naturally create an environment where Deaf children feel welcomed and valued. In turn, they are more emotionally and psychologically invested in our society and are more likely to make great contributions through civic engagement activities.

✓ **DO carefully gauge your expectations for Deaf children.** On this note, it is important to point out that modifying one's social environment, activity, or an assignment to ensure access and appropriateness does not automatically translate into lowering expectations.

It may be helpful to review criteria for Universal Design for Learning (UDL) when developing a curriculum to not only ensure access to Deaf children but for all children.

Making Connections

Check out Chapter 11 on UDL

✓ **EVALUATE the materials, tools, and instruction provided to children to ensure they are accessible to all children.** Assess what Deaf children are able to access and learn through your teaching and what concepts are not clear to them to ensure they are able to continue to navigate through their own education. Are all of your videos captioned? Are announcements made over an intercom also provided in sign language? Are assignments given that require listening to a podcast or watching a YouTube video or making an oral presentation—if so, are these accessible to the Deaf student?

✓ **TALK to the student directly.** Even if you do not sign, make sure you are communicating with Deaf students by making eye contact with them and watching them as they sign to you. Talk to students directly and let the interpreter sign. Don't worry if they need to look at the interpreter to see what you said; keep your eyes on them.

✓ **USE best practices with the interpreter.** Not sure what they are? No worries! We provided a handy checklist to use to remind yourself what to do or not do when working with an interpreter. Copy the handout on page 300 titled Strategies for Working with Interpreters and post it near your desk in the class.

SIX CAPITALS FOR BUILDING DEAF CULTURAL CAPITAL WEALTH (DCCW)

Capital	Issues	What You Can Do in the Mainstream/General Education Classroom
Linguistic	Studies show that Deaf children with native as well as early acquisition and proficiency in signed languages are better able to learn and use spoken languages (only if it is accessible). The lack of consistent linguistic input and access can account for the majority of linguistic and cognitive delays that are found among many Deaf children.	Use ASL signs with your whole class for letters, numbers, to show readiness, to ask to go to the bathroom, etc. Encourage Deaf children to teach signs to their peers. Allow Deaf children to sign their answers, even if their interpreter then says them in English. Respond directly to the children. Encourage parents to learn sign language and encourage their children to find peers who sign.
Social	Deaf children often exhibit delayed social skills development due to lack of access to their social environment and the feedback it provides. The social feedback allows children to continue to develop and adjust their understanding of self and gain confidence in this process. As their skills develop, children are able to learn how to positively navigate through relationships with peers.	Utilize Cooperative Learning groups, and make sure Deaf children are included and are an integral part. Find out what the Deaf children like, and put them with peers who share their interests. Invite Deaf children to do a Show and Tell or other similar activity about their interests and strengths (have the other kids do it too!).
Familial/ Kinship	A struggle to develop true kinship with their own families is in many ways a unique experience for Deaf children. Within some families and the larger community, there may be a sense that kinship is based on feelings of pity and low expectations, with a focus on what people feel they are lacking rather than on their significance and full human potential.	Encourage the Deaf children's families to come visit your class, to give you strategies, and to tell you what their Deaf child is good at doing. Do not view being Deaf as a problem but merely as an important part of human variation like being Latino and speaking Spanish. Invite other Deaf people into the class to talk about their challenges, successes, and what worked for them.

Capital	Issues	What You Can Do in the Mainstream/General Education Classroom
Navigational	Many Deaf children lack navigational capital for one simple reason—the hearing "norm" has a completely different skill set that is often not accessible, not applicable to, or not usable by Deaf children. Since their immediate network and community are most frequently hearing people who don't have any experience with navigational capital for Deaf children, they don't have opportunities to acquire the skill set.	Tune out sounds one day and see if you can figure out what aspects of your class or the school rely solely on auditory cues. Does your school use bells or music for transitions? Do you rely on your voice to get attention? Once you know what they are, you can work with Deaf children to come up with alternatives. Have your elementary students "experience" what it is like to be different. Ask them to go around with earplugs in, then blindfolds, then in a wheelchair; have them write with their mouths or watch a show with the sound off. Then talk about what these differences were like.
Aspirational	Because of societal views, Deaf children are often told explicitly and reminded repeatedly that they are limited in what they can accomplish. As a result of these repeated messages of inability and limitations, many Deaf children do not gain aspirational capital and, more often than not, have little resilience.	Collect resources that show successful Deaf actors, scientists, ballerinas, mathematicians, professors, and other jobs; allow any child in class to read and report on these materials. Invite guest lecturers or family members who are Deaf to come in and share their successes and challenges.
Resistant	Deaf children experience negative slights directed at them but have not yet had opportunities to observe, acquire, and learn resistant skills and strategies in order to deflect and transform the slights.	Talk to all students about their words and actions, about bullying, and about how to respond. Ask individuals in the Deaf community the best way to respond if someone talks about you, or to the interpreter instead of you, or says "Read my lips." Talk to Deaf children directly about how people can be mean and what their responses can be to change others' attitudes and behaviors.

STRATEGIES FOR WORKING WITH INTERPRETERS

☐ Thank the interpreter for their work. It's not an easy task.

☐ Ask where the interpreter should sit or stand so that the student can see the interpreter as well as you throughout the lesson.

☐ Ask what works best when you want to move around the room.

☐ Talk to the student, not the interpreter. Have eye contact with the student when you are communicating with him, even if he has to look at the interpreter's signing.

☐ Make sure both the student and the interpreter know you are more than willing to repeat what was not understood and come up with a word or signal that means they would appreciate a repeat.

☐ Avoid speaking too quickly, even when you are excited about a topic.

☐ Avoid making the interpreter teach the student; that's your job.

☐ Make sure both the interpreter and the student know that you expect the interpreter to interpret and that is it. Questions should be directed to you, and you do not want the interpreter helping with homework, giving answers to quizzes, and the like.

☐ Provide the interpreter with any written materials in advance when possible. The more time the interpreter has to look over materials, learn difficult words that will need fingerspelling, or concepts that will need explaining, the better.

☐ If there will be videos or other visual material, give the interpreter a heads-up and a chance to watch it in advance if possible. Try and get all materials captioned, but recognize that young children who do not yet read won't be accessing this material at all.

☐ Keep the interpreter in the loop, but avoid asking them to be the liaison with the family. Again, that is your job and you should directly communicate with the child's family members—for good news or bad.

☐ Find out what the process is for when the interpreter will be absent. Too often, no one thinks about this in advance, and then the student is left missing out on a whole day of instruction because there was no sub when the interpreter was home sick.

☐ Again, thank the interpreter for her work.

REFERENCES

Government Accountability Report. (2011). Deaf and hard of hearing children: Federal support for developing language and literacy. Retrieved from http://www.gao.gov/assets/320/318707.pdf

Humphries, T., Kushalnagaer, P., Mathur, G., Napoli, D. J., Padden, C., & Rathmann, C. (2014). Ensuring language acquisition for deaf children: What linguists can do. *Language, 90*(2), e31–e52.

Johnson, R. (2006). Cultural constructs that impede discussions about variability in speech-based educational models for deaf children with cochlear implants. *Perspectiva, 24,* 29–80.

Karchmer, M. A., & Mitchell, R. E. (2003). Demographic and achievement characteristics of deaf and hard of hearing students. In M. Marschark & P. Spencer (Eds.), *Oxford handbook of deaf studies, language, and education* (pp. 21–37). New York, NY: Oxford University Press.

Komesaroff, L. (2007). *Surgical consent: Bioethics and cochlear implantation.* Washington, DC: Gallaudet University Press.

Lane, H. (1999). *Mask of benevolence: Disabling the deaf community.* San Diego, CA: DawnSign Press.

Lane, H., Hoffmeister, R., & Bahan, B. (1996). *A journey into the DEAF-WORLD.* San Diego, CA: DawnSign Press.

Leigh, I. (2009). *Identity and deafness.* Oxford, England: Oxford University Press.

Mitchell, R. E., & Karchmer, M. A. (2004). Chasing the mythical ten percent: Parental hearing status of deaf and hard of hearing students in the United States. *Sign Language Studies, 4*(2), 138–163.

Schick, B., Marschark, M., & Spencer, P. (2006). *Advances in the sign language development of deaf children.* New York, NY: Oxford University Press.

Yosso, T. (2005). Whose culture has capital? A critical race theory discussion of community cultural wealth. *Race Ethnicity and Education, 8*(1), 69–91.

RECOMMENDED READINGS

* Bahan, B., Bauman, H-D., & Montenegro, F. (Directors). (2008). *Autism unveiled* [DVD]. San Diego, CA: DawnSign Press.

* Holcomb, T. K. (2013). *Introduction to American deaf culture.* New York, NY: Oxford University Press.

* Siegel, L. M. (2008). *The human right to language: Communication access for deaf children.* Washington, DC: Gallaudet University Press.

* Through Your Child's Eyes: American Sign Language. (2011). Produced by DJ Kurs in cooperation with California State University, Northridge and the California Department of Education. Retrieved from www.throughyourchildseyes.com

GO EVEN FURTHER WITH THIS TOPIC ON THE WORLD WIDE WEB

- www.VL2.gallaudet.edu
- www.gallaudet.edu/clerc_center.html
- www.nad.org
- www.rid.org
- www.deafhoodfoundation.org/Deafhood/Home.html

THE Apps WE LOVE

- iASL
- ASL Pro
- ASL Dictionary
- Hamilton Mobile CapTel
- Subtitles
- Caption Fish
- Closed Capp

19

Superb Social Skills Instruction

Michelle Dean

California State University, Channel Islands

WHAT REALLY WORKS IN SOCIAL SKILLS IN THE ELEMENTARY CLASSROOM

Strategies for Children With Social Challenges

School is a great place to make friends—children meet in classrooms, play or hang out during recess, eat together at lunch, or chit-chat after school. Unstructured social environments allow children to identify common interests, form peer groups, and work through disagreements (Spencer, Bowker, Rubin, Booth-LaForce, & Laursen, 2013). Making friends comes naturally to many children. Other children, however, have a difficult time making friends. What happens to the 8-year-old who still doesn't know how to ask someone to play? Lacking social competence, they do not know what to do during unstructured times at school. Consequently, children with social challenges struggle to make and keep friends.

It's easy to take the skills needed to socialize for granted. Think about all the skills needed to have a conversation. We show interest in and try to understand the point of view of each other, we take turns in conversation, we read body language and nonverbal cues (like eye rolling, winking, or smiling), and we adjust our own behavior to the interest of the group. For example, if everyone wants to play tag, insisting on handball is not socially appropriate. Likewise, someone who is smiling is much more approachable than someone who is furrowing their brow. For some kids though, making sense of these subtle social nuances is difficult, and they do not have all the skills needed to socialize—which are actually quite sophisticated. Rather than appearing friendly, kids who lack social competence come across as being rude, shy, or socially awkward, and consequently, they are likely to withdraw from social experiences, or be neglected or rejected by other kids (Proulx & Poulin, 2013). You've all seen these kids. They're the ones no one wants to play with!

Children with social challenges often have a hard time making and keeping friends (Kasari, Rotheram-Fuller, Locke, & Gulsrud, 2011). These kids can be fairly easy to spot—they are the kids hanging out at the edge of a group or those that are alone during free time (Bauminger, Shulman, & Agam, 2003). Children who are left out of or avoid groups have less time to practice and develop their social skills. That means that over time the gap widens between the kids who are skilled socially and the kids who are not. If we allow socially challenged children to continue to use their current repertoire of social skills—the skills that lead to rejection and/or neglect—they will continue to be left out of social groups as time progresses. And it will just get worse as they get older. In elementary school, children learn to understand the social world through play (Dunn, 2004). Adolescents, on the other hand, are more interested in hanging out and walking around and not so interested in playing games (Maccoby, 2002). Not having learned to socialize through play in elementary school will make it even more difficult to learn how to hang out in a group when these students get into middle or high school. All of the sudden, the ubiquitous "Wanna come over for a play date?" becomes so much more important!

We need to identify the kids who are having a hard time making friends and getting along with others. It's more than just helping them find a buddy, however. Social challenges can interfere with cognitive, social, and emotional development (Dunn, 2004). That means that not having friends can also affect academic achievement, getting along with teachers, and developing independence. Social incompetence is also related to long-term mental health issues (Buhs, Ladd & Herald, 2006; Mayes, Calhoun, Murray, Ahuja, & Smith, 2011). Children who are rejected in kindergarten are a lot more likely to continue to be rejected through fifth grade (Buhs et al., 2006). Experiencing years of rejection in school is difficult, and not surprisingly, can lead to school dropout, depression, and anxiety (Maag, 2006). See why we need to pay attention and intervene early? This stuff is serious!

We can't just put socially challenged children in the same room as other children and assume a simple fix. Strategies need to be tailored to the students, their specific needs, and the context in which we expect them to be social. We need to be mindful that there are a variety of reasons that cause children to have social difficulties. For example, a child with autism may have difficulty having a back and forth conversation because he or she has difficulty with perspective taking. In contrast, a noisy environment (like kids playing on the playground) may make *hear-*

Making Connections

Check out Chapter 17 on Autism Spectrum Disorder

ing the conversation difficult for a child with hearing loss. An English language learner may be familiar with textbook English, but finds kid-friendly social language (e.g., what up, dude; omg! for realz) very confusing. (I have to admit, sometimes I do too!) Each of these children may lack certain skills that are needed to have a social conversation, but the skills are different. Therefore, it is inappropriate to group these children together and teach one general social skills lesson and hope it fixes everyone's social dilemmas. At the same time, throwing all students with autism together in an "Autism classroom" makes absolutely no sense either; where exactly are these students supposed to learn social skills if they all struggle with it?

Schools are beginning to realize that social proficiency is as important as academic proficiency. Social skills interventions are an effective way to teach students socially appropriate behaviors. While there are excellent tools and resources out there, you don't need a specific social skills curriculum or a fancy (and expensive!) manual to teach social skills. There are evidence-based intervention strategies that have been effective in helping kids develop social skills. You are probably already using these strategies to teach academics, and never thought they could apply the same strategies to social skills. Therefore, the purpose of this chapter is to discuss evidence-based social skills interventions strategies and approaches that are easy to implement at school, and of course, really work.

SOCIAL STRATEGIES

Effective social skills interventions help children make friends, keep friends, and successfully manage conflicts when they arise by targeting specific skills that are socially valid—skills that are relevant to a child's everyday life (let's not use SpongeBob references with fifth graders. Minecraft or Legos . . . maybe). I know what you're thinking: If I don't have a specific curriculum that the district provides to me, how do I know what I am supposed to do? Research has taught us that high-quality social skills interventions contain a combination of the following evidence-based intervention components: direct instruction, modeling, role-play, feedback, prompting, and reward (Celeste, 2007; Chan et al., 2009). First, a social "coach" (this could be a teacher, parent, interventionist, peer, or anyone willing, able, and capable of engaging in the social intervention) introduces the targeted social behavior. Next, the coach models how to use the behavior appropriately. Make sure the child who needs the skill is given opportunities to role-play or practice the behavior. Throughout the practice sessions, the coach (yes, this is probably you!) will guide the student to use the newly learned behavior through verbal or physical prompting as needed. Finally, the coach gives the student feedback about their use of the behavior and rewards the student for using the behavior correctly. Some kids will learn new skills quickly, but others may take longer (January, Casey, & Paulson, 2011). Doesn't this all sound very similar to how to teach academics as well? If so, great! We're in familiar territory!

Another important component of social skills intervention is the environment. Effective interventionists structure the environment to facilitate social interaction and engagement. Think about it. It is easier to get to know someone when you're sitting across a table from each other than it is when you're sitting near each other at a basketball game. Environment affects the way we socialize! Because most research on social skills interventions tends to be based in clinics or controlled environments (Kasari & Smith, 2013), it is common to use "pull-out" models for the initial stages of social skills interventions at school. A student with social challenges meets with a social coach (usually a teacher or school psychologist) outside the classroom privately or in a small group, and the trainer uses a didactic approach to facilitate learning. The strength of "pull out" is that it minimizes distractions and offers a quiet setting where children can learn a new skill in a private setting. The coach and students can move through a series of social scenarios that introduce the topic and offer opportunities to practice skills. Social relationships, however, are not built in isolation. So don't limit yourself when choosing an environment. The general education classroom, the playground, or cafeteria can also be great places to learn and practice skills. When a skill is mastered in a small group or private setting, the child can test out the new skills in a natural environment (Bellini, Peters, Benner, & Hope, 2007).

Before beginning a social skills intervention, you should be clear about what skills the child needs to learn, how you intend to teach the skills, what practice opportunities will be available, and how you will measure the student's progress. Therefore, formal or informal assessments should be used to determine the child's social strengths and weaknesses, while factoring in the child's age, developmental level, and environment. On the formal side, there are standardized social skills survey instruments that parents, teachers, and the child can complete (Gresham & Elliott, 1990). Having multiple reporters fill out the survey provides a more comprehensive view of the child's social behaviors, with you observing the child at school, the parent observing the child at home, and the child describing his or her own experiences. Often school psychologists or school counselors administer these assessments, and they should be happy to share the information with you. These formal measures compare the social skills scores (social skills, problem behaviors, academic competence) of the child with social challenges to the average of a large group of children the same age.

In addition to using formal survey instruments to measure social behaviors, also watch how children socialize in natural environments like recess or lunch. In order to prevent having your perceptions of the child's social challenges cloud your observation of what the child is actually doing, observations should be systematic, with the child being observed in a certain location and at a certain time during the school day. The frequency, duration, or level of specific social behaviors should be recorded (Falkmer, Anderson, Falkmer, & Horlin, 2013; McMahon, Vismara, & Solomon, 2012). For example, if the target skill is social engagement, you would observe the child during recess and record the amount of time she was in a game, conversation, or mutually involved in an activity with other kids. Don't worry if this all seems overwhelming to you. There are professionals, such as special educators, school psychologists, and diagnosticians who do this on a regular basis. Collaborate with them, and you'll get the assessment data that you need.

🛑 BUILDING SOCIAL SKILLS AT SCHOOL: WHAT NOT TO DO

Teachers

- ✖ **STOP assuming that children *want* to be alone.** Because children with social difficulties are often isolated during recess and lunchtime, school personnel mistakenly believe that the student needs downtime and wants to be by himself or herself. Rather than *not wanting* to play, the children with social difficulties *do not know how* to play with other children.
- ✖ **STOP benching students during recess.** Benching students is a popular consequence for students who misbehave or break the rules at school. For students with social challenges, when we take away recess, we are taking away opportunities to practice social skills. Also, because students with social challenges are prone to isolation or withdrawal, benching can be viewed as a reward and, therefore, inadvertently rewarding misbehavior.

✖ **STOP assuming proximity to peers is sufficient.** Physical inclusion, on its own, does not increase social engagement (Levy-Shiff & Hoffman, 1985). In order to create an environment to promote social interactions, teachers need to structure the environment to increase socialization and to train peers and students with disabilities to socialize with each other.

✖ **STOP overlooking the girls.** Because girls are typically associated with internalizing behaviors, compliant girls with learning difficulties are easier to tolerate and to overlook (Arms, Bickett, & Graf, 2008). More attention tends to be given to boys, who are associated with externalizing behaviors. Consequently, the social difficulties of girls may be more difficult to detect than boys (Dean et al., 2014). As such, girls with disabilities are at risk for having unmet service needs (Bussing, Zima, Perwien, Belin, & Widawski, 1998) and negative outcomes (Arms et al., 2008).

✖ **STOP punishing children with social challenges for making social faux pas.** Children with social challenges are likely to misunderstand directions or violate common social norms. Instead of punishing the child, capitalize on the teachable moment and use the faux pas to inform social skills intervention.

✖ **STOP assuming social skills can only be taught in isolation.** While it is often beneficial to introduce social skills in a quiet or private setting, in order to master skills, students need to be able to practice in real-life settings. It is important to continue social training throughout the school day. Don't forget that you can use collaboration and co-teaching with a special educator to provide social skills instruction during the school day in the classroom itself.

Administrators

✖ **STOP minimizing the importance of teaching social skills.** Social competence is directly related to academic achievement and engagement and is an integral part in building independence. It is important to encourage school personnel to teach and encourage social development for all students.

✖ **STOP restricting access to play equipment.** Having a variety of toys and equipment allows children to establish a common ground, participate in activities together, and identify shared common interests. Look around. Are your playgrounds accessible for all students?

✖ **STOP discouraging adults from playing on the playground.** Adults are an excellent resource to facilitate play between students with disabilities and typically developing children. Playground monitors can promote peer engagement by starting a game or activity and inviting children to play. Students love it when their teachers play with them.

BUILDING SOCIAL SKILLS AT SCHOOL: WHAT TO DO

GO

Teachers, DO This

✓ **MAKE teaching social skills a priority.** Children with social deficits are more likely to have poor academic achievement, poor adjustment (Buhs et al., 2006), and increased loneliness and anxiety (Bauminger et al., 2003) as they move into adolescence and adulthood. Teaching social skills and providing opportunities to practice skills can improve outcomes for all students, especially those with social difficulties, who genuinely need that direct instruction. I know you're busy! But it wouldn't be that hard to incorporate social skills into collaborative group projects, now would it?

Making Connections

Check out Chapter 10 on Cooperative Learning

✓ **FIND ways to incorporate social skills into academics.** Be creative! Try to find social opportunities throughout the school day. For example, students could socialize during math. The teacher can write down math problems on one piece of paper and the answers on the other. The teacher can pass out the math problems to one side of the classroom and the answers to the others. The student assignment would be to match the problem to the answer. Have fun finding the many social opportunities throughout the school day.

✓ **UNDERSTAND how specific social difficulties impact social engagement.** Social deficits vary from child to child. Teachers need to understand what the child needs to do differently in order to build relationships and make friends. How do you do this? Watch the child during free time. Ask yourself these questions: Are they initiating conversations with others? Are they being invited to play or hang out? Are they hanging out in an area with other kids or are they alone in the corner of a library? What are the other kids doing? What does the child with social challenges need to do differently in order to join in? Maybe he needs to stop playing on the computer by himself, or maybe she needs to join a game at lunchtime. Then, think about the supports that child may need in order to try new social strategies.

✓ **USE typically developing peers.** Think about your classroom. There are always a few students who get along well with others, like to help, and are generally well liked by everyone. These students have great social skills and could be excellent peer models (Campbell & Marino, 2009). In a peer-mediated intervention, peers are trained to work with the child who has social difficulties, to socially engage, to interpret unusual social behaviors, and to accommodate play in a way that is inclusive. Researchers use the term *Peer-Mediated Intervention*. In layman's terms, this is using peers to model positive social skills. For example, a peer could help a child with social challenges participate in a game of tag, be a lunch buddy, or work collaboratively during a class project. Peer mediation has been used to increase social initiations, interactions, and to build play skills like taking turns, sharing, and other social engagement behaviors. Popular and empirically supported peer assistance strategies include peer modeling, role-play, verbal explanation, reinforcing, giving feedback, and the use of visual aids (Chan et al., 2009).

✓ **CHOOSE peers with prosocial skills.** Less socially skilled children should be in close proximity to competent children. Children who are socially excluded are at risk of being bullied, and educators should be careful to separate victims from their perpetrators (Geiger, Zimmer-Gembeck, & Crick, 2004). That said, be aware that nice kids need breaks. Be careful to not penalize a kind child by always making him or her work with the socially difficult child; vary it up. There are many students who can benefit from working on their kindness and patience skills. Share the love. Want some more ideas? Check out the websites on the Plugged In box.

Plugged In

www.circleoffriends.org

www.bestbuddies.org/

✓ **THINK about developmental appropriateness.** Socializing in preschool is very different from socializing in elementary school. In preschool, children socialize through play, and in elementary school, play becomes more complicated. Think about developmental levels and age-appropriate social skills when designing social skills intervention programs. Parents aren't always as in tune with what is developmentally appropriate for their child's age; help them out!

✓ **WORK as a team with parents.** Because of their close proximity to their children, parents are an excellent resource for modeling social behavior (Hancock & Kaiser, 2006), but they may not always know what to do. This is where you come in! Teach parents how to be supportive in helping their children practice social skills and in guiding their children through social difficulties. Working with parents helps to promote generalization (the child being able to learn new skills across a variety of settings and people) by giving the child opportunities to practice targeted skills at home and in community settings. In addition, teachers and parents working together promote consistency between home and school—that's huge.

✓ **CAPITALIZE on the moment.** Use real-life experiences and teachable moments to teach new skills and to expand on previously learned skills. Manipulate the environment to give children opportunities to practice social skills within the normal school day. For example, if a social goal is asking for something appropriately (known as *requesting*), then during a coloring activity, a teacher may pair the student with social challenges with another student. The student with social challenges will be given paper, and crayons will be given to the typically developing child. In order to color, the child with social challenges will need to ask his peer for a crayon. In turn, the typically developing peer can model appropriate requesting by asking for paper. Both children will receive natural rewards by having their requests fulfilled. A teacher should remain in close proximity to praise children for using the targeted skill and to prompt and give feedback as needed. They can also teach classroom peers how to give praise, feedback, and prompts.

Administrators, DO This

✓ **HAVE a positive attitude toward students with special needs.** As school leaders, administrator's attitudes toward students with special needs shape the school environment (Horrocks, White, & Roberts, 2008). When the principal has a positive attitude toward students with social difficulties, it sets the tone for the entire school.

✓ **EDUCATE your teachers about disabilities.** Just having a disability increases the probability that a child will have social challenges. When teachers' knowledge about disabilities is limited, it makes it difficult to set goals and expectations for the students. Training teachers about disabilities, how to make accommodations and modifications, and how to set goals and expectations will help teachers better meet the needs of the students in their class. You don't know the information yourself? No problem. Bring in professional development and make sure you stay through the whole thing.

✓ **ENCOURAGE adults to facilitate play.** Adults are an excellent resource to facilitate social engagement at school. Being aware of the isolated students, adults can structure social settings to include students with disabilities. In addition, adults can model appropriate strategies, teaching typically developing children how to engage the child with disabilities.

✓ **PROVIDE tabletop activities at recess.** Some children prefer board games or card games to ball games. One way to increase the social engagement of children with social skill deficits is to include a variety of tabletop games (a pack of Uno cards, Connect Four, chess) in the playground equipment. C'mon, wouldn't you rather supervise a rugged game of chess than a chaotic game of soccer? This is working in your favor!

Remember that it is important to identify kids who have social challenges and to intervene early. Having social challenges takes a toll on a child's development and ultimately can have long-term and life-altering consequences. So make it a priority to help kids with social challenges. You are probably already using the core components of high-quality social skills intervention to teach academics (direct instruction, modeling, guided practice, independent practice, prompting, and reward), so apply these skills to a new domain. Most importantly, teaching social skills can be fun. So get in touch with your inner child, get social, and start playing again!

ELEMENTARY SCHOOL CURRICULUM TO HELP WITH SOCIAL SKILLS

The New Social Story Book, Revised and Expanded 10th Anniversary Edition: Over 150 Social Stories That Teach Everyday Social Skills to Children With Autism or Asperger's Syndrome, and Their Peers by Carol Gray & Tony Attwood	This book was designed to be a resource for children with Autism Spectrum Disorder, but check it out. A lot of the social stories will work for any child with a social challenge.
Skillstreaming the Elementary School Child: A Guide for Teaching Prosocial Skills, 3rd Edition (with CD) by Ellen McGinnis	This is a great, evidence-based, easy-to-follow guide for teaching social skills to elementary school kids. The program includes a program book, skill cards, posters, and a student workbook. It makes planning and preparation a breeze.
The ADHD Workbook for Kids: Helping Children Gain Self-Confidence, Social Skills, and Self-Control (Instant Help . . . by Lawrence Shapiro)	This is a very helpful resource for children with inattention and hyperactivity.
Knowing Yourself, Knowing Others: A Workbook for Children With Asperger's Disorder, Nonverbal Learning Disorder, and Other Social-Skill Problems by Barbara Cooper MPS, Nancy Widdows	This is a very helpful resource to help children understand themselves, their social struggles, and to work on learning new skills.
ACCEPTS (A Curriculum for Children's Effective Peer and Teacher Skills) by Hill M. Walker	This is a great resource for teachers and coaches who are new to teaching social skills. This structured manual introduces essential social skills lessons and includes lesson plans and teacher scripts. ACCEPTS promotes teacher and peer-to-peer interaction.

FIVE QUICK STRATEGIES TO INCORPORATE SOCIAL SKILLS INTO YOUR ACADEMIC LESSON

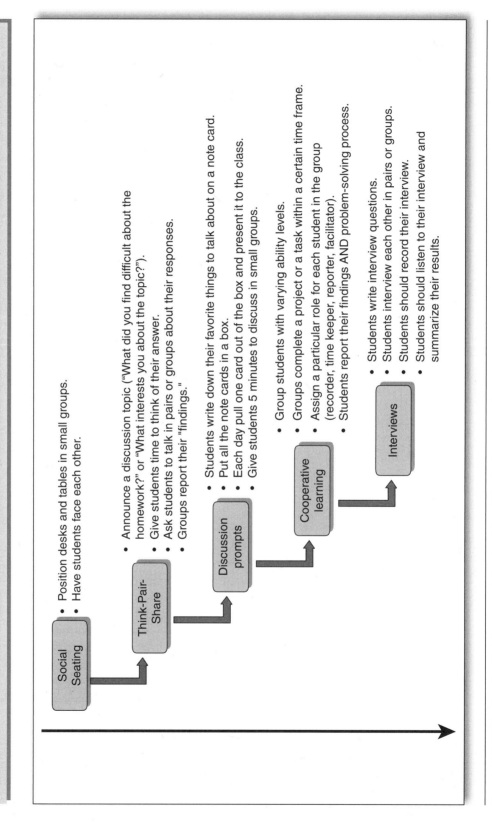

Social Seating
- Position desks and tables in small groups.
- Have students face each other.

Think-Pair-Share
- Announce a discussion topic ("What did you find difficult about the homework?" or "What interests you about the topic?").
- Give students time to think of their answer.
- Ask students to talk in pairs or groups about their responses.
- Groups report their "findings."

Discussion prompts
- Students write down their favorite things to talk about on a note card.
- Put all the note cards in a box.
- Each day pull one card out of the box and present it to the class.
- Give students 5 minutes to discuss in small groups.

Cooperative learning
- Group students with varying ability levels.
- Groups complete a project or a task within a certain time frame.
- Assign a particular role for each student in the group (recorder, time keeper, reporter, facilitator).
- Students report their findings AND problem-solving process.

Interviews
- Students write interview questions.
- Students interview each other in pairs or groups.
- Students should record their interview.
- Students should listen to their interview and summarize their results.

SOCIAL ACTIVITIES FOR KIDS

Charades	Goal: Reading body language Goal: Understanding body language and reading nonverbal cues Before beginning the game, the students write down words on a small piece of paper. The words can be book characters, movies, songs, nouns, or action words. One student draws a piece of paper and reads the word or phrase silently. Without using any words, the student acts out the words and tries to get his or her teammates to guess what is written on the paper.
The name game	Goal: Getting someone's attention before you speak Have students sit in a circle and give one student a ball. The student with the ball calls out the name of the student to whom they are throwing the ball. Then that student calls out another student's name before throwing the ball to them.
Telephone	Goal: Active listening A group of children sit in a circle. The first child whispers a word or phrase into his or her neighbor's ear. The next person will whisper the word or phrase he or she thought she heard to the second person. Then the second person whispers to a third person. The game continues to the end of the circle. The last person says the phrase they heard out loud.
Round robin story telling	Goal: Active listening, staying on topic The goal is for children to co-create a story. One child begins to tell a story. The next child takes over, building on the first person's story. This continues as each person in the group takes a turn to contribute to the story. The last person to take a turn creates the ending of the story.
Make the statue laugh	Goal: Perspective taking Students get in a circle and freeze like a statue. One student (the person who is "it") walks around the circle and, without touching, tries to make each statue laugh. The first statue who laughs is "it."

REFERENCES

Arms, E., Bickett, J., & Graf, V. (2008). Gender bias and imbalance: Girls in US special education programmes. *Gender and Education, 20*(4), 349–359.

Bauminger, N., Shulman, C., & Agam, G. (2003). Peer interaction and loneliness in high-functioning children with autism. *Journal of Autism and Developmental Disorders, 33*(5), 489–507.

Bellini, S., Peters, J. K., Benner, L., & Hope, A. (2007). A meta-analysis of school-based social skills interventions for children with autism spectrum disorders. *Remedial and Special Education, 28,* 153–162.

Buhs, E. S., Ladd, G. W., & Herald, S. L. (2006). Peer exclusion and victimization: Processes that mediate the relation between peer group rejection and children's classroom engagement and achievement? *Journal of Educational Psychology, 98*(1), 1–13.

Bussing, R., Zima, B. T., Perwien, A. R., Belin, T. R., & Widawski, M. (1998). Children in special education programs: Attention deficit hyperactivity disorder, use of services and unmet needs. *American Journal of Public Health, 88*(6), 880–886.

Campbell, J. M., & Marino, C. A. (2009). Brief report: Sociometric status and behavioral characteristics of peer nominated buddies for a child with autism. *Journal of Autism and Developmental Disorders, 39,* 1359–1363.

Celeste, M. (2007). Social skills intervention for a child who is blind. *Journal of Visual Impairment and Blindness, 101*(9), 521–533.

Chan, J. M., Lang, R. L., Rispoli, M., O'Reilly, M., Sigafoos, J., & Cole, H. (2009). Use of peer mediated interventions in the treatment of autism spectrum disorders: A systematic review. *Research in Autism Spectrum Disorders, 3*(4), 876–889.

Dean, M., Kasari, C., Shih, W., Frankel, F., Whitney, R., Landa, R., . . . Harwood, R. (2014). The peer relationships of girls with ASD at school: Comparison to boys and girls with and without ASD. *Journal of Child Psychiatry and Psychology, 55*(11), 1218–1225.

Dunn, J. (2004). *Children's friendships: The beginning of intimacy.* Malden, MA: Blackwell.

Falkmer, T., Anderson, K., Falkmer, M., & Horlin, C. (2013). Diagnostic procedures in autism spectrum disorders: A systematic literature review. *European Child and Adolescent Psychiatry, 22,* 329–340.

Geiger, T. C., Zimmer-Gembeck, M. J., & Crick, N. R. (2004). The science of relational aggression: Can we guide intervention? In M. M. Moretti, C. Odgers, & M. Jackson (Eds.), *Girls and aggression: Contributing factors and intervention strategies, Perspectives in law and psychology series* (pp. 27–40). New York, NY: Kluwer.

Gresham, F. M., & Elliott, S. N. (1990). *Social Skills Rating System.* Circle Pines, MN: American Guidance Service.

Hancock, T. B., & Kaiser, A. P. (2006). Enhanced milieu teaching. In R. McCauley & M. Fey (Eds.), *Treatment of language disorders in children* (pp. 203–233). Baltimore, MD: Paul Brookes.

Horrocks, J. L., White, G., & Roberts, L. (2008). Principals' attitudes regarding inclusion of children with autism in Pennsylvania public schools. *Journal of Developmental Disorders, 38,* 1462–1473.

January, A. M., Casey, R. J., & Paulson, D. (2011). A meta-analysis of classroom-wide interventions to building social skills. *School Psychology Review, 40*(2), 242–256.

Kasari, C., Rotheram-Fuller, E., Locke, J., & Gulsrud, A. (2011). Making the connection: Randomized controlled trial of social skills at school for children with autism spectrum disorders. *Journal of Child Psychology and Psychiatry, 53*(4), 431–439.

Kasari C., & Smith, T. (2013). Interventions in schools for children with autism spectrum disorder: Methods and recommendations. *Autism, 17,* 254–267.

Levy-Shiff, R., & Hoffman, M. (1985). Social behaviour of hearing-impaired and normally hearing preschoolers. *British Journal of Educational Psychology, 55,* 111–118.

Maag, J. W. (2006). Social skills training for students with emotional and behavioral disorders: A review of reviews. *Behavioral Disorders, 32*(1), 5–17.

Maccoby, E. (2002). Gender and group process: A developmental account. *Current Directions in Psychological Science, 11*(2), 54–58.

Mayes, S. D., Calhoun, S. L., Murray, M. J., Ahuja, M., & Smith, L. A. (2011). Anxiety, depression, and irritability in children with autism relative to other neuropsychiatric disorders and typical development. *Research in Autism Spectrum Disorders, 5,* 474–485.

McMahon, C. M., Vismara, L. A., & Solomon, M. (2012). Measuring changes in social behavior during a social skills intervention for higher-functioning children and adolescents with autism spectrum disorder. *Journal of Autism and Developmental Disorders, 43,* 1843–1856.

Proulx, M. F., & Poulin, F. (2013). Stability and change in kindergartners' friendship: Examination of links with social functioning. *Social Development, 22*(1), 111–125.

Spencer, S. V., Bowker, J. C., Rubin, K. H., Booth-LaForce, C., & Laursen, B. (2013). Similarity between friends in social information processing and associations with positive friendship quality and conflict. *Merrill-Palmer Quarterly, 59*(1), 106–113.

RECOMMENDED READINGS

* Bukowski, W. M., Newcomb, A. F., & Hartup, W. W. (1996). *The company they keep: Friendship in childhood and adolescence.* New York, NY: Cambridge University Press.

* Hartup, W. W. (2005). Peer interaction: What causes what? *Journal of Abnormal Child Psychology, 33*(3), 387–394.

* Hartup, W. W., & Abecassis, M. (2002). Friends and enemies. In P. K. Smith & C. H. Hart (Eds.), *Blackwell handbook of childhood social development* (pp. 286–306). Malden, MA: Blackwell.

* Maccoby, E. E. (1998). *The two sexes: Growing up apart, coming together.* Cambridge, MA: Belknap Press/Harvard University Press.

* Rubin, K. H., Bukowski, W. M., & Laursen, B. (2009). *Handbook of peer interactions, relationships, and groups.* New York, NY: Guilford Press.

GO EVEN FURTHER WITH THIS TOPIC ON THE WORLD WIDE WEB

- www.airbnetwork.org/remaking.asp
- www.sociallyspeakingllc.com/my-mission-for-socially/free-pdfs/101_ways_to_teach_social.pdf
- www.socialthinking.com
- www.socialskillscentral.com
- www.pbisworld.com/tier-1/teach-social-skills/

THE Apps WE LOVE

- Social Skills
- Model Me Going Places
- Responding Social Skills
- Socially Speaking
- Hidden Curriculum on the Go!

20

Fantastic Family Collaboration

Susan Auerbach

California State University, Northridge

WHAT REALLY WORKS WITH FAMILY COLLABORATION IN THE ELEMENTARY CLASSROOM

Building Authentic Partnerships With Elementary School Families

How many of you would say that "parents are the heartbeat of the school?" A principal in Los Angeles who takes the time to participate in a Parents as Authors program, considers them exactly that. "I hear the parents' stories and make a connection at such a human level," she said (Auerbach, 2011, p. 20). This leader's open, relationships-based approach is the new face of family *engagement*—an active, inclusive connection that supports families and students' learning and development—as opposed to traditional parent *involvement* focused on the school's agenda (Olivos, Ochoa, & Jimenez-Castellanos, 2011). Think of it as educators "doing with" parents through listening and empowerment versus "doing to" parents to gain their cooperation (Ferlazzo, 2011). Engagement that honors families' voices and nurtures a sense of belonging can transform today's limited home-school partnerships. So how do we make that happen?

For more than 25 years, there have been calls for American schools to partner with parents to raise student achievement (Auerbach, 2012a; Epstein, 1990). Yet preservice and inservice professional development on family engagement is minimal, and many teachers and administrators feel unprepared to work effectively with parents (Epstein & Sanders, 2006; U.S. Department of Education, 2014). There are plenty of activities in some schools. Parent Centers, Family Literacy Nights, and Coffee with the Principal have become commonplace, along with other beneficial programs and services. Yet comprehensive partnerships are rare, and schools typically plan activities without regard for parent concerns (Epstein & Sanders, 2006; Warren, Hong, Rubin, & Uy, 2009). There's often a lack of trust between parents and educators, especially at urban schools (Bryk & Schneider, 2002). Many educators blame parents for children's problems and don't recognize the "invisible strategies" that poor, minority, or immigrant families may use to support education at home (Auerbach, 2012a; Bryk & Schneider, 2002).

Fortunately, in most places, we've made progress since the days when parents were kept at a distance from educators and schools made little effort at communication. Henderson, Mapp, Johnson, and Davies (2007) contrast these "fortress schools" with gradually more welcoming "come-if-we-call," "open-door," and "partnership" schools. They say that meaningful partnerships begin with educators buying into four core beliefs: (a) all parents want the best for their children, (b) they are all able to support education in some way, (c) parents and educators can be equal partners, and (d) schools need to lead the way for partnerships. Are these beliefs the norm at your school? If not, your school may offer a few partnership activities but may be missing the genuine spirit required of true partnerships.

Genuine partnerships are collaborative relationships between equals for mutual benefit. We can take a broader view of what counts as involvement and build more *authentic partnerships* that help families and schools. Authentic partnerships are respectful alliances that value relationship building, dialogue, and sharing power to work toward common goals (Auerbach, 2012a). This chapter introduces you to research and best practices—that is, what really works—to help your school engage parents on the path to authentic partnerships.

RESEARCH HIGHLIGHTS ON PARENTS AND PARTNERSHIPS

For most educators, the main purpose of parent involvement in education is increasing student achievement. There is a lot of evidence that shows that parent involvement has a positive effect on achievement (Epstein et al., 2009; Jeynes, 2005; Jordan, Orozco, & Averett, 2002), especially home-based activities during elementary school. For example, Jeynes's (2005) study found the greatest impact came from parent behaviors like having high expectations and reading to their children regularly. Students with involved parents have better grades, test scores, graduation rates, and behavior records, regardless of family background (Henderson & Mapp, 2002). Parent programs that are sustained and culturally relevant, like the workshop series of the Parent Institute for Quality Education (PIQE), lead to changes in home routines, parent knowledge, and contact with the school that, in turn, can help student learning (Chrispeels & Gonzalez, 2004). When partnerships are *only* about achievement, however, they may not reflect the priorities of families who take a more holistic or collectivistic view of the needs of their children and communities (Cooper & Christie, 2005; Trumbull, Rothstein-Fisch, Greenfield, & Quiroz, 2001; Warren et al., 2009).

What encourages families to get involved in education? Hoover-Dempsey and colleagues (2005) say it's a combination of parents' sense of self-efficacy—a belief that their actions make a difference—and invitations for involvement from the school and teacher. If parents don't come to school, it's not because they don't care, says an urban superintendent: "Parents *do* care; they just need an invitation. They need an environment that is conducive to their engagement" (Auerbach, 2007, p. 716). School leaders need to create and sustain a family-friendly school climate (Constantino, 2003). For example, they can rethink traditional events like parent-teacher conferences and Back to School Night so these become more comfortable two-way conversations—chances to get to know and learn from each other (Henderson et al., 2007)—instead of schools and teachers simply talking to them.

Joyce Epstein's (1990) framework of six types of involvement (parenting, communicating with the school, volunteering, learning at home, school decision-making, and community involvement) has inspired many policies and programs. She urges schools to form Action Teams for Partnerships to assess current conditions, set goals, and plan activities around the six types. Parents are more likely to be involved when schools promote two-way communication, comprehensive activities, and various ways to participate (Epstein, 1990; Epstein et al., 2009; Henderson et al., 2007).

Epstein's approach, while influential, leaves out key issues like parent culture, advocacy, and power (Olivos et al., 2011). Programs that try to "fix" parenting styles or home literacy practices to meet school expectations can alienate parents; instead, programs should affirm family strengths and build on what families already do (Auerbach & Collier, 2012; Henderson et al., 2007). The National PTA's (2009) standards for partnerships stress not only Epstein's six types but also the need to speak up for every child in advocacy efforts. Family engagement goes beyond a menu of activities; it focuses on bringing parents together with educators and each other, listening to their concerns, and nurturing their leadership

(Auerbach, 2012a; Warren et al., 2009). Schools with strong "relational trust" between stakeholders—based on perceived respect, competence, and integrity—have higher rates of collaboration and achievement (Bryk & Schneider, 2002; Henderson & Mapp, 2002). Teachers and parents can pave the way by sharing their hopes and dreams for their children, stories of their own education and family history, or wish lists of what each (parent or teacher) would like the other to do or understand for a better partnership (Auerbach, 2009; Henderson et al., 2007). This leads to "reciprocal learning," where partners see themselves and others as both teacher and learner (Cooper, Riehl, & Hasan, 2010).

Building relationships and trust with parents is often easier at schools with a majority of middle-class families. Families of higher social class are more likely to attend school events, meet with educators, comply with teachers' requests, and have a partnership orientation (Auerbach, 2012a). By contrast, parents of lower social class are more likely to face barriers to meeting school requests (like lack of English fluency or child care), feel disrespected or intimidated by educators, and see learning as the school's job (Auerbach, 2007; Olivos et al., 2011).

Making Connections

Check out Chapter 16 on English Language Learners

Educators typically complain about low-income parents who are not involved enough—or about demanding affluent parents who are overly involved. Sound familiar? We need to find ways to validate all families' knowledge, caring, and goals for their children (Cooper et al., 2010)—whether they want better services for English learners in the city or for children with disabilities in the suburbs. Parents of all backgrounds want to be heard and have less bureaucratic, more personalized contact with schools (Auerbach, 2012a).

Probably the hardest part of authentic partnerships is sharing power around major school decisions. It's not enough to have parents on school governance councils if they don't represent the diversity of the school or if they lack the training needed to "minimize the knowledge gap" with educators (Sanders, 2009). "Parents can be your best allies" in school improvement, insists a principal (Auerbach, 2009, p. 16). Instead of the usual "power over," top-down approach, educators can focus on "power to" work together toward common goals (Warren et al., 2009). Investing in parent leadership development, while also training staff in the skills of collaboration, makes for more meaningful joint decision-making. Yes, it takes time—but it's worth the effort.

What will make a difference for greater family engagement? The U.S. Department of Education (2014) recommends a "dual capacity framework" for developing the knowledge, skills, and dispositions of both families and educators around partnerships. This training should be relational, collaborative, and linked to student learning as it builds awareness, confidence, and connections among stakeholders. Moving toward authentic partnerships is an ongoing journey with each new set of families that comes through your door—and it starts with respect and relationships. So how exactly does a classroom teacher begin the process of developing this kind of relationship with families? Here are some practical tips for you to get started.

 ## MOVING AWAY FROM FEAR AND BLAMING

Teachers

- ✗ **STOP assuming that if parents don't come to school, return your calls, or read with their child, they don't care about education.** Recognize that family support for education takes many forms and that some families face barriers to traditional parent involvement (Auerbach, 2007). Families are probably doing what makes cultural, economic, and personal sense to them, given their circumstances. The more you reach out and offer support to families, the more support they will be ready to give their child and your class.
- ✗ **STOP complaining about parents with fellow teachers.** It widens the gap between families and schools and perpetuates stereotypes, especially in schools with high numbers of low-income or minority students. Instead of "looking out the window" to blame others, try "looking in the mirror" to see how you can be part of the solution (Henderson et al., 2007).
- ✗ **STOP fearing parent conferences . . . parents are anxious, too!** Conferences are prime opportunities to connect with families and share ideas. Prepare for a friendly, two-way conversation about the student's learning at a time and place that is convenient for parents (not just during school hours at school). Whether doing traditional or student-led conferences, make sure there is time for you to speak directly with parents to hear their questions and concerns. If parents feel rushed, they may feel less supported and you will miss out on a chance to learn more about one of your students.
- ✗ **STOP avoiding contact with parents who are not fluent in English.** Learn their names and a few phrases to greet them in their language, smile a lot, and enlist help from bilingual adults in the school and community—including parent volunteers, if necessary. Rebecca Mieliwocki, 2012 National Teacher of the Year, created a "cheat sheet" for herself with key phrases in Spanish to keep near her when calling parents of some students. She said she always wanted to speak to the parents directly before turning to an interpreter. Making that personal connection was important to her, and should be to you.

- **STOP giving up on parent engagement because you planned a wonderful activity and only five parents came.** It takes time to cultivate relationships. Troubleshoot what may have prevented parents from coming (time? location? lack of child care or translation? unfamiliar topic?). Try a few different types of outreach next time to reach more parents, like hand-made, illustrated invitations from their children and personal phone calls from you or another parent. Flyers in the backpack are notoriously unreliable!
- **STOP *telling* parents what you'd like them to do at home; if they aren't responding, *show* them.** Demonstrate how you'd like them to read with their child or help with a new math technique, and give them a chance to practice—preferably at a small, informal event with plenty of food, fun, and presentations by students. Even better, find out what parents are already doing at home and build on that with your demonstrations.
- **STOP making Back to School Night a rushed, formal, one-sided presentation of rules, procedures, and curriculum.** This event can set the tone for a family-friendly classroom with an emphasis on student learning and building a caring community. Think interactive and fun! For example, a Canadian school reinvented the event as Meet the Family Night, with everyone (including teachers) bringing and sharing family photographs as a way to get to know each other, break down barriers, and make school a comfortable place for families.
- **STOP assuming you are the experts.** Not only are families the experts on their own children, but many of them also have expertise they could bring to the classroom if you took the time to reach out and learn.

Administrators

- **STOP allowing your staff to play the blame game with parents.** Challenge staff to reevaluate their beliefs. Model respectful, welcoming interactions with families, and nurture a culture of collaboration among all stakeholders (Auerbach, 2007, 2009, 2011).
- **STOP treating parent engagement like a task to check off on a to-do list** (Constantino, 2003). Parent engagement is an approach to leading schools; it should be an integral part of your leadership style and school operations (Auerbach, 2012a; U.S. Department of Education, 2014). See Auerbach (2011, 2012b) for stories and advice from community-oriented school leaders.
- **STOP offering one-shot family literacy workshops and occasional parent classes.** Just as professional development for teachers needs to be in-depth and ongoing, so too does parent education (Auerbach & Collier, 2012). Form an action team or task force to

plan meaningful engagement activities in response to parent interests—and join with them!

✖ **STOP relying on a small clique of active parents for input on school councils, help with volunteering, and informal feedback.** Expand parent participation with a wide range of outreach and programs and personal approaches to hard-to-reach parents (Henderson et al., 2007). If needed, urge the PTA to diversify its membership and leadership.

✖ **STOP rebuffing "difficult" parents.** Meet them on their turf where possible. Show respect, listen carefully to see their point of view, and invite them to join you in solving the problem. Such parents can become your greatest supporters (Auerbach, 2007).

GO MOVING TOWARD TRUST AND ENGAGEMENT

Teachers, DO This

✓ **CONSIDER your beliefs.** Learn about and cultivate the four core values of good home-school relations in Henderson et al. (2007) mentioned above. Does your work with families reflect these values? Can you open a conversation with other teachers about these ideas and find ways to challenge stereotypes and complaints?

✓ **GET TO KNOW your students' families and communities.** Make home visits, especially with families of a different cultural or social class background than you or with parents who don't respond to school communications (Ferlazzo, 2011). Seek parents' permission, plan the visit with an academic focus, and bring learning materials families can

Plugged In

www.pthvp.org/

keep (check out the website on the Parent Teacher Home Visit Project in the Plugged In box). Go to community events, gathering places, and businesses; consider fieldtrips that highlight local resources. The more comfortable and informed you are about what goes on outside the school walls, the better you can help parents to be comfortable in and informed about school for their kids.

✓ **MAKE home-school communication easy and comfortable.** Call, e-mail, or text home when kids do something good, especially early in the year. You'll surprise family members, who are usually expecting a problem, and open the door to better communication. Set up a separate e-mail account just for parents, let them know how soon they can expect to hear back from you, and set ground rules for online "office hours" to avoid "venting." If you don't speak the language of students' parents, call on school, district, and community resources (or go online) to help with translation—and learn some common phrases to break the ice.

✓ **DRAW ON parents as learning resources.** All classrooms, not just those in affluent communities, have parents whose knowledge, skills, and talents are relevant to the curriculum and beyond. How might a bricklayer, computer scientist, or cook contribute to a math lesson? Whose language skills, travels, or immigration experience could enrich a unit in history or geography? Inviting family members to share what they know in the classroom is real-life learning that kids will remember and parents will find affirming. At home, all families have stories and advice they can share through interactive homework, as when students interview relatives on music that was popular in their youth. Visit the National Network of Partnership Schools at the url in the Plugged In box, and get some tips on how teachers can engage parents in school work. I've included more sample tips for you on page 329 at the end of this chapter.

Plugged In

www.csos.jhu.edu/ p2000/

✓ **KEEP parent activities small, personal, informal, and hands-on.** Many parents are more comfortable with classroom or grade-level, rather than whole-school, activities. They want a chance to connect with you, other staff, and fellow parents without a lot of bureaucracy or formality (Auerbach, 2012a). How about combining a dessert potluck with a student demonstration of Readers Theater or American history Jeopardy or a workshop where family members create memory books together?

✓ **FIND ALLIES at your school who share your interest in engaging families and eliminating barriers to participation.** Plan activities together so you can share the work of finding resources, doing publicity, and other tasks; this makes it more fun and easier to fit into your schedule. Share your successes with other teachers to find more allies!

✓ **ATTEND EVENTS that your students participate in, on and off campus.** Families and students who see teachers at community events, plays, sports activities, and even birthday parties are often more willing to connect and share with those teachers. If you are making an effort to communicate and connect, they will too.

Administrators, DO This

✓ **PROMOTE the four core values of good home-school relations** in Henderson et al. (2007) mentioned above. Have an honest discussion with your staff about their attitudes and how these core values play out at your school; use lessons learned for future reflection and professional development.

✓ **MAKE SURE your school says "welcome" to parents and families** in its appearance, physical setup, operations, and climate, starting with the front office. See the many tips in Constantino (2003) for a family-friendly school.

✓ **MAKE family engagement a priority by weaving it into everything your school does.** Looking for a new antibullying program? Invite parents to help choose it. Organizing project learning around a schoolwide theme? Recruit knowledgeable family members as living resources for learning. Setting up a professional development series for your staff? Include at least one on family engagement with a panel of parent leaders. Get in the habit of asking: How can parents play a role here? How can this academic or behavioral initiative help us build better partnerships—and vice versa?

✓ **WALK THE WALK of family engagement with respectful communication, relationship building, and innovative outreach.** Greet family members on a daily basis at school and at activities for family members. Get to know your local community. Start an Action Team for Partnerships or similar task force to guide parent participation efforts and take an active role in it. Make yourself and your staff accessible for individual parents and groups who want to discuss concerns; prepare for difficult conversations with professional development, role-playing, and active listening. Model the skills of collaboration in meetings with school governance councils and community partners (Auerbach, 2012a, 2012b).

By infusing more of these ideas into your school, you'll be on your way to learning from families, expanding their participation, supporting students, and promoting more authentic partnerships.

A New Wave of Evidence
Family and Community Engagement Self-Assessment

Please rate your school or district in the following areas.

Your School or School district:

1. Recognizes that all parents, regardless of income, educational level, or cultural background, want their children to do well in school and are involved in their children's learning.

1	2	3	4
rarely	sometimes	regularly	always

2. Creates policies and programs that will support families to guide their children's learning.

1	2	3	4
rarely	sometimes	regularly	always

3. Works with parents to build their social and political connections.

1	2	3	4
rarely	sometimes	regularly	always

4. Develops the capacity of school staff to work with families.

1	2	3	4
rarely	sometimes	regularly	always

5. Links family and community engagement efforts to student learning.

1	2	3	4
rarely	sometimes	regularly	always

6. Focuses efforts to engage families on developing trusting and respectful relationships.

1	2	3	4
rarely	sometimes	regularly	always

7. Embraces a philosophy of partnership and shares power with families and communities.

1	2	3	4
rarely	sometimes	regularly	always

8. Builds strong connections between schools and community organizations.

1	2	3	4
rarely	sometimes	regularly	always

SEDL * National Center for Family & Community Connections with Schools
4700 Mueller Bvd. * Austin, Texas 78723 * 1-800-476-6861 * www.sedl.org/
connections

Source: Used with permission from SEDL.

TIPS LANGUAGE ARTS—ELEMENTARY

Student's Name _____   Date _____

TIPS: HAIRY TALES

Dear Family Partner:

In language arts I am working on using information gathered from others to write explanations. For this assignment, I am comparing today's hairstyles with those of the past. I hope you enjoy this activity with me. This activity is due _____.

Sincerely,

_____
Student's signature

FAMILY INTERVIEW

FIND A FAMILY MEMBER TO INTERVIEW.

Who is it?_____
Ask:

1) In what decade were you born? (1960s, 1970s, etc.) _____

2) What is one hairstyle that was popular when you were my age?

    For boys: _____

    For girls: _____

3) What hairstyle did you have when you were my age? _____

4) Did your family agree with your choice of hairstyle? _____

5) What is your favorite current hairstyle and why? _____

6) What is your least favorite current hairstyle and why? _____

Ask your family member to show you a picture of a hairstyle of the past. Draw a picture of the hairstyle here.

First Draft

Use the information from your interview to write a paragraph about hairstyles. Remember to:

- Give a paragraph a title.
- Be sure all of your sentences relate to your topic.
- Use descriptive words to help explain the ideas.
- If you compare hairstyles, tell how they are alike and how they are different.

WRITE YOUR PARAGRAPH HERE

Title: _____

_____
_____
_____
_____
_____
_____
_____
_____
_____
_____
_____

    Read your paragraph aloud to your family partner.
    Revise or add sentences as needed.

EXTENSION ACTIVITY

Select another topic for comparison—for example, clothing styles, ways to have fun, or rules at home or school. What topic did you choose? _____

Next to each "Q" line, write a question about your topic. Use your questions to interview a family member. Write the family member's answer next to each "A" line.

    1. Q: _____
        A: _____
    2. Q: _____
        A: _____
    3. Q: _____
        A: _____

HOME-TO-SCHOOL COMMUNICATION

Dear Parent/Family Partner,
Please give me your reactions to your child's work on this activity.
Write YES or NO for each statement.

_____ My child understood the homework and was able to complete it.
_____ My child and I enjoyed the activity.
_____ This assignment helped me know what my child is learning in language arts.
Any other comments: _____
Parent's signature: _____

Epstein, J. L., Salinas, K. C., Jackson, V., & Van Voorhis, F. L. (revised 2000). Teachers Involve Parents in Schoolwork (TIPS) Interactive Homework for the Elementary Grades. Baltimore: Johns Hopkins University, Center on School, Family, and Community Partnerships.

REFERENCES

Auerbach, S. (2007). Visioning parent engagement in urban schools: Role constructions of Los Angeles administrators. *Journal of School Leadership, 17*(6), 699–735.

Auerbach, S. (2009). Walking the walk: Portraits in leadership for family engagement in urban schools. *School Community Journal, 19*(1), 9–32.

Auerbach, S. (2011). Learning from Latino families. *Educational Leadership, 68*(8), 16–21.

Auerbach, S. (2012a). Conceptualizing leadership for authentic partnerships: A continuum to inspire practice. In S. Auerbach (Ed.), *School leadership for authentic family and community partnerships: Research perspectives for transforming practice* (pp. 29–52). New York, NY: Routledge.

Auerbach, S. (2012b). Conversations with community-oriented educational leaders. In S. Auerbach (Ed.), *School leadership for authentic family and community partnerships: Research perspectives for transforming practice* (pp. 233–247). New York, NY: Routledge.

Auerbach, S., & Collier, S. (2012). Bringing high stakes from the classroom to the parent center: Lessons from an intervention program for immigrant families. *Teachers College Record, 114*(3), 1–40.

Bryk, A. S., & Schneider, B. (2002). *Trust in schools: A core resource for improvement.* New York, NY: Russell Sage Foundation.

Chrispeels, J., & Gonzalez, M. (2004). *Do educational programs increase parents' practices at home? Factors influencing Latino parent involvement (Family Involvement Research Digest).* Retrieved from www.hfrp.org/publications-resources

Constantino, S. (2003). *Engaging all families for student success: Creating a positive school culture by putting research into practice.* Lanham, MD: Scarecrow Education.

Cooper, C. W., & Christie, C. A. (2005). Evaluating parent empowerment: A look at the potential of social justice evaluation in education. *Teachers College Record, 107*(10), 2248–2274.

Cooper, C. W., Riehl, C. J., & Hasan, L. (2010). Leading and learning with diverse families in schools: Critical epistemology amid communities of practice. *Journal of School Leadership, 20*(6), 758–788.

Epstein, J. L. (1990). School and family connections: Theory, research and implications for integrating sociologies of education and family. In D. G. Unger & M. B. Sussman (Eds.), *Families in community settings: Interdisciplinary perspectives* (pp. 99–126). New York, NY: Haworth Press.

Epstein, J. L., & Sanders, M. (2006). Prospects for change: Preparing educators for school, family, and community partnerships. *Peabody Journal of Education, 81*(2), 81–120.

Epstein, J. L., Sanders, M. G., Simon, B. S., Salinas, K. C., Jansorn, N. R., & Van Voorhis, F. L. (2009). *School, family and community partnerships: Your handbook for action* (3rd ed.). Thousand Oaks, CA: Corwin.

Ferlazzo, L. (2011). Involvement or engagement? *Educational Leadership, 68*(8), 10–15.

Henderson, A., & Mapp, K. (2002). *A new wave of evidence: The impact of school, family, and community connections on student achievement.* Retrieved from http://www.sedl.org/connections/resources/evidence.pdf

Henderson, A. T., Mapp, K. L., Johnson, V. R., & Davies, D. (2007). *Beyond the bake sale: The essential guide to family-school partnerships.* New York, NY: New Press.

Hoover-Dempsey, K. V., Walker, J., Sandler, H., Whetsell, D., Green, C., Wilkins, A., & Closson, K. (2005). Why do parents become involved? Research findings and implications. *Elementary School Journal, 106*(2), 105–130.

Jeynes, W. (2005). A meta-analysis of the relation of parental involvement to urban elementary school student academic achievement. *Urban Education, 40*(3), 237–269.

Jordan, C., Orozco, E., & Averett, A. (2002). *Emerging issues in school, family and community connections: Annual synthesis 2001.* Austin, TX: Southwest Educational Development Laboratory.

National PTA. (2009). National standards for family-school partnerships. Retrieved from http://www.pta.org/files/National_Standards_Implementation_Guide_2009.pdf

Olivos, E. M., Ochoa, A. M., & Jimenez-Castellanos, O. (2011). Critical voices in bicultural parent engagement: A framework for transformation. In E. M. Olivos, O. Jimenez-Castellanos, & A. M. Ochoa (Eds.), *Bicultural parent engagement: Advocacy and empowerment* (pp. 1–20). New York, NY: Teachers College Press.

Sanders, M. (2009). Collaboration for change: How an urban school district and a community-based organization support and sustain school, family, and community partnerships. *Teachers College Record, 111*(7), 1693–1712.

Trumbull, E., Rothstein-Fisch, C., Greenfield, P. M., & Quiroz, B. (2001). *Bridging cultures between home and school: A guide for teachers.* Mahwah, NJ: Lawrence Erlbaum.

U.S. Department of Education. (2014). The dual capacity framework for building family-school partnerships. Retrieved from http://www.ed.gov/family-and-community-engagement

Warren, M., Hong, S., Rubin, C. L., & Uy, P. S. (2009). Beyond the bake sale: A community-based relational approach to parent engagement in schools. *Teachers College Record, 111*(9), 2209–2254.

RECOMMENDED READINGS

* Delgado Gaitan, C. (2004). *Involving Latino families in schools: Raising student achievement through home-school partnerships.* Thousand Oaks, CA: Corwin.

* Dyches, T. T., Carter, N. J., & Prater, M. A. (2012). *A teacher's guide to communicating with parents: Practical strategies for developing successful relationship.* Upper Saddle River, NJ: Pearson.

* Marsh, M. M., & Turner-Vorbeck, T. (Eds.). (2009). *(Mis)understanding families: Learning from real families in our schools.* New York, NY: Teachers College Press.

* Ridnover, K. (2011). *Everyday engagement: Making students and parents your partners in learning.* Alexandria, VA: Association for Supervision and Curriculum Development.

* Sileo, N. M., & Prater, M. A. (2012). *Working with families of children with special needs: Family and professional partnerships and roles.* Upper Saddle River, NJ: Pearson.

GO EVEN FURTHER WITH THIS TOPIC ON THE WORLD WIDE WEB

- www.communityschools.org/
- www.hfrp.org/family-involvement
- www.ncpie.org/
- www.csos.jhu.edu/p2000/
- www.pthvp.org/
- www.schoolcommunitynetwork.org/docs/FET_Booklet.pdf

THE Apps WE LOVE

- BuzzMob
- Teacher App & Grade Book
- Collaborize Classroom
- Remind101
- TeacherKit
- HomeworkNow
- Class Messenger

Index

A SAGE Company

Corwin is committed to improving education for all learners by publishing books and other professional development resources for those serving the field of PreK–12 education. By providing practical, hands-on materials, Corwin continues to carry out the promise of its motto: **"Helping Educators Do Their Work Better."**